ALI

Muhammad Ali

The Record

61 FIGHTS | 56 VICTORIES | 21 YEARS | 12 COUNTRIES | 4 CONTINENTS | 3 HEAVYWEIGHT TITLES | 2 NAMES

Against a swirling backdrop of personal, social and political upheaval, Ali's record in the ring stands as nothing less than history's Greatest.

CASSIUS CLAY vs ARCHIE MOORE

NOVEMBER 15, 1962
Memorial Sports Arena
Los Angeles
TKO / ROUND 4

CASSIUS CLAY vs CHARLIE POWELL

JANUARY 24, 1963
Civic Arena
Pittsburgh, Pennsylvania
KO / ROUND 3

CASSIUS CLAY vs DOUG JONES
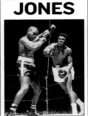
MARCH 13, 1963
Madison Square Garden
New York City
W / 10 ROUNDS

CASSIUS CLAY vs HENRY COOPER
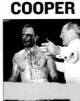
JUNE 18, 1963
Wembley Stadium
London, England
TKO / ROUND 5

CASSIUS CLAY vs SONNY LISTON

FEBRUARY 25, 1964
Convention Hall
Miami Beach, Florida
TKO / ROUND 7

MUHAMMAD ALI vs SONNY LISTON

MAY 25, 1965
St. Dominic's Arena
Lewiston, Maine
KO / ROUND 1

MUHAMMAD ALI vs FLOYD PATTERSON

NOVEMBER 22, 1965
Convention Center
Las Vegas, Nevada
TKO / ROUND 12

MUHAMMAD ALI vs GEORGE CHUVALO

MARCH 29, 1966
Maple Leaf Gardens
Toronto, Canada
W / 15 ROUNDS

October 28, 1962: Cuban Missile Crisis ends . . . November 22, 1963: JFK shot in Dallas . . . February 21, 1965: Malcolm X shot in New York . . . December 31, 1965: 180,000 U.S. troops in Vietnam . . .

MUHAMMAD ALI vs AL LEWIS

JULY 19, 1972
Croke Park Stadium
Dublin, Ireland
TKO / ROUND 11

MUHAMMAD ALI vs FLOYD PATTERSON

SEPTEMBER 20, 1972
Madison Square Garden
New York City
TKO / ROUND 7

MUHAMMAD ALI vs BOB FOSTER

NOVEMBER 21, 1972
Sierra-Tahoe Hotel
Stateline, Nevada
KO / ROUND 8

MUHAMMAD ALI vs JOE BUGNER

FEBRUARY 14, 1973
Convention Center
Las Vegas, Nevada
W / 12 ROUNDS

MUHAMMAD ALI vs KEN NORTON

MARCH 31, 1973
Sports Arena
San Diego, California
L / 12 ROUNDS

MUHAMMAD ALI vs KEN NORTON

SEPTEMBER 10, 1973
The Forum
Inglewood, California
W / 12 ROUNDS

MUHAMMAD ALI vs RUDI LUBBERS
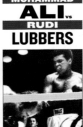
OCTOBER 20, 1973
Senayan Stadium
Jakarta, Indonesia
W / 12 ROUNDS

MUHAMMAD ALI vs JOE FRAZIER

JANUARY 28, 1974
Madison Square Garden
New York City
W / 12 ROUNDS

September 5–6, 1972: Terrorists kill 11 Israeli athletes at Munich Olympics . . . January 22, 1973: Roe v. Wade . . . January 27, 1973: Paris Peace Accords officially end Vietnam War . . .

CASSIUS CLAY vs ALEX MITEFF

OCTOBER 7, 1961
Freedom Hall
Louisville, Kentucky
TKO / ROUND 6

CASSIUS CLAY vs WILLI BESMANOFF

NOVEMBER 29, 1961
Freedom Hall
Louisville, Kentucky
TKO / ROUND 7

CASSIUS CLAY vs SONNY BANKS

FEBRUARY 10, 1962
Madison Square Garden
New York City
TKO / ROUND 4

CASSIUS CLAY vs DON WARNER

FEBRUARY 28, 1962
Convention Hall
Miami Beach, Florida
TKO / ROUND 4

CASSIUS CLAY vs GEORGE LOGAN

APRIL 23, 1962
Memorial Sports Arena
Los Angeles
TKO / ROUND 4

CASSIUS CLAY vs BILLY DANIELS

MAY 19, 1962
St. Nicholas Arena
New York City
TKO / ROUND 7

CASSIUS CLAY vs ALEJANDRO LAVORANTE

JULY 20, 1962
Memorial Sports Arena
Los Angeles
KO / ROUND 5

Catch-22 by Joseph Heller published . . . February 20, 1962: John Glenn first American in orbit . . . October 1, 1962: James Meredith first black student at University of Mississippi . . .

MUHAMMAD ALI vs JOE FRAZIER

MARCH 8, 1971
Madison Square Garden
New York City
L / 15 ROUNDS

MUHAMMAD ALI vs JIMMY ELLIS

JULY 26, 1971
Astrodome
Houston, Texas
TKO / ROUND 12

MUHAMMAD ALI vs BUSTER MATHIS

NOVEMBER 17, 1971
Astrodome
Houston, Texas
W / 12 ROUNDS

MUHAMMAD ALI vs JÜRGEN BLIN

DECEMBER 26, 1971
Hallenstadion
Zürich, Switzerland
KO / ROUND 7

MUHAMMAD ALI vs MAC FOSTER

APRIL 1, 1972
Nihon Budokan
Tokyo, Japan
W / 15 ROUNDS

MUHAMMAD ALI vs GEORGE CHUVALO

MAY 1, 1972
Pacific Coliseum
Vancouver, Canada
W / 12 ROUNDS

MUHAMMAD ALI vs JERRY QUARRY

JUNE 27, 1972
Convention Center
Las Vegas, Nevada
TKO / ROUND 7

Armstrong first man on the moon . . . May 4, 1970: Four Kent State students killed by National Guard . . . June 17, 1972: Five men arrested for break-in at DNC offices in Watergate Hotel . . .

MUHAMMAD ALI vs KEN NORTON

SEPTEMBER 28, 1976
Yankee Stadium
New York City
W / 15 ROUNDS

MUHAMMAD ALI vs ALFREDO EVANGELISTA

MAY 16, 1977
Capital Center
Landover, Maryland
W / 15 ROUNDS

MUHAMMAD ALI vs EARNIE SHAVERS

SEPTEMBER 29, 1977
Madison Square Garden
New York City
W / 15 ROUNDS

MUHAMMAD ALI vs LEON SPINKS

FEBRUARY 15, 1978
Las Vegas Hilton
Las Vegas, Nevada
L / 15 ROUNDS

MUHAMMAD ALI vs LEON SPINKS

SEPTEMBER 15, 1978
Superdome
New Orleans, Louisiana
W / 15 ROUNDS

MUHAMMAD ALI vs LARRY HOLMES

OCTOBER 2, 1980
Caesars Palace
Las Vegas, Nevada
L TKO / ROUND 11

MUHAMMAD ALI vs TREVOR BERBICK

DECEMBER 11, 1981
Queen Elizabeth Sports Center
Nassau, Bahamas
L / 10 ROUNDS

1976: Supreme Court reinstates death penalty . . . August 16, 1977: Elvis Presley dies . . . March 28, 1979: Three Mile Island meltdown . . . November 4, 1980: Ronald Reagan elected

Row 1

CASSIUS CLAY vs TUNNEY HUNSAKER

OCTOBER 29, 1960
Freedom Hall
Louisville, Kentucky
W / 6 ROUNDS

CASSIUS CLAY vs HERB SILER

DECEMBER 27, 1960
Auditorium
Miami Beach, Florida
TKO / ROUND 4

CASSIUS CLAY vs TONY ESPERTI

JANUARY 17, 1961
Auditorium
Miami Beach, Florida
TKO / ROUND 3

CASSIUS CLAY vs JIM ROBINSON

FEBRUARY 7, 1961
Convention Hall
Miami Beach, Florida
TKO / ROUND 1

CASSIUS CLAY vs DONNIE FLEEMAN

FEBRUARY 21, 1961
Auditorium
Miami Beach, Florida
TKO / ROUND 7

CASSIUS CLAY vs LAMAR CLARK

APRIL 19, 1961
Freedom Hall
Louisville, Kentucky
KO / ROUND 2

CASSIUS CLAY vs DUKE SABEDONG

JUNE 26, 1961
Convention Center
Las Vegas, Nevada
W / 10 ROUNDS

CASSIUS CLAY vs ALONZO JOHNSON

JULY 22, 1961
Freedom Hall
Louisville, Kentucky
W / 10 ROUNDS

September 26, 1960: First televised presidential debate, between Nixon and Kennedy . . . November 8, 1960: JFK wins presidency . . . April 17, 1961: Bay of Pigs invasion . . . November 10, 1961:

Row 2

MUHAMMAD ALI vs HENRY COOPER

MAY 21, 1966
Highbury Stadium
London, England
TKO / ROUND 6

MUHAMMAD ALI vs BRIAN LONDON

AUGUST 6, 1966
Earls Court Arena
London, England
KO / ROUND 3

MUHAMMAD ALI vs KARL MILDENBERGER

SEPTEMBER 10, 1966
Waldstadion
Frankfurt, Germany
TKO / ROUND 12

MUHAMMAD ALI vs CLEVELAND WILLIAMS

NOVEMBER 14, 1966
Astrodome
Houston, Texas
TKO / ROUND 3

MUHAMMAD ALI vs ERNIE TERRELL

FEBRUARY 6, 1967
Astrodome
Houston, Texas
W / 15 ROUNDS

MUHAMMAD ALI vs ZORA FOLLEY

MARCH 22, 1967
Madison Square Garden
New York City
KO / ROUND 7

MUHAMMAD ALI vs JERRY QUARRY

OCTOBER 26, 1970
Municipal Auditorium
Atlanta, Georgia
TKO / ROUND 3

MUHAMMAD ALI vs OSCAR BONAVENA

DECEMBER 7, 1970
Madison Square Garden
New York City
TKO / ROUND 15

January 15, 1967: Packers defeat Chiefs in Super Bowl I . . . April 4, 1968: Martin Luther King assassinated in Memphis . . . June 5, 1968: Robert F. Kennedy shot in Los Angeles . . . July 20, 1969: Neil

Row 3

MUHAMMAD ALI vs GEORGE FOREMAN

OCTOBER 30, 1974
Stade du 20 Mai
Kinshasa, Zaire
KO / ROUND 8

MUHAMMAD ALI vs CHUCK WEPNER

MARCH 24, 1975
Coliseum at Richfield
Richfield, Ohio
TKO / ROUND 15

MUHAMMAD ALI vs RON LYLE

MAY 16, 1975
Convention Center
Las Vegas, Nevada
TKO / ROUND 11

MUHAMMAD ALI vs JOE BUGNER

JUNE 30, 1975
Merdeka Stadium
Kuala Lampur, Malaysia
W / 15 ROUNDS

MUHAMMAD ALI vs JOE FRAZIER

OCTOBER 1, 1975
Araneta Coliseum
Quezon City, Philippines
TKO / ROUND 14

MUHAMMAD ALI vs JEAN-PIERRE COOPMAN

FEBRUARY 20, 1976
Roberto Clemente Coliseum
Hato Rey, Puerto Rico
KO / ROUND 5

MUHAMMAD ALI vs JIMMY YOUNG

APRIL 30, 1976
Capital Center
Landover, Maryland
W / 15 ROUNDS

MUHAMMAD ALI vs RICHARD DUNN

MAY 24, 1976
Olympiahalle
Munich, Germany
TKO / ROUND 5

April 8, 1974: Hank Aaron breaks Babe Ruth's record with 715th home run . . . August 9, 1974: Nixon resigns . . . April 1, 1976: Apple Computer Company is launched by Jobs and Wozniak . . . July 2,

ABOVE IT ALL Throughout his career Ali, here
having laid out Cleveland Williams in three rounds
in the Astrodome in 1966, transcended boxing.

photograph by NEIL LEIFER

"'WHO'S THE GREATEST?'
HE ASKED THE CHILDREN,
AND THEY ALL SHOUTED
HIS NAME. 'WHO UPSET
THE WORLD?' AND THEY
SHOUTED HIS NAME. 'I AM
THE CHAMPION,' HE
TOLD THEM, 'AND THAT
MEANS ALL OF US
ARE CHAMPIONS.
I SHOWED YOU NOW
WHAT WE CAN DO.'"

◆

HUSTON HORN - *Sports Illustrated 3/9/64*

"OH, YES, HE KNOWS THE BUTTERFLY'S SECRET. KNOWS IT AND DOESN'T EVEN KNOW HE KNOWS IT. IN ORDER TO TRANSFORM HIMSELF, A MAN MUST FIRST BE ABLE TO LOSE, ABLE TO KEEP LETTING HIS OLD SELF DIE. PART OF SUCH A MAN WILL NEVER GROW OLD."

◆

GARY SMITH - *Sports Illustrated 11/15/89*

KARL TARO GREENFELD   STEVEN HOFFMAN
Editor   *Designer*

RICHARD O'BRIEN *Senior Editor*   GEORGE WASHINGTON *Picture Editor*

KATHERINE PRADT *Copy Editor*   JOSH DENKIN *Associate Designer*

BEN REITER *Reporter*   MICHELE BREA *Associate Picture Editor*

photograph by HERB SCHARFMAN

CONTENTS

16 .... INTRODUCTION BY RICHARD HOFFER

20 .... Rise 1943 - 1963
22 .... "WHO MADE ME—IS ME!" • By Huston Horn
46 .... "I'M SOMETHING A LITTLE SPECIAL" • By Cassius Clay

52 .... Rumble 1963 - 1966
54 .... ALI TAKES A CROWN AND A CAUSE • By Angelo Dundee with Tex Maule
74 .... THE WORLD CHAMPION IS REFUSED A MEAL • By George Plimpton

80 .... Exile 1966 - 1969
82 .... TAPS FOR THE CHAMP • By Edwin Shrake
106 ..... FOR ALI, A TIME TO PREACH • By Tex Maule

114 ..... Return 1969 - 1973
116 ...... MAN IN THE MIRROR • By George Plimpton
142 ..... AT THE BELL . . . • By Mark Kram

150 ..... Kings 1973 - 1974
152 ...... CRAFTY WIN FOR MUHAMMAD • By Mark Kram
170 ..... BREAKING A DATE FOR THE DANCE • By George Plimpton

180 ..... Thrilla 1974 - 1976
182 ..... MANILA—FOR BLOOD AND FOR MONEY • By Mark Kram
204 ..... "LAWDY, LAWDY, HE'S GREAT" • By Mark Kram

212 ...... Greatest 1976 - 1981
214 ..... ONCE MORE TO THE MOUNTAIN • By Pat Putnam
234 ...... ONE MORE TIME TO THE TOP • By Pat Putnam

240 ..... Statesman
242 ..... "THE FIGHT'S OVER, JOE" • By William Nack
264 ..... ALI AND HIS ENTOURAGE • By Gary Smith

WHAT LIES AHEAD Ali after
KOing Brian London in Earls
Court Arena, London, in 1966.

INTRODUCTION

BY RICHARD HOFFER

I F MUHAMMAD ALI was in his time the most famous person in the world, it was as much a tribute to his talent for provocation as for his boxing. He was a glorious athlete, of course, his white-tasseled feet a blur to match his whizzing fists. But his legacy as a global personality owes more to that glint in his eye, to his capacity for tomfoolery, his playfulness. He was a born prankster, pie-eyed in his eagerness to produce surprise, and the world won't soon forget his insistence on fun. ✦ Fighting in the far corners of the earth, when that was still done, he was for years our most popular ambassador, advancing the American doctrine of self-satisfaction. ✦ His practiced malarkey—the doggerel of doom, the ritual belittlement—didn't so much enliven the sport of boxing as it created a whole new platform of entertainment. Really, there was boxing, and there was Ali, and everybody knew the difference. In time his artful application of nonsense would be revealed as a veneer, covering a mission of greater importance. But watching him emerge, half man/half message, in Manila, Zaire or even Cleveland was to witness a one-man comic relief effort. He was a carnival unto himself, a buffet of buffoonery, a traveling circus, the highest embodiment of self-confidence.

We can see now that Ali was always much more than that, although that was enough for some folks. You might say he was a forward settler in the discovery of new American truths, his stands on religion and war as dangerous as any he took in Madison Square Garden. Like any cultural adventurer of the time, he suffered for his independence. He bloomed during a time when America was just reawakening to the advantages of individualism, and the country could be hard on nonconformists. Keep in mind that less like-minded citizens effectively deprived him of his sport for three years, basically because he had "no quarrel with them Viet Cong." But, still, there was no better pioneer than him, somebody who could challenge history, getting away with it in the end, forgiven all.

He had the extraordinary ability to bend everyone to his will. Maybe not at first, of course. He was just too idiosyncratic, too full of himself to be immediately appreciated. Purists did not take to his limericks, did not understand why he had to hype his bouts with prefight poetry. "Who would have thought/When they came to the fight/That they'd witness the launching/Of a human satellite." Where was the modesty in that? And was it really good sportsmanship to walk around proclaiming one's own greatness, one's beauty, even? But Ali—he was, of course, still Cassius Clay then—saw no possibilities for showmanship in humility, no fun there. And so he performed with a bravado that struck all the old-timers as simply obscene, the rest of us as wonderful.

And he hung his hands down at his sides, leaned back to avoid punches, amused himself with a shuffle, as if his improvisation was all that could possibly keep him interested in the task at hand. This was aggravating to fans of convention, people who thought athletes—and dare we say black athletes—ought to know their place. And changing religion, raising matters of race, this was hardly the path to mainstream acceptance in the early 1960s. But you couldn't watch it, the only slightly orchestrated chaos of Ali, and be unamused yourself, not for long. His exuberance, the sheer joy of being Muhammad Ali, had a way of demolishing all resistance. Pretty soon you were glad he was Muhammad Ali too.

None of this would have counted for much if he hadn't been a pretty good fighter as well. To celebrate his personality is not to diminish his achievements in the ring.

His early career, before he was blackballed at the age of 25 for refusing induction, was an astonishment, so much invention, so much flair, boxing as gleeful as he was articulate. But he really got interesting at the age of 28—his athletic sweet spot just taken from him—when he returned after his three-year exile, more flat-footed but more hardened, too. His gifts weren't quite the same in his comeback, and he was forced to become a man of substance as well as style. That murderers' row he faced—Joe Frazier, George Foreman, Ken Norton—gave him the opportunity for immortality, as it turned out.

Also the chance to uncork ever more surprises. The fight in Zaire with Foreman, who was so big and brutal that many believed Ali was finally marching to his doom, became an instant classic when Ali developed his rope-a-dope strategy, on the fly, and allowed the big man to punch himself out. It was comical, it was brilliant and it was original. But then, completing his trilogy with the stoic Frazier in Manila, he took an altogether different route, waging a drastic war of attrition, each man fighting as near to death as is possible. No critic could cling to his complaints of clowning, having seen Ali dredge up such desperate courage to outlast Frazier.

The variety of foils—whether the bully Sonny Liston, the warrior Frazier or the implacable menace of Foreman—allowed Ali a showcase few fighters had before or since. And, as his escapades took him from continent to continent, an audience no fighter or even entertainer would ever again enjoy. We can only fully understand his distinction as history rolls on, failing year after year to deliver his replacement. Boxing has never really been the same since he departed. Nor has the world. Will there ever again be a single person who can hopscotch the globe and rally the troops with his hysterical call to anarchy?

Of course Ali long since ceased being Ali, his featherweight feet stuck in the sands of Parkinson's. That elastic mug of his, always stretched out in some display of mock outrage or surprise, rigid for a long time now. And his antic voice, muted by disease, has been a long time without rhyme. Every athlete faces that inevitable irony but, in Ali's case, it seems unnecessarily tragic. He ought to have been able to make his customary noise, anyway.

But he never acknowledged the decline. In fact, he embraced it, as if it brought him closer to the mortals he used to float above, like that butterfly he always imagined himself. And maybe he actually became more Ali than ever before. Refusing to acknowledge any self-sacrifice—this was the toll required to entertain us all those glorious years; he didn't mind—he was amazing, steadfast in his bravery, resolute in his religion, still able to lean down and produce a quarter from behind some kid's ear. In his long debilitation we discovered what he knew all along, that he really is the greatest. ◆

Rise

{ 1943 – 1963 }

"WHO MADE ME—IS ME!"

BY HUSTON HORN

*Cassius Marcellus Clay Jr. was a bubbling young
boxer whose nerve was colossal and whose modest
aim was to win the heavyweight crown*

SI, SEPTEMBER 25, 1961

THE CLAPBOARD HOUSE AT 3302 GRAND Avenue, Louisville, is a commonplace dwelling one story high and four rooms deep. The ornamental frame of the front screen door was curlicued by hand with a scroll saw, and the concrete steps to the gray front porch are painted in stripes, red, white and blue. ✦ "Don't bother your head about that house," says Cassius Marcellus Clay Jr., 19 going on 20, the lyrical young man, lyrically named, who grew up there. "One of these days they're liable to make it a national shrine. Only by that time I'll be long gone, man, living it up on the top of a hill in a house that cost me $100,000. You'll find me out by the swimming pool, and I'll be talking to a bunch of little boys sitting in a circle around my feet. 'Boys,' I'll say to them, 'I was just a poor boxer once, as I reckon you already know. Only I was a very fine boxer, one of the finest that ever lived. And right there's how come I could move out of that little house down there on Grand Avenue and build this big one up here on the hill.' " ✦ For the present, of course, Cassius Clay is still just a boxer, still just an unsophisticated Olympic gold medalist (he won the light

READY TO RUMBLE In 1954, the 12-year-old Cassius Clay already had his eyes on the prize. **23** heavyweight championship in Rome a year ago) who has turned professional and hasn't run out of luck. How very fine a fighter he is remains to be seen, but for Cassius, munificently backed as he is by 11 influential businessmen, it is merely a matter of months before he fulfills the prophecy fluorescently and unconventionally spelled out in a sign in a tavern he leases in Louisville's east end. Cassius himself composed it with stick-on letters, and it reads:

WORLD-HEAVY-WT.
CHAMIONSHIP
FLOYD-PATTERSON,
V.S.
CASSIUS-CLAY. ★
➔19-62

What the sign refrains from concluding, Cassius is glad to supply: When the epic fight is over, proud Floyd Patterson the Champion will skulk from the ring as poor Floyd Patterson the Ex. Cassius Clay will thereupon settle the world heavyweight boxing crown on his own handsome head, and from that day forward will wear it for all it is worth—which, for him, is everything.

"Like last Sunday," said Cassius, the unashamed, unequivocating materialist, not long ago. "Some cats I know said, 'Cassius, Cassius, come on now and let's go to church; otherwise you won't get to Heaven.' 'Hold on a minute,' I said to them, 'and let me tell you something else. When I've got me a $100,000 house, another quarter million stuck in the bank and the world title latched onto my name, then I'll be in Heaven. Walking around making $25 a week, with four children cryin' at home 'cause they're hungry, *that's* my idea of Hell. I ain't studying about either one of them catching up with me in the graveyard.' "

Thus freed from the ordinary man's care for life's hereafter, bachelor Cassius Clay is a free spirit swinging through the here and now with an ebullient, epigrammatic personality. When held to the light, the colors dance off that personality as from the imprisoned patterns of a *millefiori* glass paperweight. "Everything in this life is made to suit the women," says Cassius the social philosopher. "If the women come, the men got to follow, ain't that so? So to get a good gate, I wear these pretty white shoes and these shiny white trunks and the women says, 'Land, ain't he nice and neat.' The women don't like the sight of blood either, so I make sure they never see none of mine by not getting hit." Cassius the phrasemaker may say, "It's either get rich in three hours or get poor in eight." He means by this that training to be a boxer may be tedious and inconvenient but it beats working. Cassius the humorist sometimes discusses his ring strategy this way: "I like to hit a guy with two fast left jabs, a right cross and then a big left hook. If he's still standing after that—and if it ain't the referee that's holding him up—

I runs." But the most typical Cassius is the boy with the big innocent eyes and the monumental, rodomontade conceit. Says this one, "I got the height, the reach, the weight, the physique, the speed, the courage, the stamina and the natural ability that's going to make me great. Putting it another way, to beat me you got to be greater than great."

Putting it that way, it figures that such heavyweight favorites as Patterson and Sonny Liston could easily establish themselves as greater than great against Clay, for Cassius is not the awesomely proficient fighter that he says he is. (No one really believes *he* believes all he says.) But if the overenthusiastic self-appreciation he expresses sounds somewhat precocious at this stage of his career, it must be recognized that he is still physically and mentally immature. He has been boxing (and marveling at his own talent) since he was 12 years old, or for more than a third of his lifetime, but he is still a boy with some growing up to do and still a boxer with some learning to do. Says a friend of his named Archie Moore, "Cassius has quite a bit of hard-knock studying ahead of him."

CASSIUS HAS, IN FACT, FOUGHT ONLY EIGHT TIMES PROFESSIONALLY, and in every case his opponents were chosen not because they would draw a big crowd but because it could be reasonably concluded in advance that they would either keel over or succumb to the blind staggers after a few fast rounds with the boy wonder. So far the has-beens or never-weres he has fought have accommodated Clay's matchmakers. But the ninth, Alex Miteff, who will fight Clay October 7 on national television in Louisville, may fail to acquit himself the same way. "Frankly," says Cassius, whose most creditable victory to date was that Olympic triumph over a bamboozled left-handed Pole, "there ain't one of these professionals has been a real match for me yet, and old Miteff don't scare me either. But let's face another fact, I couldn't last one round with any of them if I was fighting like I did as an amateur. That shows I'm learning, and learning fast."

However fast Cassius is learning now, he and his parents, aided by hindsight, tend to embroider the theme that he was marked for heavyweight supremacy from the day he was born, Jan. 10, 1942. "He came into this world with a good body and a big head that was the image of Joe Louis," says his father, Cassius Marcellus Clay Sr. (The Cassius Clays inherited their name from forebears who were the slaves of C.M. Clay, a Kentucky politician and a kinsman of Henry Clay.) "That made me real proud. I loved Joe Louis. When he was fighting, all the world stood still to listen to the radio, you dig? It ain't like that no more."

Cassius' mother, Odessa, says, "I remember when people used to say, 'My oh my, your boy sure looks like he's going to be a boxer,' and him only six months old. I'd say, 'Aw, go on.' " Young Cassius showed other signs of fulfilling the promise his parents and neighbors saw in him. His first words as a baby were "gee-gee"—which became his nickname—because, Cassius says today, "I wanted to let folks know I was on my way up to the Golden Gloves." Cassius gained weight fast by eating Wheaties, the Breakfast of Champions, out of a serving bowl ("Eating and sleeping, that's the hardest work that boy ever did," says his father); he became the neighborhood marbles champion ("Where I learned to shoot my right") and an expert rock fighter ("where I learned to duck").

One day when Cassius was 12 he reported to a policeman that his new bicycle had been stolen. "I betcha we paid almost $60 for that wheel," Odessa Clay still likes to say, tormenting herself. The policeman, whose name was Joe Martin, was giving boxing lessons in a community gymnasium operated by Louisville's Department of Recreation. Martin was sorry about Clay's swiped bike, but, as he confesses today, he felt less like finding it than teaching the powerfully built, aggressive little boy to box. So persuasive was his sales pitch that Cassius practically gave up cycling on the spot and showed up the next day at the gym, towing his 10-year-old brother, Rudolph Valentino Clay (who, on the basis of evidence presented on television, considers himself aptly named). "We never saw hide nor hair of that wheel again," says Mrs. Clay, a little disconsolately, "and precious little more of my boys."

Joe Martin, 55, wears Louisville Police Department Badge No. 474 and collects coins from parking meters to earn his monthly salary of $408. (Teenager Clay draws a monthly allowance of $400 from his sponsors.) Martin has done more than any other man to develop Cassius' talent, but he is no longer associated with the boy and, should Cassius ever become rich and famous, Martin's chest may well swell up but his pocketbook won't. "In the past 20 years I guess I've taught 10,000 boys to box, or at least tried to teach them," says Martin. "Cassius Clay, when he first began coming around here, looked no better or worse than the majority. About a year later, though, you could see that little smart aleck— I mean, he's *always* been sassy—had a lot of potential. He stood out because, I guess, he had more determination than most boys, and he had the speed to get him someplace."

DURING THE SIX YEARS CASSIUS FOUGHT AS AN AMATEUR IN Louisville, most of that time under the tutelage of Martin, he appeared in 141 fights, an average of close to one match every fortnight. Of these, he lost only seven. Eventually, Cassius won six Golden Gloves titles in Kentucky, and in 1960 won the national Golden Gloves heavyweight title in New York City. ✦ Cassius will half-heartedly admit that his ascension was not all his own doing, but then he adds: "Man, it's like everything else. All the time somebody is telling me, 'Cassius, you know *I'm* the one who made you.' I know some guys in Louisville who used to give me a lift to the gym in their car when my motor scooter was broke down. Now they're trying to tell me they made me, and how not to forget them when I get rich. And my daddy, he tickles me. He says, 'Don't listen to the others, boy; *I* made you.' He says he made me because he fed me vegetable soup and steak when I was a baby, going without shoes, he says, to pay the food bill, and arguing with my mother, who didn't want me eating them things so little. My daddy also says he made me because he saved me from working so I could box—I've never worked a day in my life—and he made me this and he made me that. Well, he's my father and he's the boss, and I have to pay attention. If I had a child who got rich and famous, I know I'd want to cash in too, like my daddy, and I guess more teenagers ought to realize what they owe their folks. But listen here. When you want to talk about who made me, you talk to me. Who made me is *me*."

Whoever it was ("Let's just say he fell off the Christmas tree, a gift-wrapped champion," says Joe Martin sourly), Cassius was on his own when he proved at the Olympics that he was

Even at four Cassius, with younger brother Rudy, was hardly camera shy.

the best amateur boxer in the business. With the frilly, hands-down, showboat style he affected as an amateur and the elaborate dance patterns he used to flit away from danger, he cha-cha-chaed through three rounds with the Polish boy and reduced him to bloody defenselessness. Given a gold medal and, in his mind, a green light to become an international celebrity, he spent the rest of his time in Rome making himself one of the best-known, best-liked athletes in the Olympic Village. "You would have thought he was running for mayor," said one teammate. "He went around introducing himself and learning other people's names and swapping team lapel pins. If they'd had an election, he would have won it in a walk." Says Cassius: "Don't get the wrong idea about all the hand-shaking I did over there. I'm not friendly because I want people to help me; I'm friendly because that's how I am."

One day after winning the gold medal (which Cassius has since worn so much, caressed so much, and displayed so much that its thin 22-carat-gold plate has worn down to the silver beneath) the champion was interviewed by a Soviet newspaperman. "This Commie cat comes up," Cassius relates, "and says, 'Now how do you feel, Mr. Clay, that even though you got a gold medal you still can't go back to the U.S. and eat with the white folks because you're a colored boy?' I looked him up and down once or twice, and standing tall and proud, I said to him: 'Tell your readers we've got qualified people working on that problem, and I'm not worried about the outcome. To me, the U.S.A. is still the best country in the world, counting yours. It may be hard to get something to eat sometimes, but anyhow I ain't fighting alligators and living in a mud hut.' This cat said, 'You really mean that?' and I said, 'Man, of course I mean it. Who do you think I am?' Poor old Commie, he went dragging off without nothing to write the Russians." (Cassius, who can sometimes be discreet and practical beyond his years, has avoided any discussion of segregation since he became the business property of Southern white men. "I don't join any groups or nothing because it might embarrass my sponsors," he says. One day recently at a root beer stand in New Orleans, he was served in a paper cup while his white companion merited a heavily frosted glass mug. "Only thing I got to say," said Cassius, "is when I get a nightclub someday like I hope to, my ticket taker is going to be color-blind. All he will look at is your money.")

A S SOON AS CLAY RETURNED FROM ROME TO HIS HOME AND THE patriotic paint stripes his father had applied to the front steps, he was approached by assorted trainers and managers hoping to take over his professional career. At the time, however, Cassius was thinking about signing a contract with Louisville's Billy Reynolds, a millionaire vice-president of the Reynolds Metals Co. who had known him for two years. Surprisingly, however, Cassius turned down the lucrative 10-year contract Reynolds was offering—mostly because Joe Martin was to figure in Reynolds's plan as a sort of right-hand adviser. For personal reasons—jealousy and so on—Cassius Sr. and Martin nurse a mutual animus, and the senior Clay refused to approve the contract.

In less time than it took to count Reynolds out, a new proposal was made to the Clays. Where before there had been but one rich man, now there were 11, seven of whom had made their first million or better. All Louisville executives with the exception of one New Yorker, the 11 had combined themselves into a syndicate with pooled assets of some 25,000 tax-deductible dollars. Their contract offered Cassius a $10,000 bonus to sign, a $4,000 no-strings guarantee for two years, liberal training allowances and 50% of all earnings.

For a young boxer's first contract, the money offered was singularly impressive, and so were the men putting it up. Principal organizer of the syndicate was Bill Faversham Jr., who had boxed at Groton and Harvard. Faversham, a vice president of Louisville's Brown-Forman distillery (Old Forester, Jack Daniel's) and a big, bustling man of breezy temperament, sold the syndicate idea to such other Louisville friends as W. L. Lyons Brown, a onetime boxer at the Naval Academy and the Brown of Brown-Forman; William Cutchins, the president of Brown-Williamson Tobacco Co. (Raleighs, Viceroys); and Vertner D. Smith Jr., the chairman of a liquor distributing company.

By a most curious set of circumstances, as syndicate members enjoy pointing out, Cassius Clay's mother once cooked for Vertner Smith's wife, and Cassius Clay's aunt, says Lyons Brown, "cooks for my double first cousin." But even without these imponderables, Cassius and his parents were inclined to accept the terms; "the way they talked, the way they carried themselves, the amount of money they had" was enough.

Because none of the syndicate men have had any previous firsthand experience with professional boxing, it is easy to suppose that they have undertaken the development of Cassius' career for much the same reason that other men buy race horses. Even Cassius, though somewhat in awe of his sponsors (a few of whom he has never met), speculates cheerfully that all they want "is to get their change back and a chance to impress their friends by saying, 'That's my boy; after the fight I'll take you back to the dressing room to meet the new champ.'" Regardless of the motive, it is logical to suppose that nothing much better could have happened to Cassius Clay.

"In Cassius," said Bill Faversham the other day, "we saw a good local boy with a clean background from start to finish. With the proper help and encouragement, he could bring credit to himself and his home town. There are plenty of wolves who would leap at the chance to get their paws on Cassius, to exploit him and then to drop him. We think we can bring him along slowly, get him good fights and make him the champion he wants to be."

In its measured, orderly program to bring Cassius up from the bottom, the syndicate began more or less at the top. For what was described as a "most reasonable fee," Cassius began his professional training under the direction of Archie Moore, the light-heavyweight champion of three-fiftieths of the U.S. and the rest of the world. For six weeks last fall, Cassius thrived in the company of the urbane Archie at his San Diego camp. "Then I got homesick," says Cassius. "I was too far away out there." Says Archie, "Well, that's the way of the boxer; they're restless types, especially when they're young like that and unmarried, so I didn't stand in his way. He was coming along real good, though."

Marv Jenson, LaMar Clark's manager (and Gene Fullmer's, too) and a reputable critic, has said of Clay, "He has the fastest hands I've ever seen on a heavyweight anywhere." Archie Moore doesn't lay it on so thick. "He's not as fast as Patterson," says Moore, who, unlike Jenson, has seen Floyd's hands banging away at his own face. Angelo Dundee, a Miami trainer next hired to coach Cassius, says, "Clay's fast enough, don't kid yourself."

"In fact," says Dundee, a warm little Italian of protruding eyes and ears, "I can say a lot of nice things about Cassius—but I can also run down a list of 20 things he does wrong, and I'll hold him back until he shakes them off."

Dundee was not impressed, for instance, last winter when Clay came to Miami spouting such slogans as "People say Cassius Clay fights like Sugar Ray," and coupling with that vanity bits and pieces of style he had picked up from Archie Moore. Said Dundee to Cassius one day, "You, my friend, are neither Sugar Ray Robinson nor Archie Moore, and you've got a long way to go before you will even resemble them. Who you are is Cassius Marcellus Clay Jr., and that's the man I'm going to teach you to fight like. A guy is never going to get anywhere thinking he's somebody else."

WITH THIS SOLEMN PRONOUNCEMENT UNDERSTOOD (OR accepted, or tolerated) by Cassius, Dundee went to work. "I started to smooth him out and put some snap in his punches," says Angelo. "I told him to forget the Olympic head hunting and to dig into the body. I told him to get down off his dancing toes so he could put some power behind his fists." Cassius, serene in his confidence, charitably agrees that "Dundee has done a lot for me," but adds typically, "What has changed the most is my own natural ability."

This summer, after a six-week vacation in Louisville, following a home-town fight with knockout specialist LaMar Clark (whom Clay knocked out), Cassius returned to Miami and Dundee, 15 pounds overweight. He checked into the Sir John Hotel, a rambling, pinkish construction that folds itself around a mint-green swimming pool, in Miami's downtown colored quarter. The next morning, in a plaid madras sport coat, starched khaki pants and "ready" yellow shoes, he swaggered out to greet his public.

Nat & Sonny's Downtown Barber Shop comes to animated life when Cassius swings in the door. "Look who the cat dragged in," says Sonny in a bless-my-soul tone of voice. Cassius gives the collected company the big wave, and when asked whom he'll fight next, his answer is "Johansson in a couple of weeks, and Floyd Patterson, I guess, this winter."

"Sure enough?" says a gullible soul.

"Get him out of here before Floyd walks in and hears him carrying on," says the manicure girl, and Cassius tosses a wink in her direction and waltzes out the door, turning down the sidewalk, laughing, laughing.

"Here comes the boxer, look at that," says a little boy by the curb to his sister. "How you know that?" says Cassius Clay. "I see you skipping along, shadowboxing," the boy says proudly. "What's your name?" he asks Clay. "Sonny Liston, that's me," says Cassius, "and I'm liable to getcha if you don't watch out."

Three blocks along he struts into The Famous Chef café, where he often eats his meals. "Don't you come in here, Cassius Clay, showing off and acting silly. Say now, you hear what I told you?" This is Dorothy, the boss's daughter, says Clay, and it's plain she has his number. "How you like that," says Cassius. "I ain't opened up my mouth yet, and she stands there telling me to hush. Let me have orange juice, four eggs and grits, honey."

Cassius lopes over to the jukebox and drops in the dime that stimulates rock-'n'-roller Dee Clark to unleash Clay's favorite tune, *Your Friends*. "When you are down and out," laments Dee Clark, "there's not a friend in this world to help you out. But when you, when you get on your feet again, everyone will want to be your friend."

"I like to sit here eating and wait for somebody to come up and want to borrow money," Cassius explains. "I don't have to wait long. They'll say, 'Cassius, let me have 10 till payday, my brother.' I don't have to say nothing, just go over and play that record. Then the cat will say, 'You trying to tell me something?' and I'll say, 'Oh, no, my brother, I just wanted to hear that pretty tune. I think there's so much truth in the words, don't you?' "

After his breakfast Cassius wants to go shopping for a new suit and shoes. He takes a cab. "I wonder what my mother is doing with my Cadillac this morning," he says in a loud voice. The cab driver doesn't hear. "How much did that watch cost you?" he asks his companion. Cassius confides that when a wristwatch was given him recently by a Negro civic club in Atlanta, he found a concealed price tag. It cost only $49.50. He mentions it because, gift or not, it didn't cost enough. He rambles on in a loud voice for the driver's benefit: "Sure is a pretty day; day just like this I won that gold medal in Rome last summer. . . . Reminds me of the day they had the parade for me in

In 1961, Clay worked out with future foe Jimmy Ellis (left) and Joe Martin Jr.

Louisville, too. The mayor, everybody was there, man, to welcome me home. Then I went up to Frankfort to see the governor." When Cassius still gets no rise from the driver, he tries a joke he has heard from another boxer. "One day I was fighting Sugar Ray Robinson. Man, I had him scared silly for two rounds. He thought I was dead." The driver is silent and Cassius looks out the window, glumly.

BECAUSE HE GETS HIS HOTEL ROOM ON A SPECIAL RATE THROUGH Angelo Dundee, a friend of the management, Cassius does not get an air conditioner. Sometimes at night, in the stifling heat of his room and in the dim light of an economy-watted lamp, he becomes restless and reflective. "The hardest part of the training is the loneliness," he says. "I just sit here like a little animal in a box at night. I can't go out in the street and mix with the folks out there 'cause they wouldn't be out there if they was up to any good. I can't do nothing except sit. If it weren't for Angelo, I'd go home. It's something to think about. Here I am, just 19, surrounded by showgirls, whisky and sissies, and nobody watching me. All this temptation and me trying to train to be a boxer. It's something to think about.

"But it takes a mind to do right. It's like I told myself when I was little. I said, 'Cassius, you going to win the Olympics some day, and then you're going to buy yourself a Cadillac, and then you're going to be world champ.' Now I got the gold medal, and I got the car. I'd be plain silly to give in to temptation now when I'm just about to reach out and get that world title."   ✦

Rise

GIVE 'IM FIVE Before facing Henry Cooper in London in 1963, Clay predicted a fifth-round KO. Though decked by Hammering Henry, Clay made good on the prediction.

READY TO ROLL Mother and
son tried out young Cassius's
Cadillac. What a ride lay ahead.

A proud Cassius Sr. posed with sons Rudolph (left) and Cassius Jr. in front of the Clay house.

With his 1963 bout against Charlie Powell just hours away, Clay was lost in reflection.

"When a baby he would never sit down. When I would take him for a stroll in his stroller, he would always stand up and try to see every thing. The only thing he was afraid of when a Baby was a fur piece. He tried to talk at a very early age. . . . He learn to walk at 10 months old. When he was one year Old he would love for some One to rock him to sleep, if not, he would sit in a Chair and Keep Bomping his head on the back of the Chair until he would go to sleep."

—ODESSA CLAY'S NOTES ON HER SON,
REPORTED BY JACK OLSEN,
"Growing Up Scared in Louisville," SI, 4/18/1966

NO KID GLOVES Clay KO'd Gary Jawish for the 1960 Inter-City Golden Gloves championship.

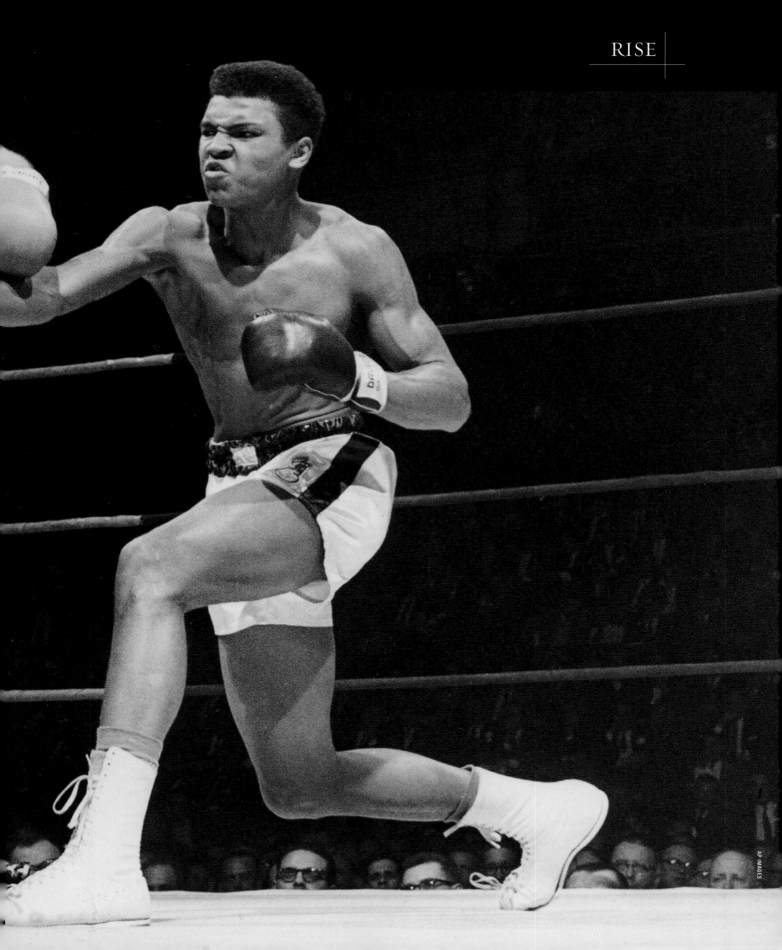

GOLDEN BOY Clay crowned his amateur career with the Olympic light heavyweight title, beating Zbigniew Pietrzykowski of Poland (far right) in the final.

The champ posed with fellow U.S. gold medalists Eddie Crook (left) and Skeeter McClure.

"At 18, Clay was the best of our boxers in Rome, but he never caught a really hard punch. Could he take it if hurt? 'Man,' says Clay. 'I don't want *ever* to get hurt.' "

MARTIN KANE, *"Three for Some Guests,"* SI, 9/19/1960

When in Rome, Cassius was a classicist: He came, he saw, he conquered—in the ring and out.

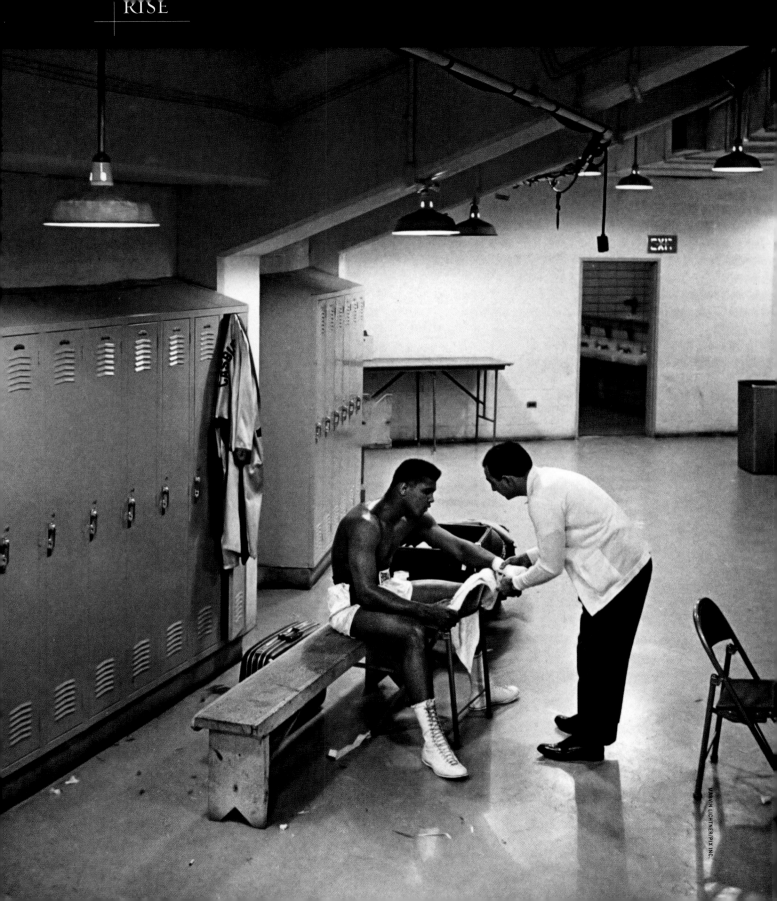

IN GOOD HANDS Upon turning pro, Clay began training under the guidance of Angelo Dundee, who would become a central figure in the champ's entourage.

POOL SHARP Always ready to dive into any promotional stunt, Clay, in his first year as a pro, came up with the idea of shooting this watery workout in Florida.

WONDER YEARS Young Stevie Wonder, along
with Dionne Warwick (between Clay and
Wonder) and Ronnie Spector (arms crossed)
caught the fighter in full voice in 1963

Before taking on Henry Cooper in England, young Cassius made time for his first SI cover.

" 'How tall are you?' said Cassius Clay to Douglas Jones the other day. 'Why do you ask that?' said Jones, warily. 'So's I can know in advance how far to step back when you fall in four,' said Cassius merrily, and waltzed away with his knot of laughing admirers."

HUSTON HORN,
"A Comeuppance for the Cocksure Cassius," SI, 3/25/1963

As the Louisville group learned, there was no such thing as a bored room when Clay presided.

"I'M SOMETHING A LITTLE SPECIAL"

BY CASSIUS CLAY

As he was emerging as the most engaging—and bombastic—athlete of his era, SI asked the future champ to pontificate on his favorite subject: himself

SI, FEBRUARY 24, 1964

I F I WERE LIKE A LOT OF GUYS—A LOT OF HEAVYWEIGHT boxers, I mean—I'll bet you a dozen doughnuts you wouldn't be reading this story right now. If you wonder what the difference between them and me is, I'll break the news: You never heard of them. I'm not saying they are not good boxers. Most of them—people like Doug Jones and Ernie Terrell—can fight almost as good as I can. I'm just saying you never heard of them. And the reason for that is because they cannot throw the jive. Cassius Clay is a boxer who can throw the jive better than anybody you will probably ever meet anywhere. And right there is why I will meet Sonny Liston for the heavyweight championship of the world next week in Miami Beach. And jive is the reason also why they took my picture looking at $1 million in cold cash. That's how much money my fists and my mouth will have earned by the time my fight with Liston is over. Think about that. A Southern colored boy has made $1 million just as he turns 22. I don't think it's bragging to say I'm something a little special.

FLIP SCHULKE/BLACK STAR

POSITIVELY 5TH STREET The young Clay was the picture of beaming optimism in his Miami gym. **47**

Where do you think I would be next week if I didn't know how to shout and holler and make the public sit up and take notice? I would be poor, for one thing, and I would probably be down in Louisville, my hometown, washing windows or running an elevator and saying "yes suh" and "no suh" and knowing my place. Instead of that, I'm saying I'm one of the highest-paid athletes in the world, which is true, and that I'm the greatest fighter in the world, which I hope and pray is true. Now the public has heard me talk enough and they're saying to me, "Put up or shut up." This fight with Liston is truly a command performance. And that's exactly the way I planned it.

Part of my plan to get the fight has made me say some pretty insulting things about Sonny Liston, but I might as well tell you I've done that mostly to get people to talking about the fight and to build up the gate. I actually have a certain amount of respect for Liston; he's the champion, isn't he? That doesn't mean I think he's going to stay champion. I have too much confidence in my own ability to think I'm beaten before we start. I do mean he is a strong, hard puncher, and he's not a fighter anybody can laugh at. When I walk into a room where he is and see him staring at me with that mean, hateful look, I want to laugh, but then I think maybe it's not so funny. I'm pretty sure the way he acts is just a pose, the same way I have a pose, but that look of his still shakes me. I wonder what's really going on in that head of his, and I wonder what poor, humble Floyd Patterson was thinking when he had to climb into the ring with Liston.

But I am not fooled by what Liston did to Patterson once they started to fight. Liston didn't do anything except hit Floyd while he stood there and took it. Now don't think for even a little bit I'm going to stand around for Liston to do with as he pleases. The way I plan for things to go is to stay out of his way during the early rounds, and I count on him to wear himself out chasing me. I'll circle him and jab him and stick and fake, dogging him most of the time and tying him up when he gets too close. He won't be able to hurt what he can't even hit.

Otherwise, I'll fight him the same as I've fought the others. I've been criticized for leaning away from the other man's punches instead of ducking, but I'm not going to change my style. Leaning away is a faster reflex than ducking, and I'll go on doing it until somebody proves it's a mistake—and that somebody has got to be another boxer, not a trainer. They also tell me I carry my hands too low—that it's show-off and dangerous. Well, I just answer, Have you ever seen a mirage on the desert? You can walk along looking for a drink of water, and suddenly you see a lake and you jump in. All you get is a mouthful of sand. Mr. Liston will get a mouthful of leather the same way.

So I'm saying I will win this fight in the eighth round because I think Liston will be worn out by then. If he's not, I sure can go on longer until he is. I'm 22 and he's 34 or 36 and I just don't believe he can outlast me. If I don't win the fight in any round—and "if" is a big word—if I don't win, I still think I will have given Liston a good fight and there is bound to be a rematch. That wouldn't bother me too much, either, because that way I'll be able to have another big payday. I'll just start hollering, "Look out, world, here I come again. I didn't feel too good that night, but now I'm on my way back." I don't think I'd have too much trouble drawing another crowd.

I don't seem to have trouble drawing a crowd anywhere. I can even do it on the sidewalks of New York, where people are used to everything. But when I get a crowd around me, somebody always wants to know if I'm really like the way I act. Well, of course I'm like I act or else I couldn't act this way. But what I have done is to exaggerate the natural way I am. I wouldn't sit around my house shouting and carrying on if it was just me and my folks, but I would if there was anybody else there to hear me. I do that for the reasons I've already said: to attract attention and to get rich. I don't really love to fight, you see, but as long as I'm doing it, I sure don't want to do it for free. I've been boxing since I was 12 years old, and I'm getting mighty tired of training and always having somebody trying to pop me in the mouth. But I probably won't ever get tired of the money. I love money, and we're going to go on like that for a long, long time. The fame and pride of doing something real well—like being the world champion—is a pretty nice thing to think about sometimes, but the money I'm making is nice to think about *all* the time. I suppose it's the one thing that keeps me going.

I REMEMBER ONE DAY IN LOUISVILLE I WAS RIDING A BUS READING IN the paper about Patterson and Ingemar Johansson. It was right after I had won the Olympic gold medal in Rome and had turned professional, and I was confident then I could beat either one of them if I had the chance. But I knew I wouldn't get the chance because nobody much had ever heard of me. So I said to myself, How am I going to get a crack at the title? Well, on that bus I realized I'd never get it just sitting around thinking about it. I know I'd have to start talking about it—I mean really talking, screaming and yelling and acting like some kind of nut. I thought if I did that people would pretty soon hear enough of that and insist I meet whomever was champion. I would be like Gorgeous George, the wrestler, who got so famous by being flashy and exaggerating everything and making people notice him.

You can see how it has turned out—just the way I wanted it to. I started off slow because I was feeling my way, but pretty soon I caught on to what reporters like to hear and what would make the public pay attention. I told this man I was going to knock that boy down in the sixth round, and then I did. I said I am the greatest, I am a ball of fire. If I didn't say it, there was nobody going to say it for me. Then people commenced to say, "What's that loudmouth talking about?" and it grew and it grew. And pretty soon other people were saying I'm the greatest, and I said, "Didn't I tell you so in the first place?" And you know what? The more I talked, the more I convinced myself. I believe in myself so much by now it's embarrassing.

All the time I was building myself up, of course, I was fighting and winning. I don't pretend I fought a lot of great boxers in the beginning, because I certainly did not. I fought a bunch of bums exactly like Liston and Patterson did when they were starting out. But every time I won a fight, I also made a lot of fresh enemies. One thing people can't stand is a blowhard, and the more I blew, the more people would come out to see me get beaten. I said I was pretty (I'm not as pretty as I let on), I said I was fast, I said I was terrific, and it got so you couldn't keep people away. And those that got in would yell, "Take away his pink Cadillac, the bum," and "Bash in his pretty nose," and "Button his fat lip." Well, that's just fine. I don't really care what people say about me personally as long as they buy a ticket to come see me. After they pay their money, they're entitled to a little fun.

After the Doug Jones fight in Madison Square Garden last year, for instance, people who thought Jones should have had the decision got so mad they didn't know what to do. They were booing and screaming and trying to get at me as I walked out of the ring. So I just yelled right back at them to shut up or I'd beat their ears off, and all the way to the dressing room I was thinking, "Cassius, you are even better than Gorgeous George. You have just made a whole lot more enemies and every one of them will be back for your next fight. Only then the tickets are going to cost more."

Of course, the real way I built up my fame was by predicting the round I would knock out some guy. I forget now when I first started doing that and how many times it has worked, but I know it has worked most of the time. How do I do it? I do it by trying extra hard and the other boxer helps by worrying extra hard. Sometimes, though, I tell reporters who don't know me that I hear voices in the night saying, "You'll win in five, no jive," or something. I did that in England when I fought Henry Cooper and the reporters' eyes got big and round and they wrote down every word. Those English were sure I was crazy. The only voices I hear, of course, are people telling me I can't do what I say.

Already they're saying I can't get Liston in eight. Maybe I can and maybe I can't, but you better believe he's wondering about the same thing right this minute. If I do get him like I say, there won't be anybody who will care, because they'll be for Liston anyway. It's easier to like an ugly old man than it is to like a loudmouth kid, and everybody wants him to teach me a lesson. But just as sure as I do the teaching and win, people will say, "Aw, so what? Liston was nothing anyway." People are hypocrites, if you don't know that already.

Folks ask me what I'll do if I win and what I'll do if I don't win, but I don't have the answer yet. I have to go into the Army pretty soon, and after that I don't know. Maybe I'll build a big housing project and get married and settle down and think about being rich. But I'm not too worried. I think I can make it in something else the same way I've made it in boxing. If things go wrong in the fight, I'll just wait a while. Summertime comes, flowers start blooming, little birds start flying and you wake up, get up and get out. You change with the times. ✦

ON THE RISE At the Rome Olympics in 1960, Clay won gold—and his first taste of fame.

Rumble

{ 1963 - 1966 }

ALI TAKES A CROWN AND A CAUSE

BY ANGELO DUNDEE
WITH TEX MAULE

Ali was the calm in the eye of the storm as he embraced the Black Muslims, changed his name and beat Sonny Liston—twice
SI, AUGUST 21, 1967

CASSIUS CLAY HAS ALWAYS HAD A GENIUS FOR creating excitement before his fights, but I doubt that even he will ever be able to match the uproar he brought about before the first championship fight with Sonny Liston in Miami Beach. ✦ Not many people gave him a chance against Liston. Sonny had demolished Floyd Patterson twice and was generally regarded as a superman. Some columnists even said that the fight should be canceled, warning that Liston might do permanent injury to poor little Cassius. None of this had any effect on Clay. He was the same fighter in the gym he had always been, and he was as confident of beating Liston as he had been of beating any of the fighters he had met during the three years I trained him before the championship match. ✦ He took the psychological play away from Liston early, with the help and encouragement of Drew Brown. I don't know how much effect all their antics had on Sonny, but they did one thing—they began to destroy the image of the superman that Liston had used to psych most of

SO PRETTY Clay peppered the older Liston with short, sharp shots—and danced off with the title. **55**

NEIL LEIFER

his opponents. Liston had a thing going for him. He always tried to look bigger and meaner than life. I mean, he would come into the ring for a workout wearing a hood and a robe with a couple of towels under the shoulders, so that he looked even bigger than he was. In training he'd go through the routine with the medicine ball, letting Willie Reddish pound him in the stomach with it, and if you didn't know better you had to believe he really was superhuman. Any fighter in good condition can take a medicine ball in the belly. It's so big it distributes the impact. A fist in a glove, thrown as hard, is a different thing.

Aside from the antics Clay went through to bug Liston, he created additional excitement by admitting—or proclaiming—for the first time that he was a Muslim. The first I heard about it was when Bill McDonald, the promoter, came to the gym in a sweat one afternoon. "There are rumors around town that Clay is a Black Muslim," he told me, very excited. "This can kill the gate! You have to get him to deny it, Angie. Tell him what he's doing to me."

I told him to talk to Clay himself, and he and Cassius went off together for about half an hour. Then McDonald left, very unhappy. I asked Clay what happened.

"He says if I am a Muslim he may have to call the fight off," Clay said. He wasn't disturbed. "Look like they may not be a fight, Angie."

I don't know if his announcing his membership in the Muslims hurt the gate or not, but I knew Clay well enough to know that once he had made his mind up no one would ever change it. Funny thing is that I should have suspected it earlier. There were some Muslims hanging around the gym before the fight, but I didn't recognize them. Once Malcolm X came in, and McDonald wanted to get him out of the gym right away, before any reporters saw him. He left quietly.

After Clay told reporters that he had joined the Muslims, I used to sit in the gym next to a big guy named Sam Saxon and tell him it was a shame what was happening to Clay and how much I hoped that he would give up the Muslim idea. I thought he was just off on a kick and that he would get over it, and I told Saxon that. Saxon would nod and smile a little and not say anything. Then one day while I was talking to him, another man came up to him and called him Captain Sam, and that was the first I knew that he was a Muslim.

It was at this time, too, that Cassius decided he would be called Muhammad Ali. That was all right with me. My name was Mirena before I had it changed legally to Dundee. Joe Louis's real name is Barrow. I could give you a dozen or more instances of fighters who have changed their names.

I did suggest to Muhammad that he keep Cassius Clay as a ring name and use Muhammad Ali in private. I pointed out that he had built up a big reputation as Cassius Clay and it would be foolish to change, but he said that Elijah Muhammad had given him the name of Muhammad Ali and that he was going to use it. I didn't try to argue with him.

By the time of the weigh-in, he had managed to get everyone on edge. He had heckled Liston at the airport and at his training quarters. He had turned McDonald gray, and he had made most of the writers forget the image of Liston as the unbeatable monster. The scene at the weigh-in was his own idea, and I was as surprised as everyone else when he brought it off. I knew when it started that it wasn't serious, though. He was yelling and screaming and trying to get at Liston, and I was holding him back—with one finger. He believes his own scenes after a while, and when they took his pulse rate and blood pressure both of them were way up. For a little while the commission doctor threatened to call off the fight, but I had Dr. Ferdie Pacheco check him at his house later in the afternoon and everything was normal. He laughed and said, "Did I have Liston shook up? I shook him up, didn't I?" He shook up Liston and a lot of other people.

THE NIGHT OF THE FIGHT HE WAS ICE-COLD. HE CAME IN A LITTLE early and stood in the aisle and watched his brother in a preliminary. The photographers were shooting pictures of him, with the flashes going off in his face, and I wanted them to stop. But he said it didn't bother him. Nothing really bothers Ali. He can be the most completely undisturbed man I have ever known. ✦ After he reached the dressing room, Sugar Ray Robinson came in to wish him luck. Ali was loosening up, dancing around and shadowboxing, and he was relaxed and happy. He went into the shower room and said his prayers, the way you see him do it now before a fight. That was the first time I ever noticed him doing this.

When I started wrapping his hands, Reddish came in to watch. Willie put in his little bit to psych Muhammad, but it didn't work.

"My man is going to get you," he said.

Ali laughed at him.

"Man, I'll get *him*," he said.

Liston didn't really present much of a problem. I was confident from the time the bout was made that we could take him. I told Ali to dance and move and make him miss, and he did that and Liston didn't reach him at all in the first three rounds. Ali would feint a punch and then not throw it. Sonny would react and Ali would give him a target to shoot at and he'd shoot and miss. Liston had to plant himself to punch, and in those first few rounds he was throwing his left hand so hard that his fist turned when he missed. When you punch that hard and miss you wear yourself out, and that's what happened to Liston. He found out he couldn't hit Ali, and that made him more mad and tired him even more.

Sonny also found out that Ali could hit him and dance away, and he turned desperate after that. Ali throws punches that break people up. He turns his hand just as it lands, and it punishes. He was breaking Liston up. I always thought that Liston was made to order for Ali, and he showed it in Miami Beach. Liston had to be able to hit you with the left jab. If he could do that and set and punch, he could take you. But he was big and slow, and I knew if he missed many punches he would get tired and discouraged.

The only real problem in that fight was in the fourth round, when some of the coagulant they put on a cut near Liston's eye got on Ali's forehead and then into his eyes from the sweat coming down. He came back to the corner and said that his eyes were burning, that he wanted to take off his gloves and stand up and tell everyone that there was foul play, but I wouldn't let him. "This is a championship," I told him. I shoved him into the ring at the bell. "Stay away from him," I hollered. "Run!"

I knew he wasn't kidding. His eyes were red and watering. I had been running plain water over them to clear them. I tasted the water in the bucket to make sure there wasn't anything in it and then I put my finger in the corner of his eye. Then I put it in my own eye and it stung. So I figured it had to be something on Liston's face that caused it.

Before the fight, oddly, Liston had tried to give Ali the evil eye. He was built up, as usual, with two towels under his robe and the big hood to make him look more impressive, but he didn't impress Ali at all. He tried to stare Ali down, and Ali laughed at him. "I ain't no Patterson," he told Liston. "I got *you,* sucker."

By the end of the sixth round Liston knew he was whipped. His shoulder might have been hurt, but it wouldn't have made any difference if it had been healthy. He knew he was in the ring with a better man. When it was all over, Ali was the heavyweight champion of the world. The group gave me a $20,000 bonus for the fight, which was the first real money I made out of training Ali.

ALI WENT OFF TO TOUR AFRICA, AND I WAS BUSY WITH THE other fighters I train. We signed to fight Liston again, in Boston, and when Ali came back from Africa I got a shock. He'd had a good time in Africa, understandably. But when he came into the gym he weighed 245 pounds and he was fat. He'd had a ball in Africa, but he paid for it. He was ashamed of the way he looked; he used to walk to the gym in a rubber suit, trying to sweat off the weight, but it came off hard. I think one of the things that ruins a fighter is ballooning between fights and then having to work to take the weight off again. This was the only time it happened to Ali. He is proud of the way he looks and he doesn't let himself gain much weight between fights. The Africa tour was a special thing.

We took it slow and easy at first. I didn't want to burn him out trying to get the fat off. Actually, I think the extra weight brought on the hernia that postponed the second Liston fight. When it happened, it was a complete surprise. We were in Boston, and it happened on a Friday evening. I'm a football nut and Boston College was playing Miami that night. I was watching the game on television with Johnny Crittenden, a Miami sportswriter. Luther Evans was doing the color on the show and he came on between the first and second quarters and said that the Clay-Liston fight was off because Clay had just been taken to the hospital with a severe hernia. I thought he must be kidding, but he said it again and I ran out and jumped into a cab and said, "Take me to the hospital." The cab driver looked at me like I was nuts. "There are 20 hospitals in Boston. Which one?" he said.

I had to go back to the hotel and find out which hospital they took him to. By the time I got there they had a police guard outside his room to keep out all the people who wanted to get in. By the time he got over the operation and started working again the fight had been moved to Lewiston. I figured that the thing Ali had to do in the second fight was remind Liston what had happened to him in the first fight.

"The thing that sticks in my craw," I told Ali, "is that he thinks he can lick you. You got to take that confidence away from him early. You got to bring back memories of Miami Beach." So our plan was to get off fast and then coast and make Liston fight our fight.

As usual, the scene before the fight was pretty hectic. One afternoon me and some other people went out to the arena in Ali's red Cadillac to check the ring and see if it was regulation. It was a good thing we did, because the ring they had in Lewiston was a wrestling ring, as bouncy as a trampoline. Eventually they had to ship in a boxing ring from Baltimore. A ring as soft as the first one would have cut Ali's speed down and been a big advantage for Liston.

Anyway, after we went out there in the red car and checked out the ring, some writers had it that a bunch of Muslim opponents had been out casing the place, hoping to shoot Ali and get revenge for the assassination of Malcolm X. I think if I had been Ali I might have skipped the whole thing, but nothing bothers him. One thing he got out of being a Muslim was a sure faith that Allah is taking care of him.

Physically, he was in perfect shape. He had no ill effects from the hernia operation, and he trained real well. He is not an impressive gym fighter. I don't like my fighters to go in for vicious workouts in the gym. I like them to *train* in the gym, not fight. If they have to fight for their lives every afternoon in the gym, it only shortens their careers. Ali and Jimmy Ellis had ideal workouts. They were always trying to outthink each other, and they learned from each other all the time. They didn't try to make punching bags out of each other. I could tell when Ali was ready by his moves. The sharper he got, the better he moved and the easier he made the moves. When he came back from Africa, before he got the hernia, he could barely move at all. He got decked by a sparring partner, Chip Johnson, because he couldn't get out of the way. When they had finished the round, Johnson said to Ali, "It was an accident, man. You was off balance."

"No I wasn't," Ali said. "I just ain't ready. You hit me."

He never kidded himself about things like that. So he knew very well that he was ready in Lewiston, and he did just what we had decided he should do. He walked out of his corner and—blip!—he hit Sonny a good shot in the mouth and knocked him right out of whatever plan he had for this fight. I guess Liston would have liked to wait and stalk and make Ali commit himself, but after Ali gave him that token of what had happened in Miami Beach he came after the champ. And he got tagged with a perfect right hand and was knocked out. That punch was a counter over a left jab that missed, leaving Liston coming in off balance with his head down. The right caught him flush on the side of his face. He never saw the punch.   ✦

Rumble

THE AFTERMATH Ali, with TV announcer Steve Ellis, described his shocking first-round KO of Sonny Liston in their second bout.

SWING AND A MISS Clay shocked the champion with his elusiveness and stung him repeatedly with sharp jabs and flashing combinations.

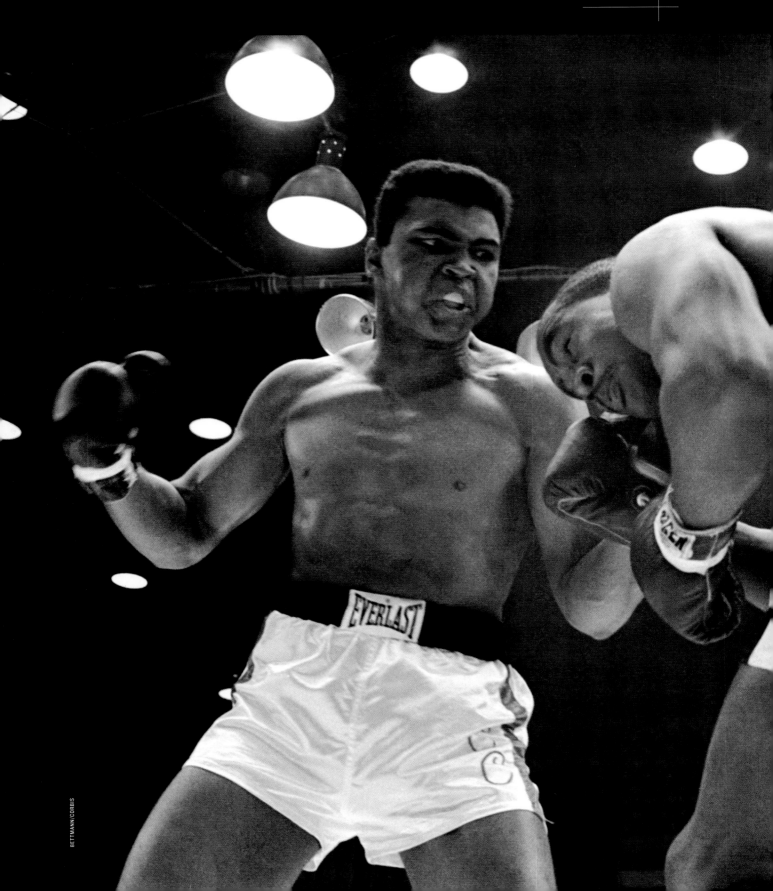

"The Fifth Street Gym in Miami Beach is an inelegant establishment on the second floor of a two-story building. It is small, hot and, these days, crowded with spectators who will endure almost any hardship to watch Cassius Marcellus Clay prepare himself mentally as well as physically for his challenge for the heavyweight championship of the world."

TEX MAULE, *"The Sting of the Louisville Lip,"* SI, 2/17/1964

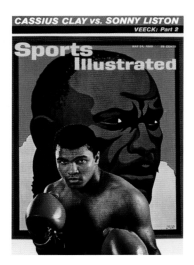

It was monkey business as usual for the challenger as he prepared to face Sonny Liston for the title.

Ali was champ now, but as the rematch approached, Liston still loomed large in the public's mind.

BAITED Ali, wielding a bear trap, did not amuse the stolid Liston (in car).

WORLDS
HEAVYWEIGHT
CHAMPIONSHIP
FEB. 25 - 19[
LAY VS LISTO[
PRICES
$ 20.00
50.00
100.00
150.00
200.00
250.00

THE LIP *Giving new meaning to the term "gate mouth," a pop-eyed Clay hyped the fight.*

Fresh off two first-round KOs of Floyd Patterson, Liston saw Clay as another easy payday.

"Liston, the champion after a couple of unsettling knockouts of Floyd Patterson, was considered indomitable. He fit in with America's principal value at the time: Bigger is better. He was a 9-to-1 favorite at one point and the expert opinion was that the ringside physician had better have some postmortem experience."

—RICHARD HOFFER,
"A Lot More Than Lip Service," SI, 11/29/1999

The challenger, far from awed, never missed a chance to mock Liston's brooding-killer image.

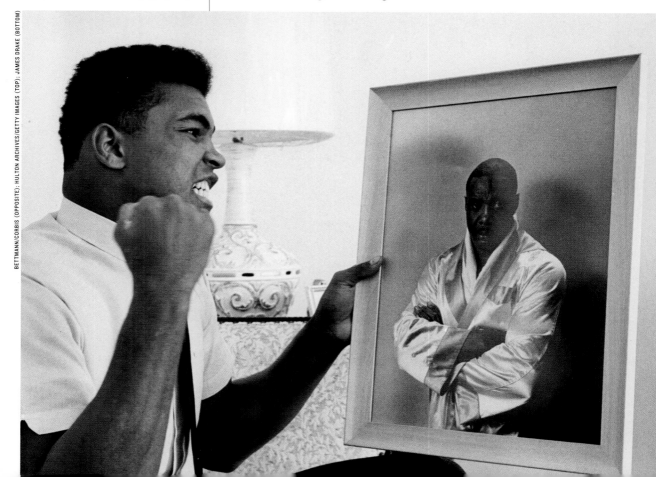

"In winning, the incomparable Clay, that child of scorn, showed that he will possibly be champion for as long as he wants, that he has everything going for him except a true knockout punch and, perhaps—for who can divine the strange things that move this man—he has that, too."

GILBERT ROGIN,
"Champion As Long As He Wants," SI, 11/29/1965

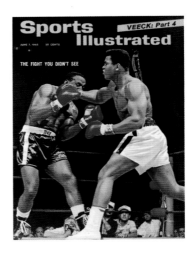

In the rematch with Liston, Ali came out aggressively, setting the stage for a controversial finish.

SI's cover referred to the "phantom" punch that sent Liston to the canvas in Lewiston, Maine.

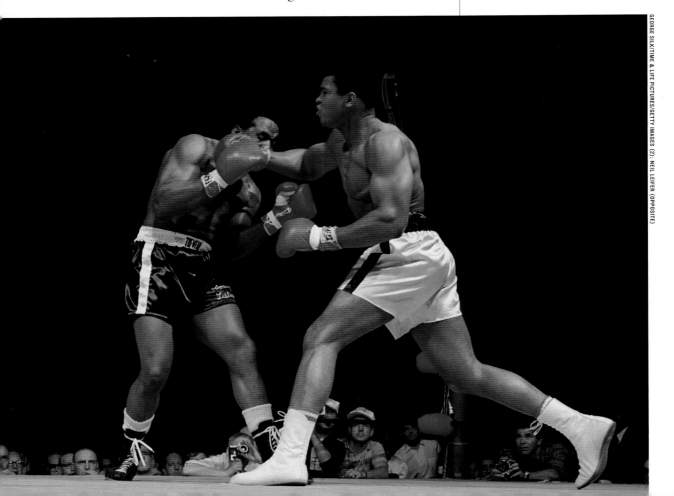

GET UP! Shouting for Liston to rise, Ali produced one of boxing's most iconic images.

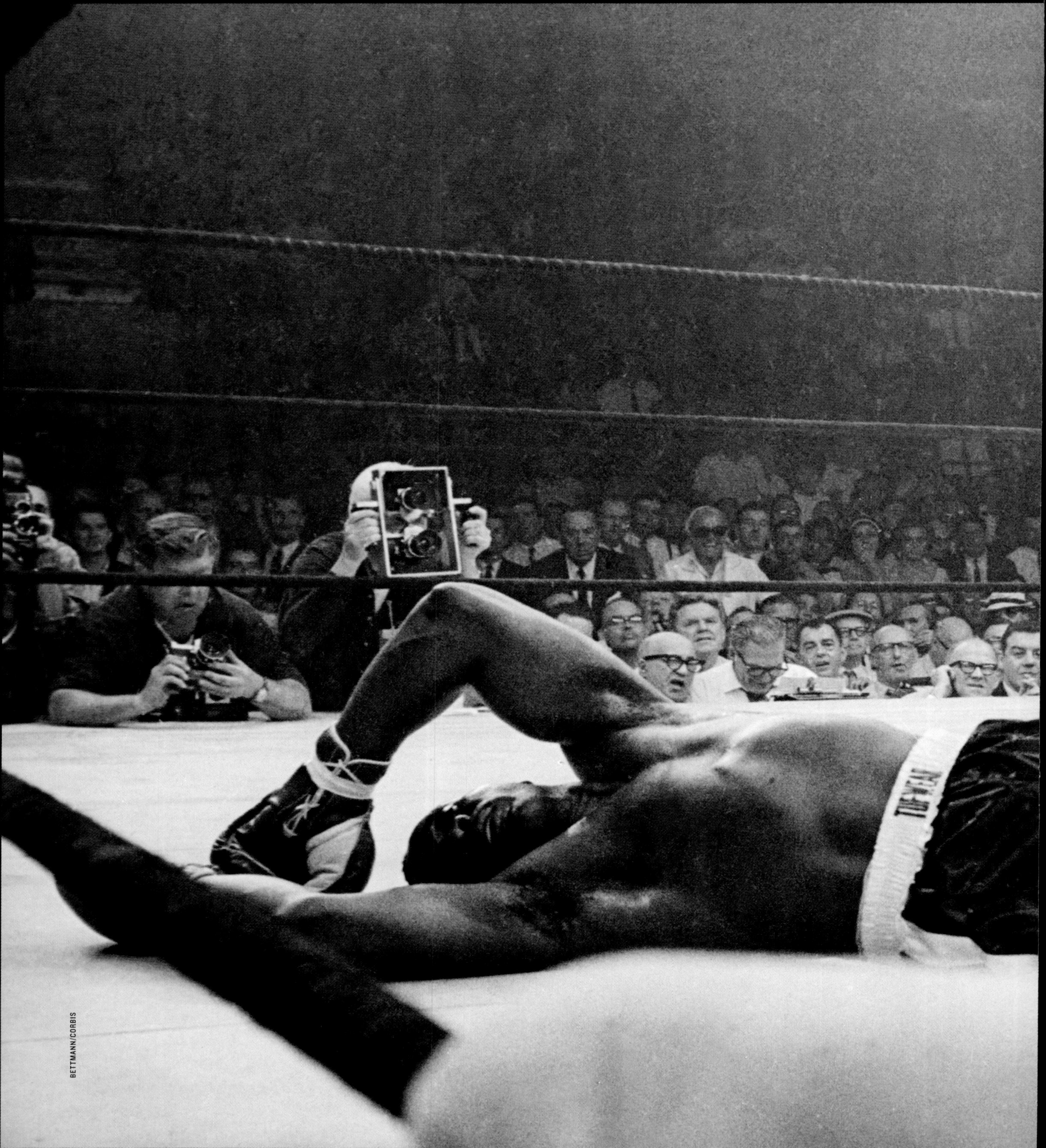

BETTMANN/CORBIS

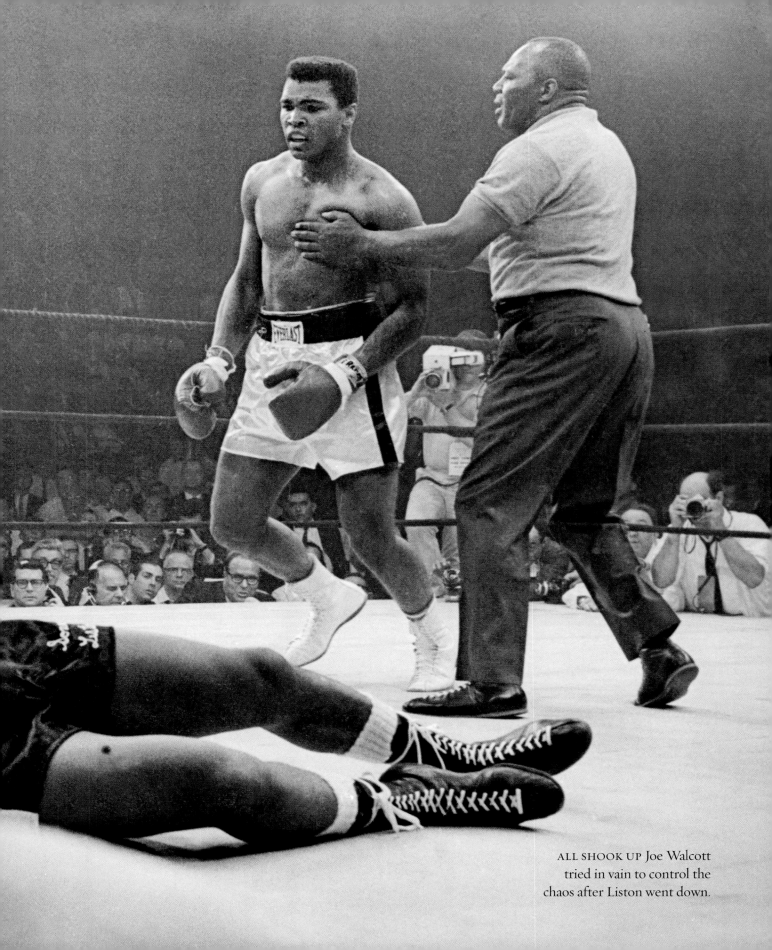

ALL SHOOK UP Joe Walcott
tried in vain to control the
chaos after Liston went down.

MAINE EVENT The Ali legend was partially forged in his rematch with Liston in a Lewiston hockey arena amid bomb threats and heavy security.

THE WORLD CHAMPION IS REFUSED A MEAL

BY GEORGE PLIMPTON

*The young heavyweight champion of the world stopped
for a bite to eat on the Florida-Georgia border—and
was told to eat out back with his kind*

SI, MAY 17, 1965

BUNDINI BROWN SAID, "LET'S STOP AND EAT. I'm empty." No one said anything. It was dark outside, the pine forests stretching back from the road, their thin trunks showing up as sticks of gray in the headlights. Four or five miles up the road the Muslim driver slowed down and turned the champion's bus into a truck stop near the Florida-Georgia border. Yulee, the name of the place was. The big gas pumps, which displayed the Pure Firebird gasoline emblems, stood in pools of light from overhead standards, and there were a few diesel truck trailers parked across the macadam-topped lot. The restaurant had a small neon light in the window. The champion's brother, Rudy, said: "You're goin' to watch a man face reality—that's what you're goin' to see." ✦ Bundini, whose name is pronounced without the first *n*, climbed down from the bus and headed for the restaurant. With the bus motor switched off it was quiet outside and warm, with the day's heat still rising from the blacktop. The reporters walked with Brown, holding

IN THE PICTURE Malcom X was behind the young champ—figuratively and literally—in 1964. **75** themselves stiffly, hoping there would be no shame. There were four of them—invited by the champion to join his entourage for the trip north in his private bus, a ramshackle vehicle he calls Big Red, from Miami to Chicopee Falls, Mass., where he intended to do his prefight training.

The champion and his group and the sparring partners left the bus, but they stood back near the pumps. Cody Jones, the sparring partner they call The Porcupine for his swept-up hair style, stared up at the steel standards, watching the moths flutter in the strong flat light.

Bundini led a procession across the lot to the restaurant. He was wearing a blue denim jacket with BEAR HUNTING in red script across the back. He is the champion's trainer—an effervescent figure responsible for much of the flamboyant activity in the champion's camp. He has led a full life—in the CCC when he was 11, the merchant marine at 13. At 15, having falsified his age, he was fighting with the naval forces in the Pacific—at Bougainville, among other places. His real name is Drew Brown. Sometimes he says Bundini means "lover" in Pakistani and, at other times, when he is more serious, he says it means "wise man" in Hindustani. He is one of the few in the champion's entourage, other than sparring partners, who is not a member of the separatist Black Muslim sect. The Muslims have tried without success to fetch him. Elijah Muhammad, the Muslim leader, wrote him a letter in which he was reported to have said, "If I had 10 men like you I could conquer the world." Sometimes, on the bus, the Muslims called him "The Integrator," scornfully, though all of them, the champion particularly, have difficulty getting the epithet acid enough. They appreciate Bundini and like him too much.

The restaurant had a screen door that squeaked and the people inside, six or seven couples sitting in the booths, looked up when Bundini and the others came in. He sat down at the counter, the reporters on stools to either side. The waitress looked and the group and put her hands together. The manager came out from behind the counter. "I'm sorry," he said. "We have a place out back. Separate facilities," he said. "The food's just the same." Through the serving window the reporters could see two negro cooks looking out. "Probably better," the manager said with a wan smile. He talked at the reporters as if Bundini was not there. Bundini's face began working. The reporters could not look at him, so they began intimidating the manager, whipping whispered furious words at him. He stayed calm, tapping a grease-stained menu against his fingertips. "In this county—Nassau County—they'd be a riot," he said simply. In the booths the people continued eating, watching over their forks as they lifted the food and put it into their mouths.

Bundini said: "The heavyweight champion of the world and he can't get nothing to eat here." He spoke reflectively, and he spun around on his stool and stood up.

The screen door squeaked again and slapped shut. The champion stood in the room, leaning forward slightly and staring at Bundini. He began shouting at him. "You fool— what's the matter with you—you damn *fool*." His nostrils were flared, his voice almost out of control. "I tol' you you ought to be a Muslim. Then you don' go places where you're not wanted. You clear out of this place, nigger, you ain't wanted here, can't you *see*, they don' want you, nigger. . . ." He reached for Bundini's denim jacket, hauled him toward him and propelled him out the door in an easy furious motion, Bundini so preoccupied that he offered no resistance. He stumbled out on the macadam as if he had been launched from a sling.

The champion rushed after him, pushing him for the bus, still vilifying him. Then he broke away from Bundini and began leaping among the gas pumps and out across the macadam under the flat, eerie light, circling among the trailers, one with a multi-thousand-

The ebullient Bundini Brown was the irrepressible heart of the Ali entourage.

dollar yacht balanced in its cradle—a lunatic backdrop for the champion's frenzy that suddenly became as gleeful as a child's. "I'm *glad*, Bundini!" he shouted. "I'm glad—you got *showed*, Bundini, you got *showed*."

Bundini's shoulders were hunched over and he was looking at his feet. "Leave me alone," he kept repeating. "I'm good enough to eat here!" he shouted suddenly. "I'm a free man. God made me. Not Henry Ford."

The champion whooped with delight. He leaped high in the air and circled Bundini as if he had him quarried. "Don' you know when you not *wanted*? Face reality and dance!" he shouted.

Bundini cried back at him, "I'll be what I was, what I always been—in my heart I'm a free man . . . no slave chains 'round *my* heart." He broke past the circling champion and escaped into the bus.

The rest of the group stood by and watched the champion, still capering and shouting, begin to wind down. His brother stalked about, his face lit with excitement, repeating like a litany: "A man has seen reality, seen re-al-i-ty." One of the reporters went to look in through a window at the room in back. It was off the kitchen, a table with just enough room for six chairs. An old magazine lay tossed in a corner. When the champion had calmed down, the tree-frog buzz began drifting across the macadam lot from the dark pine and swampland.

But when the bus was reloaded, and the Muslim driver got it moving again along Route 17, the turmoil started afresh. The champion leaned over the top of his seat and kept railing at Bundini, a constant castigation: "Uncle Tom! Tom! Tom! Tom!" and when Bundini

Ali could be harsh to Bundini, called by the Muslims in camp "the Integrator."

attempted to answer the champion leaned over and muzzled him with a red pillow.

The champion shouted: "This teach you a lesson, Bundini!" He leaned over and pushed down on Bundini's head. "You bow your head, Bundini."

"Leave me alone!" Bundini shouted. "My head don' belong between my knees. It's up in the stars. I'm free. I keep trying. If I find a water hole is dry, I go on and find another."

The exchange was carried on in full volume, the rhetoric high-blown and delivered carefully, as if the lines were from a memorized morality play.

"You *shamed* yourself back there," the champion shouted.

"*They* were ashamed!" Bundini said.

"What good did that do, except to shame you?"

"That man," said Bundini. "That manager. He'll sleep on it. He may be no better, but he'll think on it, and he'll be ashamed. I dropped a little medicine in that place."

The champion whooped. "Tom! Tom! Tom!" He whacked a series of quick blows at Bundini with the red pillow. "You belong to your white master."

"To a fool it may seem like that!" Bundini shouted at him. "But to a man who's been around the world he know the world is a black shirt with three white buttons."

"Bougainville!" the champion shouted scornfully. "If I hadn't pull you out of that place back there, those crackers'd *killed* you!"

It got to Bundini finally, and he began to cry. He is a man with his emotions close to the surface, and with his face wide and mobile, his grief is unbearable to watch, his face a perfect reflection of the mask of tragedy. The champion looked at him.

"Hey, Bundini," he said softly. He mopped at Bundini's face with the red pillow—clumsy but affectionate swipes.

"Leave me alone," Bundini said, barely audible.

The champion tried to make him laugh. He made funny sounds at him, the routines the two did in unison at the training camp. "Hey, Bundini," he said. "What sort of crackers was they back in that restaurant?"

Bundini did not want to answer.

"I'll tell you what kind of crackers. They was soda crackers. And if they're soda crackers, that makes you a graham cracker. That's what you are—a *graham cracker*."

Bundini did not say anything.

The champion gave a great whooping laugh and belted Bundini on the top of the head with the red pillow. Bundini's shoulders began shaking, now from laughter.

"Champ," he said, "les' just train and fight—none of the other stuff. Why you make us come this way?" he said resignedly. "We could have flown over all these miserable miles."

"Don' fly over it, Bundini," the champion said, in an odd shift of doctrine, which is part of the paradox of him and makes him so difficult to judge. "You fight it out, Bundini," he said, ". . . like your aunts and uncles have to do."

Bundini looked at him, and not far down the road, seeming to take his counsel, he said again: "I'm empty. I want to eat. A Howard Johnson's coming up."

"We'll stop," the champion said grimly. He was again a Muslim. "This is Georgia, Bundini. You haven't been *showed*?" he asked incredulously.

When the bus was parked in the lot, this time the sparring partners joined Bundini and the reporters, a grim group moving up the path for the restaurant with its bright windows and the illuminated orange-peaked cupola roof; behind, the Muslim contingent stood by the bus, with the champion's brother once again calling out, his voice tense with excitement, "You facing reality, Bundini, reality."

The restaurant, which was nearly full, went silent at the group's entrance, and a cocktail ensemble playing *Tea for Two* was nearly deafening over the Muzak; in the booths forks and spoons were poised, perhaps not surprisingly: the group was apprehensive, considering what happened in Yulee, very grim and walking stiffly, eyes flicking everywhere to see where the first rebuff would come from, a formidable group, too, with the boxers part of it, tattoos showing on their broad arms. A sheriff, if he had been sitting there, might well have stepped up and arrested the whole troupe on suspicion.

The group gathered around a long table and sat down. A waitress appeared with a stack of menus. "You all look *hungry*," she said brightly. She began passing out the menus.

Bundini began giggling. "My," he said. "No one mind if I sit at the head of the table?" The seats were rearranged, and Bundini pointed out the window at the Muslims standing by the bus. "I'm going to eat three steaks standing up so's they's can see," he said.

The champion came in after a while, striding through the restaurant, the people watching him, and those with children getting ready to push them up for autographs.

"What you doin' here," Bundini said smugly. "This place only for integrators."

The champion smiled at him and sat down. He had his meal and when his coffee came he said: "Bundini, I'm goin' to integrate the coffee." He poured some cream into it. "When it's black, it's strong."

Bundini shook his head. The two were smiling at each other. "Champ," said Bundini once again. "Les' just train and fight—none of the other stuff." ◆

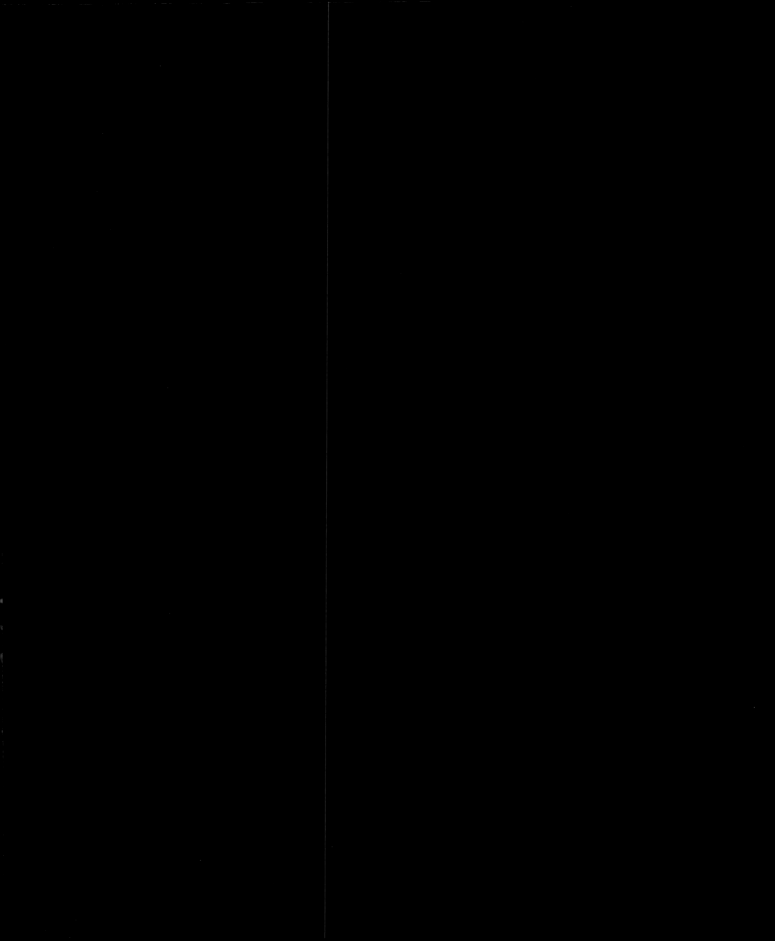

Exile

{ 1966 – 1969 }

TAPS FOR THE CHAMP

BY EDWIN SHRAKE

Ali refused the symbolic step forward that would put him in the Army—his religious beliefs forbade it. Here began the eclipse of boxing's brightest star

SI, MAY 8, 1967

AS HE LOOKED AT HIMSELF IN THE MIRROR behind the coffee-shop counter at the Hotel America in Houston early last Friday, on perhaps his final morning as heavyweight champion, Muhammad Ali was wondering how history would reflect upon him. The idea that he is a historical figure, a leader of his people, a Muslim Davy Crockett, had become an obsession and a consolation to Ali as the time approached for him to refuse to be inducted into the armed forces of the United States. ✦ Three days earlier, at lunch in another hotel, he had said, "I've left the sports pages. I've gone onto the front pages. I want to know what is right, what'll look good in history. I'm being tested by Allah. I'm giving up my title, my wealth, maybe my future. Many great men have been tested for their religious belief. If I pass this test, I'll come out stronger than ever. I've got no jails, no power, no government, but 600 million Muslims are giving me strength. Will they make me the leader of the country? Will they give me gold? Will the Supreme Being knock down the jails with an earthquake, like He could if He want? Am I a fool to give up my wealth and my title and go lay in prison? Am I a fool to give

WALK THE LINE Ali was grim as he left the Houston Customs House after refusing induction.   **83** up good steaks? Do you think I'm serious? If I am, then why can't I worship as I want to in America? All I want is justice. Will I have to get that from history?"

Now, as he poked a fork at four soft-boiled eggs and drank a tall glass of orange juice and a cup of coffee, Muhammad Ali—or Cassius M. Clay Jr., as it says on the legal documents that his lawyers carry into court in two cardboard boxes—was being moved by the clock toward his most fateful encounter since the night in 1964 when he knocked out Sonny Liston in Miami Beach. That one got him the heavyweight championship, and this one could lose it for him. "But not in the eyes of the people," he said. "The people know the only way I can lose my title is in the ring. My title goes where I go. But if they won't let me fight, it could cost me $10 million in earnings. Does that sound like I'm serious about my religion?"

"Come on, Champ, come on," said his New York attorney, Hayden Covington. "We've got 25 minutes."

"If we're one minute late, they're liable to shove you behind bars," his Houston attorney, Quinnan Hodges, said.

"All right, man, all right," said Ali. "If you want to go, let's go."

They went out onto the street and packed the entourage into two taxicabs for the ride to the Armed Forces Examining and Entrance Station on the third floor of the U.S. Custom House at 701 San Jacinto Street in Houston. The morning was cool and gray, elephant-colored, with a touch of mist coming down. Earlier, Ali had said he would walk to the induction center from the Hotel America, a distance of about a mile, or from his apartment in South Houston, six miles out into a Negro district. But "the champ don't feel up to it, anyhow," said Bundini Brown, Ali's sometime assistant trainer. The night before, Ali and Brown had been up until nearly 2 a.m., talking. Ali was working off his vast energy.

"It was like the night before a fight," Bundini said. "The champ had got to talk and talk until he can fall asleep without tossing and turning."

Ali was still in the shower when Covington and Hodges went up to fetch him at 6:30 a.m. He dressed quickly, putting on a tailored blue suit, reassuring his lawyers he would not be late. "He was a lot cooler than we were," Hodges said.

AT THE INDUCTION CENTER THERE WAS A CROWD OF REPORTERS and photographers but only a few curious spectators standing on the steps and on the broad walk that led into the building. Ali got out of his cab shortly before 8 a.m. When the lights of the television cameras went on, Ali shoved Bundini away from him. Although he is largely in sympathy with the Muslims, Bundini is not a convert, and they did not want his face appearing at the champion's shoulder. Ali pushed through the crowd, paused on the steps to smile for the cameras and entered an elevator in the lobby. There was such a crush of people that many of the 26 pre-induction examinees who were reporting that morning for Houston's

Board No. 61 could not get on the elevator, causing the examination schedule to begin 15 minutes late. One of the PIEs, John McCulloch, 22, of Sam Houston State College, was forced back against the wall by the wake of the champion's following. Clutching his canvas overnight bag—an item Ali did not bother to bring, since he knew he would not be leaving on the 6 p.m. bus for Fort Polk, La.—McCulloch said, "I feel kind of sorry for the old guy. He can't get away from all this mess."

On the third floor Ali was taken down the hall past a barrier guarded by soldiers. After roll call he began his physical examination. A mental examination was not required, because the results of Ali's previous mental exam were available to processing personnel. "It was great, the way he came in," said Ron Holland, a PIE transfer from Escondido, Calif. " 'You all look very dejected,' he told us. 'I'm gonna tell you some jokes.' He was very cheerful. He cheered us all up. He talked about Floyd Patterson. I asked him about that Russian who is supposed to be such a good boxer, and he said, 'We'll take care of him.' He told us his mind was made up. He said if he went into the Army and the Viet Cong didn't get him, some redneck from Georgia would. He was in good spirits. I got his autograph. I've been in this examining center before, and this was the first time I've been treated so well. I think the Army was trying to impress the champ. He even told me to hang around and he'd see that I got out of the building all right in case there was a riot or something outside."

ALI HAD BEEN PREPARING FOR WEEKS FOR THE MOMENT when he would refuse to take the symbolic one step forward that would put him into the service. He had decided at least two weeks earlier on his course of action. ✦ The refusal to take that one step forward, Ali had been told, was the only way he could get his case judged in court in a civil suit. In any controversy with the government, a citizen must, in legal terms, "exhaust his administrative remedies" before he can be heard in a civil proceeding by a federal judge. Ali's request for a draft exemption on the grounds that he is a Muslim minister had been denied not in court but by the Selective Service Board of Kentucky, by National Selective Service System Director Lieut. General Lewis Hershey, and by Judge Henry Gwiazda, Dr. Kenneth W. Clement and Commissioner Charles Collatos, members of the three-man National Selective Service Appeal Board. Until Ali actually showed up for induction and refused to take the one step forward that is, in effect, an oath, his administrative remedies were not exhausted—which explains why there had been so many appeals, requests and suits filed by Covington and Hodges.

Ali, under the guidance of Muslim Leader Elijah Muhammad and Elijah Muhammad's son, Herbert, hired Covington in August of last year. Covington, 56, is a distinguished attorney who wears rimless glasses, combs his white hair in a flowing sweep and gives the impression he should be hooking his thumbs into a pair of galluses in the Clarence Darrow manner when he leans over the rail of a jury box. A member of the Jehovah's Witnesses, he has argued many of their cases, and on a single day in 1943 he got 13 decisions handed down in his favor by the U.S. Supreme Court. Covington is the son of a Texas Ranger. He grew up in Sulphur Springs, Texas, on the Mexican border, went to law school in San Antonio and has practiced in Manhattan since 1939. A month ago he brought in prominent Houston trial lawyer Hodges, 45, as associate counsel. Ali calls them Big Boss and Little Boss. They both call him Champ.

"I'm a southern white Episcopalian from the University of Virginia and the University of Texas," Hodges says. "But it doesn't matter what I think of the Muslims. I'm a lawyer first, and I know the champ is not only a sincere Muslim but a nice person. The first time I talked to him, a cute white girl walked up and held out her hand to him. 'Oh, break it, break it,' she said. It embarrassed him and he walked off. Later I was talking to him and said something would 'enhance' our position. 'What's that word, lawyer?' he said. If he had an education, there'd be no limit to that man."

Ali returned to Houston from a trip to Chicago, Louisville and Washington, on the Monday night of his final week before reporting for induction. Covington and Hodges met him at the airport. He got into the back seat of a white convertible and asked to be driven to his apartment. "This won't blow my hair, will it?" he asked, laughing. "Hey, lawyers, I been in jail. I went to a jail in Washington, just checking the place out. They live nice in that jail. They got a gym, TV, good food. The prisoners heard I was there and the warden asked me to speak before they tore up the place. Then I went into the streets and spoke to thousands. I signed autographs for two and a half hours. I got thousands coming to the faith. What does it take to make me a minister? Why they want to put a man like me in the Army? If I have to die, I'll die. Most people die for nothing. I'll at least be dying for something."

Cruising along through the warm, blue Houston night, Ali directed the driver to stop at a bowling alley. "I'll show you what people think of me," he said. Inside were a few whites and about 50 Negroes. Ali walked among them, kissing babies, shaking hands, always looking over his shoulders to see who was coming up next. Rather disappointed with his reception, he went back to the car and was driven to Texas Southern University, where roughly 100 Negro students had gathered on the sidewalk, not knowing they were to be visited. More than a week before, they had been throwing bottles and bricks through car windshields in a protest inspired by Stokely Carmichael. This evening Ali jumped out of his car, threw up his arms and shouted, "I'm ready to rumble."

The students gathered around him, while Hodges and Covington waited in the car.

"Burn their babies," a student said.

"Stokely, he tell the word to burn Whitey," said another.

"I'm telling you religion," Ali said.

"Naw, not religion. We want to burn Whitey."

"Don't do nothing violent. We're not violent," said the champion.

"This is rebellion, man. They take you in the Army, they see a rebellion."

"Stokely say burn their babies."

"We don't want violence," Ali said.

"Are you married?" Ali asked a girl.

"Yeah, man. I'm married to the SNCC," she answered.

After a few more minutes of listening to shouted slogans, Ali returned to the car. "They're a bunch of young fools," he said. "I don't want any of this violence. I hear there'll be demonstrations Friday morning in New York, Chicago, London, Egypt. There are 16,000 Muslims in Cleveland who'll demonstrate. Jim Brown's organization called me about that. Nearly every Negro is a Muslim at heart. The trouble is, first thing you got to do to be a Muslim is live a righteous life. Most people, white or black, don't want to do that."

Ali got out of the car at the Ardmore Apartments, where he rents a little two-bedroom air-conditioned white-brick cottage. He said good night to his attorneys and knocked on the door of his legal residence. Reggie Shabazz, who works for Ali, was staying there, but he was not in and Ali had no key. He took a cab and went to the Hotel America.

THE NEXT DAY AT NOON ALI WENT TO LUNCH AT THE EXCLUSIVE Houston Club with Hodges, Covington, U.S. Attorney Morton Susman, Assistant U.S. Attorney Carl Walker and a local Muslim minister, Raymond X (né Watlington). Susman, a Jew, and Walker, a Negro, were to take the government side in Ali's final pre-induction appeal, with two native white Texans defending Ali, an irony that was duly remarked upon. While the lawyers discussed ground rules, Ali launched into a typical speech about his religion.

"Blacks and whites are dying in Vietnam so those people over there will have the freedom to worship as they want," he said. "So how come I can't do it here?" He is not necessarily opposed to the war in Vietnam, merely to his own presence in the armed services.

Ignoring the stares from the luncheon crowd at the Houston Club, Ali finished his meal and went up one flight to the kitchen to shake hands with the help. "I want the baddest man in the house," he said. "Who wants to fight me?" Raymond X, a tiny, sharp-faced man with a thin mustache, smiled. "Oh, my, he's sweet," he said. "He comes out to preach at our mosque on Polk Street."

How many members did the local mosque have? "A hundred," said Raymond X. A hundred? "Well, almost," he said. "Of course, all of them don't always attend. They're like members of any church, I guess. Some of them attend just often enough to stay members."

Could whites attend? "Oh, my, I don't have that authority. Permission would have to come from Chicago. I'd hate to go back to the ranks, you understand."

On the sidewalk again, Ali loped off in his swinging, bouncing stride, with little Raymond X trotting after him. The champion went to the airport and flew to Chicago to close up his suite at a motel, put his Cadillac into a garage and deposit some money in his bank. While in Chicago he discussed the house he wants to buy. It would have a Muhammad

Ali museum in the basement and a movie screen to show his fights to his grandchildren. He talked about being a leader of his people, like a few of his heroes—Columbus, Jesus, Wyatt Earp and Davy Crockett, all of whom, he says, stood up for what they believed. He is not a Joe Louis fan. The former heavyweight champion has criticized Ali for not going into the Army as Louis did in a different time and a different war. "Louis is the one without courage," said Ali. "Louis, he doesn't know what the words mean. He's a sucker."

Ali returned to Houston and met with Covington and Hodges for lunch at the Rice Hotel on Thursday. Covington was talking about his big day in 1943 with the 13 favorable Supreme Court decisions. "Big Boss, this is '67, no longer are you in heaven," Ali said, laying his head against Covington's shoulder and snoring. "Oh," he said, "when this is over, all I want to do is fall down on the islands of Japan and listen to that native music."

They were on their way to the Federal District Court of Judge Allen Hannay. Covington and Hodges were seeking a restraining order to prevent the Selective Service boards of Kentucky and Texas, as well as General Hershey, from reporting Ali as delinquent until his request for an exemption could be ruled on in federal court as a civil matter. Under normal procedure, when Ali refused to take the one step forward, he was to be reported as delinquent, which could result in a criminal charge. Eventually he would be indicted and arrested. That was what Ali's attorneys wished to avoid.

WAITING FOR THE 2 P.M. HEARING, ALI CHATTED IN THE hall outside the courtroom with a score of fans. Wearing a blue suit, a Muslim tie clasp and wraparound sunglasses, he said he wanted to give Patterson another chance at the championship. "Liston, they'd say he's too old if I beat him again. The Cat [Cleveland Williams]? He's a nice fellow. Next thing, I'll be fighting football and basketball players. Chamberlain? Ti-i-i-m-ber-r-r. I can whip all those folks. I turned down $500,000 to play the life of Jack Johnson because he wasn't the right type of person. I'd want to control my own scripts. I don't like movies. I like real-life drama. Like what's going on here today. This is history you're witnessing. Why, people are betting money on this just like a fight."

In the courtroom it began to look like a fight crowd. Promoter Harold Conrad came in from New York. Bundini Brown sat in the first row. Ali sat at a table, leaning back in a green leather swivel chair. After Covington had made his opening argument and Susman and Fred Drogula, a federal attorney from Washington, had responded, Ali was called to the stand. Generally, an attorney will spend hours preparing his client for testimony. The practice is called woodshedding. Ali was prepared in less than a minute. All Hodges told him was "Tell the truth, and don't get belligerent if you are cross-examined."

Judge Hannay seemed very interested in having Ali in his witness box. In the hall Ali told some Texas Southern students who spoke of protest, "I don't want you suffering just because I suffer. Don't get hurt. They're talking about filling the jails." To Judge

Hannay, Ali was courteous, always saying "sir." But his testimony made the judge blink.

Ali told how he had been approached by the Muslims in Miami in 1961 and had finally been sold on the religion shortly before the Liston fight in 1964. He said "Old McDonald" (promoter Bill McDonald) had tried to make him renounce his religion but he had refused. He claimed that he had packed his bags and climbed aboard his bus to leave Miami Beach, even though he was owed $64,000, before McDonald relented.

After that demonstration of his sincerity, Ali testified, he was given the Muslim name of Muhammad Ali—meaning "one who is worthy of praise." Ali then became a minister of his religion, one that is known as the Lost Found Nation of Islam in North America. Ali told the judge there were 75 Muslim mosques in the U.S. and said that he had spoken at 18 of them. Also, he said, he had spoken at a number of colleges. He said his job is as a Muslim minister, at which he spends 160 hours per month, and his sideline is being the heavyweight champion of the world. Unfortunately for Ali, none of that was at issue in court that day. Susman and Drogula kept repeating that Ali had not exhausted his administrative remedies yet, and Judge Hannay agreed.

But not before he heard Ali testify that "Jesus was a righteous prophet of Allah who came 2,000 years too soon. He didn't leave Earth and go up to Heaven on a cloud. He's no spook in the sky. His body is embalmed to last 10,000 years and is buried in the East. But of course, Judge, all Shriners, Masons and Muslims know about that."

Ali discussed his ex-wife and the money it cost him to divorce her when he realized she was not a devout Muslim. He said Columbia Records had broken a $100,000 contract because he insisted they use the name Muhammad Ali. He said he had been guaranteed $350,000 to fight in Tokyo and $1 million to fight in Lebanon. He said he is thick with Nasser and Faisal. About serving in the armed forces, he said, "It's against the teachings of the Holy Koran. I'm not trying to dodge the draft. We are not supposed to take part in no wars unless declared by Allah or by The Messenger [Elijah Muhammad]. Muhammad was a warrior 1,400 years ago but he was a holy warrior fighting in the name of Allah. We don't take part in Christian wars or wars of any unbelievers. We are not Christian or Communist."

Fascinated, the judge bent forward and asked, "In a conflict between Communism and Christianity, which side would you take?"

"Neither side, Judge," replied Ali.

After Bundini Brown had testified to Ali's sincerity, the champion's party loaded into an airport limousine, went to Hodges' office and then began a customary romp through the streets. At Foley's Department Store, Ali ate a bowl of vegetable soup and bought a pecan cake and a half dozen oatmeal cookies. A little girl with long hair and a frilly dress, looking very much like the Alice who went to Wonderland, asked Ali for his autograph. "I see you wrestle," the girl said. "She must have seen the Terrell fight," said Ali.

Leaving Foley's, Ali looked up at a new 40-story office building. "See that? Well, that's about as high as a pyramid I saw. It would start way down there in that other block and go up to the top of that building in a perfect point. Now, how they do that?"

"They must have had a hammer and a saw," the reporter said.

Ali chuckled. "I know how," he said. "In Egypt I heard it from a wise old man whose granddaddy told him. It had to do with compression. They'd dig a hole, put a rock on top of it, pump the hole full of air, and whoosh! That stone shot right up to the top."

"With the help of 6,000 slaves," Bundini said.

"President Nasser and I saw that pyramid," said Ali, closing the discussion.

THE NEXT MORNING, WHILE ALI WAS CLOSED OFF IN THE examining room at the induction station, three or four whites who had come down from Long Island to work at an Indian reservation in Oklahoma were protesting out front with 11 Negroes, several dressed up in African suits and sandals. It was hardly the mass protest Ali had predicted. ✦ The photographers and reporters, who outnumbered the protesters 10 to 1, immediately demonstrated one basic flaw in modern journalism. They photographed and interviewed all the protesters, thus giving weight to what was a very puny demonstration by a very scraggly-looking bunch. There have been few demonstrations or protests of any sort in Houston—a fact the city is smugly proud of and one that could change suddenly and explosively this summer. "We integrated this city quietly, without any fuss, by agreement, and we have no trouble" is what one hears in Houston.

Weary of watching the protesters, Bundini Brown asked a white friend to go with him across the street to a place called the Brown Derby Lounge. Inside the Brown Derby, the friend asked the barmaid for two soft drinks. "Señor, we don't serve no colored people," said the barmaid in a Tex-Mex accent that Bundini could not comprehend.

Down the block at the Texas State Hotel, Bundini said, "You got awful peculiar laws in Texas. The white folks serve me here in this hotel, but that Mexican wouldn't. Well, I understand. I got no malice in my heart toward anybody. Neither does the champ. He's got the right medicine for the black man, you know. He loves people. He helps the little people. When he goes up to a wino, that man straightens up. If the champ walked by, the wino would just get worse, thinking nobody loved him. The champ offers people respect. That's better than just offering love. Love can turn into hate. Respect turns into shame for not doing better or into pride if you do good.

"The champ wants to clean up the black man, to wipe out prostitution and dope addiction, to give the black man respect. So what difference does it make what the champ calls himself? If he wants to call himself Two and say he's a member of the Boop Boop tribe, that's his business. America is supposed to mean freedom, isn't it? What white people can't understand is that the hurtingest thing in the world is to be black and live in a ghetto. If you live in a ghetto, you prove you're a man by throwing bricks. If you're intelligent, they don't respect you for it. They think you're crazy. The champ is trying to teach respect. I'm not a Muslim, but sometimes I talk like one."

In front of the induction center five Negro students were burning their draft cards while a score of others, coming in at noon, marched in a circle carrying placards and a Black Power flag. They sang songs about black nationalism. They chanted, "Keep the faith." They read from the writings of Malcolm X—"Whoever heard of a revolution where they lock arms and sing *We Shall Overcome*?" and, "America is a house on fire. Let it burn, let it burn." They shouted racist clichés: "blue-eyed devils," "send them to their graves," "Molotov cocktails," "Black Power," "Whitey's war."

Up on the steps stood G-men wearing red bands in their left lapels and carrying walkie-talkie radios. Morton Susman sat on the steps, his radio muffled in a cardboard folder, looking slightly embarrassed by the squawking. The protesters kept marching in a circle, waiting for Ali to come out, looking for a leader. Ali was inside, eating his box lunch, tossing aside the ham sandwich.

WHEN THE MOMENT CAME, HE REFUSED THREE TIMES to step forward at the call of his name. Navy Lieutenant C.P. Hartman called him into his office and warned him he was committing a felony punishable by five years in prison and a fine of $10,000. Ali then returned to the big room and again refused to answer to his name, whereupon he was asked to write, "I refuse to be inducted into the armed forces of the United States." He signed his name, making the refusal official. Susman was notified, though he was hardly surprised. The procedure is for Lieut. Colonel J.E. McKee, commanding officer of the induction station, to notify the Selective Service Board of Texas, which notifies the Kentucky board, which notifies Hershey, who refers the matter to the Justice Department, which hands it back to Susman, who goes before a federal grand jury to request an indictment. That process will require from 30 to 60 days, in Susman's estimate. The government is obviously not anxious to rush Ali off in manacles.

Covington and Hodges have filed further legal actions. Even if a federal court rules that Ali is not a minister and he is found guilty of violating the Universal Military Training and Service Act, it could be two years or more before Ali enters prison. But he has been prejudged, as he knew he would be, by boxing authorities. "That's what really hurts," said Hodges. "In the law, a man is innocent until he is proven guilty. Muhammad Ali has not even been charged with a crime yet, and they're all leaping in to strip him of his title."

Ali had little to say about it except for a prepared statement. He was under orders from Elijah Muhammad to keep his mouth shut. He went back to the Hotel America and called Herbert Muhammad. Then he curled up on his bed and phoned his mother in Louisville. "Mama," he said, "I'm all right. I did what I had to do. I sure am looking forward to coming home to eat some of your cooking." ✦

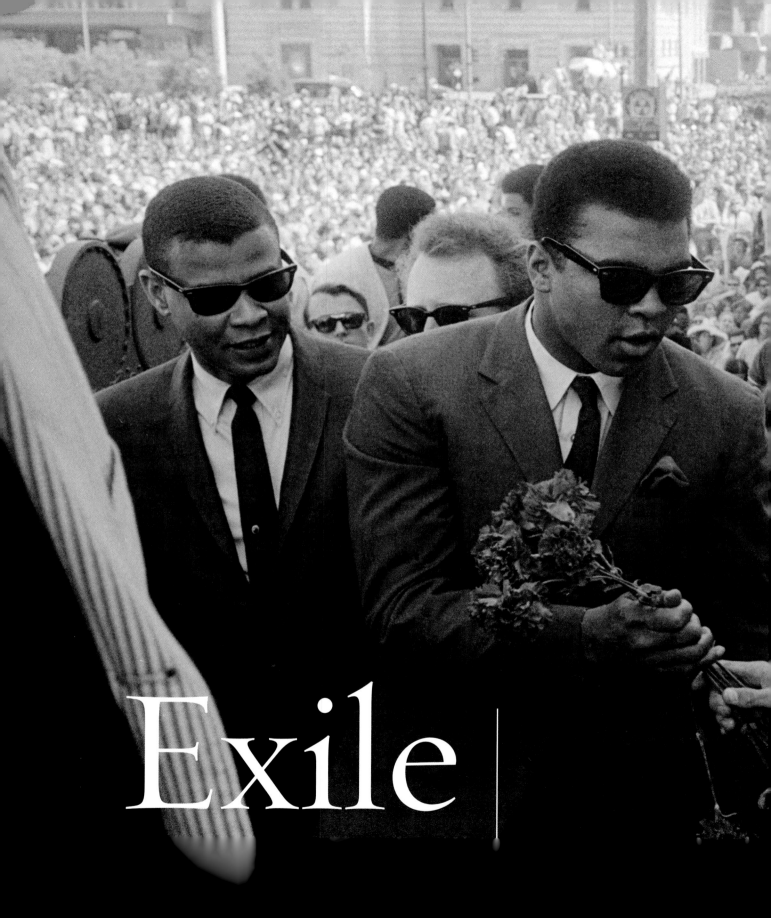

Exile

FLOWER POWER In 1968 the world's most famous fighter was embraced by a crowd of draft protesters in San Francisco.

Ali and his second
wife, Belinda, were
wed on Aug. 17,
1967, in Chicago.
She was 17.

A 1968 *Esquire* cover portrayed
Ali as a martyr for the movement against the Vietnam War.

In 1969 Ali struck a regal pose
as he contemplated a comeback
that would restore his crown.

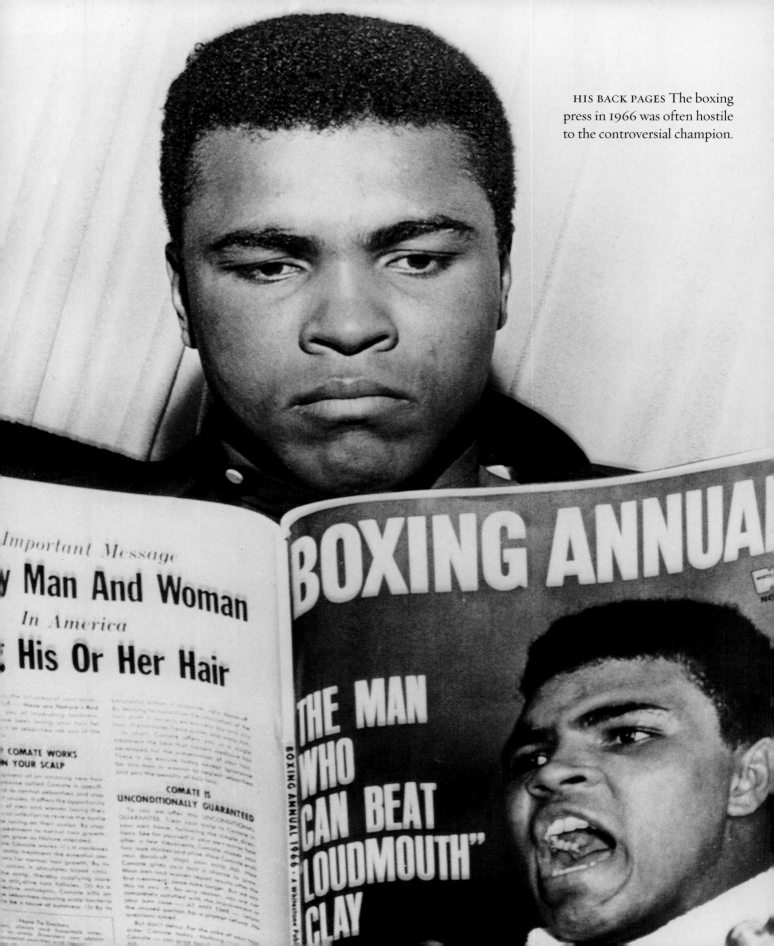

HIS BACK PAGES The boxing press in 1966 was often hostile to the controversial champion.

RING MASTER Ali was the focus at the weigh-in for his 1967 bout against Zora Folley, his last fight before his exile.

GLOVES OFF During his exile, Ali would perfect throwing cultural and political punches.

THOMAS HOEPKER/MAGNUM PHOTOS (3); GORDON PARK/LIFE MAGAZINE/TIME INC. (BOTTOM LEFT)

Ali's long-anticipated return to the ring spiced up life—and LIFE—for fans across the U.S.

Keenly aware of his own magnetism, Ali was never more at home than before a camera.

" 'The Negro's been lynched, killed, raped, burned, dragged around all through the city hanging on the chains of cars, alcohol and turpentine poured into his wounds. That's why the Negroes are so full of fear today. Been put into him from the time he's a baby. Imagine! Twenty-two million Negroes in America, suffering, fought in the wars, got more worse treatment than any human being can even imagine, walking the streets of America in 1966, hungry with no food to eat, walk the streets with no shoes on, existing on relief, living in charity and poorhouses, 22 million people who faithfully served America and who have worked and who still loves his enemy are still dogged and kicked around.' "

ALI TO JACK OLSEN,
"Learning Elijah's Advanced Lesson in Hate," SI, 5/2/1966

Martin Luther King (with Ali here in Louisville in 1967) supported Ali's stance on the draft.

AP IMAGES (TOP); THOMAS HOEPKER/MAGNUM PHOTOS; TONY TRIOLO (OPPOSITE)

No matter his legal status, Ali was always ready to spend time with his fans, as here in Chicago.

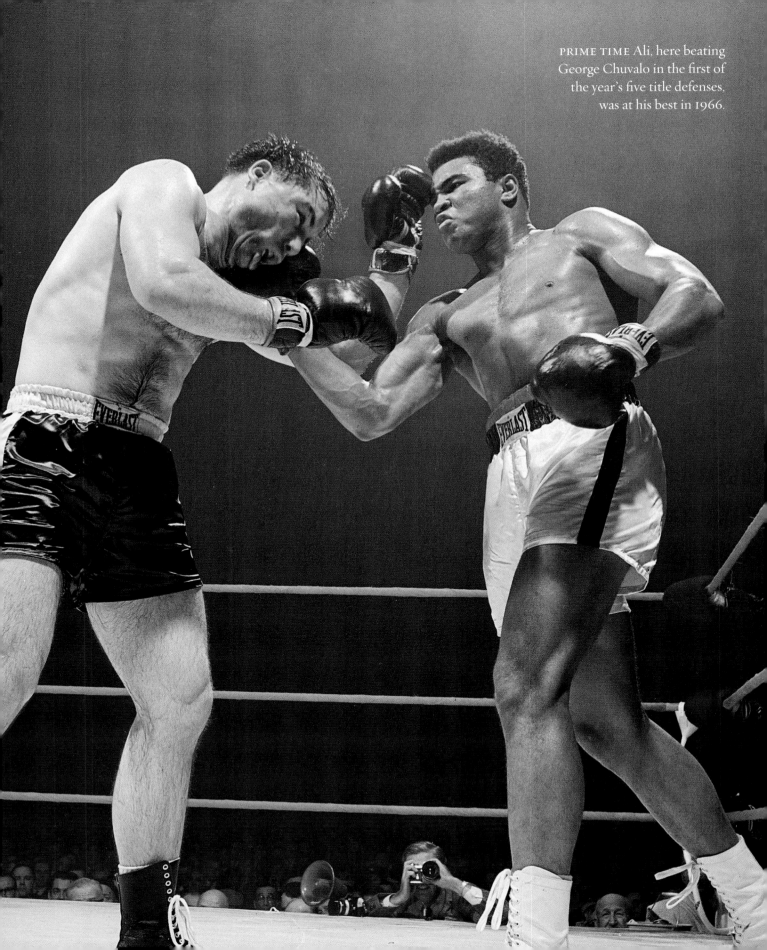

OUTSPOKEN The name of the newspaper said it all as Ali faced the press amid the ongoing legal struggle over his draft status.

"I envy Muhammad Ali. He faces a possible five years in jail and he has been stripped of his heavyweight championship, but I still envy him. He has something I have never been able to attain and something very few people I know possess. He has an absolute and sincere faith."

BILL RUSSELL WITH TEX MAULE,
" 'I Am Not Worried About Ali,' " SI, 6/19/1967

Ali's stance galvanized blacks in the U.S., who may not previously have spoken against the war.

Black athletes including (front, from left) Bill Russell, Jim Brown and Lew Alcindor supported Ali.

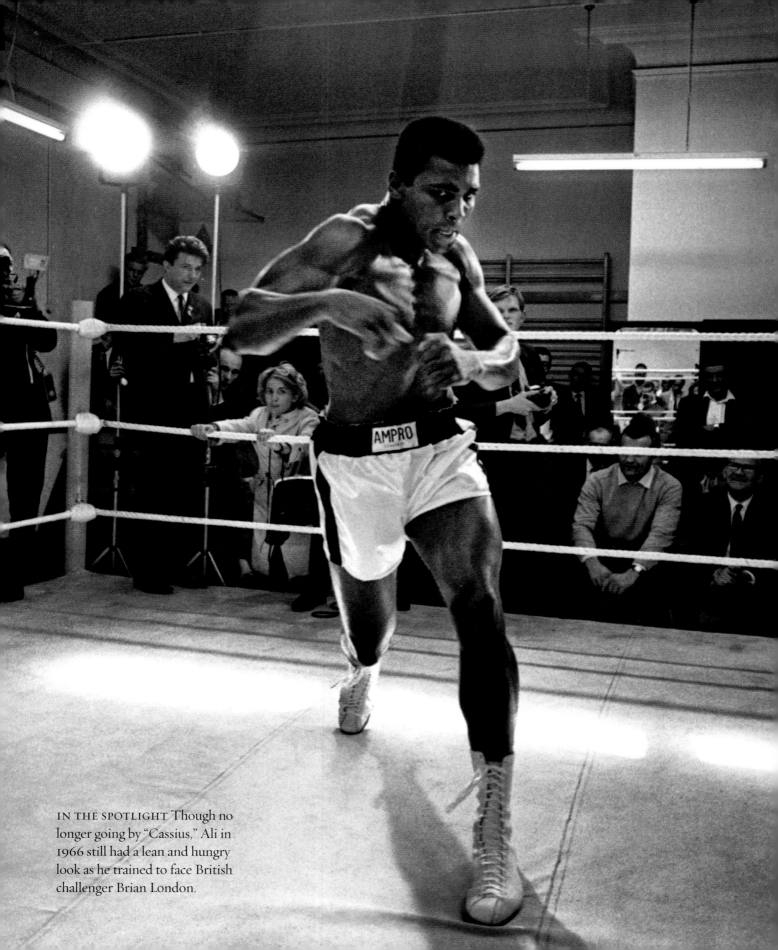

IN THE SPOTLIGHT Though no longer going by "Cassius," Ali in 1966 still had a lean and hungry look as he trained to face British challenger Brian London.

Ali, turning 25, took a break from training to take on a real heavyweight—a 578-pound cake.

Down goes Ali! With a little help, the fighter beat the count during a ski lesson in Vermont.

Voted Fighter of the Year in 1966, Ali would box just twice in '67 before going into exile.

FOR ALI,
A TIME TO PREACH

BY TEX MAULE

Whether sermonizing in public or holding forth at home, Muhammad Ali remained as controversial and colorful as he ever was in the ring
SI, FEBRUARY 19, 1968

MUHAMMAD ALI, NÉ CASSIUS CLAY, who is the heavyweight champion of the world to everyone but a few misguided officials of the World Boxing Association and Madison Square Garden, spends his time these days laboriously preparing lectures or exuberantly giving them. He lives in a small house in what was a middle-class white section of Chicago but is now rapidly becoming a middle-class Negro section. ✦ On a cold, wet afternoon a fortnight ago he sat at the dining room table in the house he bought from Herbert Muhammad, his manager. He was wearing a dark blue undershirt, blue jeans and white sweat socks, and before him on the table were a Bible, a Koran and a book by Elijah Muhammad, *Message to the Black Man in America*. On the floor was a tape recorder loaded with a tape of a speech Elijah had made in Chicago to his Black Muslim followers some time before. Ali has nearly a hundred of these tapes, which he plays over and over, making notes on what Elijah says.

TEACHINGS OF MUHAMMAD The deposed champ addressed a Black Muslim gathering in 1968. **107**

He had been transcribing notes from a yellow legal pad to three-by-five cards, in preparation for a lecture, and now he stopped and stretched hugely. The muscles in his arms and shoulders are immense; the mature Ali is a big man, bigger than Sonny Liston ever was.

"I been up since 5:30," he said. "Been working on this lecture I got to give at UCLA. This one runs 54 cards and I can hold an audience spellbound for an hour and a half with it."

He riffled through the cards admiringly, stopping now and again to read a phrase.

"I got six lectures I can give now," he said. "Took me two and a half months' hard work to get them ready. Sometimes I get up at 5:30 in the morning, work straight through to 3:30 the next morning and get mad 'cause I can't keep my eyes open to study more. I didn't study too good in high school, and now I'm ashamed and I'm making up for it. I find a word I don't know, I look it up in the dictionary."

He regarded the top card of the 54 and began reading from it. At first he read in a quick monotone, but quickly the charm of his own prose and his extraordinary sense of the dramatic took hold, and in a few moments he was delivering what amounted to a sermon. He has the same flair as a speaker that he had as a fighter.

"Take Lazarus," he said, staring hypnotically across the room as if he were addressing a multitude. "He was *charmed* by the wealth of the rich man. He didn't *get* any of it but he loved to be around it, loved to see it and feel it and smell it. Even when he was offered a home in *paradise*, he couldn't *bear* to leave all the wealth behind him. And Lazarus was *hated* and *despised* by the rich men."

He broke off suddenly and grinned.

"I got this down like I did boxing," he said. "Got to have the power and the speed and the stamina. I haven't got this lecture memorized, but I will by the time I have to give it."

He leafed through the Bible on the table, stopping occasionally to read a sentence or two.

"I'm going through the Bible looking for parables and comparing it with the Koran," he said. "Then I read Elijah Muhammad's book and I take what I understand out of that and that's how I get the subjects for my lectures. Like I find a parable about the wolf and the sheep trying to integrate together and I find other things to go with that, maybe out of some of these tapes of Elijah's. The time has come now for the black man to help the black man. The Negro needs a program of self-development, and I'm developing myself now."

HE PAUSED TO REFLECT UPON THIS. ✦ "INTEGRATION," HE SAID. "It's like that wolf and sheep trying to integrate together. God didn't *mean* it that way. He made brown and black and red and yellow and white and meant them to be separate. Like I saw a little red ant wandering around on the ground. Maybe he was lost or maybe he was looking for something to eat. Anyway, he walked into a nest of black ants, and the next thing you know they carried him out of their nest dead. Red ants stay with red ants, black with black. Sharks stay together, dolphins stay together. You don't see them trying to integrate. You say maybe in another 5,000 years or so all the races going to be the same, but it ain't so. You say we'll all be the same color, maybe the color of that dog's ear over there." He pointed to a small stuffed dog with long honey-colored ears.

"I don't want to be that color," he said vehemently. "And I don't want my children to be that color. A man naturally wants his children to look just like him. I don't want no child with a speckled black and white skin and blue eyes and you don't want no black child. You want your child to look like *you*."

ALI TURNED TOWARD THE DOOR TO THE KITCHEN AND CALLED out: "Belinda! Come here, wife, I want you to meet someone." ✦ Belinda came into the dining room shyly. She was wearing the ankle-length dress the Muslims prescribe for their women, but even the voluminous folds of that garment could not conceal the fact that she is pregnant. ✦ "I got a 17-year-old wife, she been watching me since she was 13," Ali said proudly. "She been trying to act like me all that time. She even looks like me, same color and everything."

"Ali!" Belinda cried, feeling her face tentatively as if she could discover any resemblance by touch. "I'm prettier," she said. She was right.

She returned to the kitchen, and Ali went on.

"Now in about five months we're gonna have a child, maybe two. Doctor says she maybe going to have twins. But the child is gonna *look* like me, 'cause its mother looks like me. And that's the way I want it, and that's the way any man wants it."

He picked up another stack of cards from the table and glanced through them. "Here's a lecture I made up proving God is a human being," he said. "Christians say God is a mystery. The dictionary say a mystery is something that is unknown. And the Christians divide God up into three parts—the Father, the Son and the Holy Ghost—contrary to the laws of nature and mathematics. Call Him a spirit. Can a spirit talk to us in His own language? They call Him a spirit but they call Him He, His, Him. He walks and talks and sits. Elijah Muhammad teaches God is a man and we are made in His image."

He put the cards down.

"Takes me at least six days to make an outline," he said. "Hard work, 16, 18 hours a day. But this is all I want. If I was walking down the highway with a quarter in my pocket and a briefcase full of truth, I'd be so happy. This is eternal work. If someone told me tomorrow that he would guarantee me the heavyweight championship for the next 15 years, five fights a year, half a million dollars after taxes from each fight, or he would make me a well-versed minister of Elijah Muhammad making $200—or $150—a week, I'd be a minister. And not because I'm already a rich man, because I'm not."

He opened a notebook and began to write down figures.

"Here's where it all went," he said. "First wife, she cost me $125,000 with lawyers' fees and all. Then I've spent probably $45,000 helping my mother and father. Bought them a house and I gave my mother a Cadillac, too. My brother, he's trying to get a little house. I've spent $25,000 on him. I paid Covington [Hayden Covington, the attorney who represented him in his case with the draft board] $68,000 and he say I owe him another $200,000. Other lawyers, $50,000. My home cost about $26,000 and I spent another $35,000 getting it all fixed up, say a total of $75,000. Cars, $45,000. Then my own personal use, maybe $30,000, not much because you never saw me drink or smoke or party. After a fight it was just me and a few friends sitting around and talking about the fight."

He added the figures up and said, "All that comes to $463,000. Now, in all my years of fighting, my share of the purses came to $2,300,000, and the government took about 90% of that in taxes. All my taxes are paid up. But you can see that don't leave me much."

If the government did, indeed, take 90% of Ali's earnings, his calculations leave him some $233,000 in the hole.

"People ask me, 'Champ, how you gonna eat?' " he went on. "I say, look out there at that little robin pecking and eating. Look up at all the stars and the planets in the heaven. They are not held up there on the end of long steel poles. The Lord holds them in their orbits and the Lord feeds the birds and the animals. If the Lord has this power, will the Lord let His servant starve, let a man who is doing His work go hungry? I'm not worried. The Lord will provide."

ALI HAS ANOTHER HEARING IN HIS LONG BATTLE WITH THE draft board set for next week in Houston. He has appealed for reclassification on the grounds that he is a minister and a conscientious objector to war. He is not specifically concerned with the war in Vietnam. ✦ "I'm against *all* war," he said. "I'm not following anybody. I said this before all this draft-card-burning stuff. I still got my draft card. I made a speech at a white college in Buffalo, N.Y., and when I got to the room where I was gonna talk, they had 34 signs stuck up on the walls and behind the platform. Signs said things like 'LBJ, how many kids did you kill today?' So I told the man who invited me there I wouldn't talk until they took all the signs down. They took them down. I'm not criticizing the government I'm asking to give me justice. I'm against all war."

If Ali's appeals fail, he faces up to five years in the penitentiary, and he considers this possibility with philosophical calm.

"The Koran says you must be tested," he said. "God will try you. He tried Job and He tried Abraham and He tried Elijah Muhammad, too. Elijah spent three years in prison during the war, studying. If I was in jail tomorrow, I'd study and preach to the other prisoners. The loneliness and the confinement and the food, that would all be a test. But a man who believes in a Supreme Being does not fear."

He shrugged the huge shoulders and smiled. "I'm prepared," he said. "I'm thinking ahead. You see that pretty young wife. I'll have one child, maybe two before I go to jail. Then, during the years I'm in jail, they'll be getting bigger, so when I get out I'll already have them and I won't be starting at 30. And my wife will still be young.

"I don't know if I'll be able to fight," Ali said. "I mean I'll have to see what the food is like. Right now I'm 219, so I'm not far out of shape. I work so hard on the sermons and studying, I don't have time to do any exercise. The other day I ran four miles just to check my wind, and my wind was good but I got awful tired. If it was urgent, I could get in fighting shape in maybe three weeks. Seven weeks would be better."

JIMMY ELLIS, ALI SAYS, IS THE BEST OF THE PRETENDERS TO HIS throne. ✦ "He used to give me hell for four or five rounds in the gym," he said. "He moves good, hits good with the right hand. And he's had all that experience as my sparring partner. He can whip the other ones. Joe Frazier? He's like this." ✦ Ali got up and imitated Frazier, moving in with his hands up near his face. ✦ "He gets hit," he said. "Jerry Quarry I don't know," he said. "But I think Ellis will beat him."

He was up now, moving around the room, shadowboxing.

"People criticize me for holding my hands down," he said, holding his hands down. "Defense ain't in the hands. It's here in the legs."

"Move, move," he said, moving. "Stay just out of range." He held his hand up six inches from his nose.

"Here's where a man can reach," he said. "Move, make him miss, move in, pow, pow, move out. Long as I know how far he can reach, I'm going to be too far away. Don't make any difference where my hands are. You notice, if I get in trouble, I get my hands up." He brought his hands up by his face and ducked and wove, watching himself in the living room's wall-sized mirror.

After a moment he sat down on a long couch facing the mirror and a built-in color television set. A cartoon featuring the Road Runner was on and he watched it for a moment.

"That's cute," Ali said. "I like that. Always trying to catch the Road Runner and never getting him. It's cute."

The phone rang and he picked it up and listened a moment. "Sell it," he said. "It isn't doing me any good."

He hung up and turned away from the TV set. "That's my bus," he said. "I paid $14,000 for it and it's been in the garage for six months. I got no use for it. Man offered me $12,000 and I might as well take it."

He got up and went into the kitchen and made himself a cheese sandwich, which he ate with great gusto.

"I only eat one meal a day," he said. "Since I don't get much exercise, I got to watch it. I don't eat beef. I eat lots of fish. Beef brings up the animal instinct in a man. I eat beef when I'm fighting."

A stairway leads down from the kitchen to a den in the basement of the house. The floor of the den is cluttered with the reminders of Ali's days of glory—a pair of boxing gloves, a big scrapbook, two suitcases full of letters he has received from Muslims all over the world. He looked at the disarray.

"This is my past," he said. "All of it down here, out of the way. Here's my shoes. Boxing gloves. Things like that I got no use for now. They won't let me fight here and they won't give me my passport to fight anywhere else. If I was a cab driver I could drive my cab while I'm waiting on this case. I got a million dollars in contracts in Europe, but they won't let me go. They think I'm going to run away? This is my country. I got 22 million people suffering here. I'm not about to go away and never come back to America."

BACK UPSTAIRS IN THE LIVING ROOM, HE STOOD AND BEGAN TO dance in the effortless, fluid style that distinguished him as a fighter. He jabbed and moved sideways, avoiding a glass-topped coffee table in front of the couch. ✦ "He does that all the time," said Belinda, who had just entered the room. She added, "One of these days he's gonna break my mirror doing that." ✦ Ali stopped for a moment, then held his hand up dramatically. ✦ "Ladies and gentlemen," he intoned, "here we are in Yankee Stadium and every seat is filled. And in this corner, at 223 pounds, right out of Alcatraz, is Muhammad Ali. He is 31 years old, and can he still have that same old power and speed after five years in prison?"

He changed to Muhammad Ali and stood up, shaking his hands over his head.

"And in this corner," he said, again the announcer, "we got Joe Frazier. He been the heavyweight champion for five years and he has won 13 straight fights and he is a *young* man. Can he beat Ali, the real champion?"

He pantomimed ringing a bell and came out of his corner moving sideways, fast, around the living room, pumping his left hand with wonderful speed.

"Ali sticking and moving," he said. "Pow, pow, he hit Frazier with two left jabs. He's moving and sticking. Pow, pow, pow, he hit Frazier three more lefts. He's in and out. He missed a right!" Ali threw a clumsy overhand right.

"Now he's sticking and moving some more," he said, sticking and moving. "Frazier hit him in the stomach with a right hand. Frazier moving in on him. Oh, oh! Frazier hit him in the head with a right hand and Ali is *down*!"

He fell on his stomach, shaking the house, and began to count dramatically.

"One, two, three," he was on his hands and knees and was shaking his head dazedly.

"Four, five, six," now on one knee but obviously hurt. "Seven, eight," he was up, wobbly.

"Referee wiping off Ali's gloves," he said. "And here Frazier come after Ali, but Ali is moving and sticking again." Ali began to move and stick, getting stronger and quicker, and by the time he rang the imaginary bell to end the round he was clearly in control again.

The second round did not last long.

"Ali looks like the old Ali," he said. "Pow, pow, pow, pow! Four left jabs to Frazier's head. Pow, pow, pow, pow, pow!" He pumped blows with both hands as fast as he could punch. "A machine gun combination! Frazier is hurt! POW! Ali hit him with a left hook! POW! And a right hook! POW! POW! A right and a left to the head and Frazier is down!"

He danced back to a neutral corner and counted slowly to six.

"Frazier is up and Ali is after him," he said, going after the phantom Frazier. "He's got him backed into a corner. Pow, pow, pow, pow, pow, pow, POW! Frazier is helpless." He backed away from the corner between the mirror wall and the front window and held up his right hand.

"They stopping the fight," he said. "And still champion of the world—Muhammad Ali!"

He was puffing slightly and sweating and Belinda regarded him with a wife's jaundiced eye. "He's always doing that," she said. "He's crazy."

LATER, IN HIS CAR DRIVING TOWARD DOWNTOWN CHICAGO, ALI was relaxed and becoming sleepy. ✦ Someone asked him if he ever thought of himself as Cassius Clay and he shook his head. ✦ "Cassius Clay?" he said as if it were the name of someone dimly recalled from his childhood. "Now and then someone call me Cassius Clay, but they don't mean harm by it. I don't make a thing of it unless it's on national television with millions watching, then I correct them. But most of the time I let it go, 'cause if I gave everyone who does it a lecture I wouldn't have much time to do anything else."

He pulled into a service station and a small, middle-aged black man came out.

"What can I do for you," he said and did an exaggerated double take. He peered doubtfully for a moment.

"You Cassius Clay?" he asked.

Ali grinned and nodded, then said, "What's my name?"

The little man slapped his fist into his palm and thought for a moment. Then his face brightened.

"Allah," he said. "Allah."

"Muhammad Ali," Ali said gently. "Muhammad Ali. That's who I am. The preacher."

That's who he is. And he is still the heavyweight champion. ✦

Return

{ 1969 - 1973 }

MAN IN THE MIRROR

BY GEORGE PLIMPTON

*Though millions saw Muhammad Ali
return to the ring after years of exile, none
had a closer view than this old friend*
SI, NOVEMBER 23, 1970

THEY HAD BEEN THERE FOR 13 DAYS, IN A cottage by a small dun-colored lake in suburban Atlanta; thick woods in back, with the autumn foliage still and heavy from a rain that had come through the night before. The railroad tracks were half a mile or so back through the woods, the freight trains going by once in a while— heavy and long loads, they must have been, because the whistle would die mournfully off in the distance while the wheels of the last cars clicked slowly and distinctly across the sidings on the far side of the ridge. ✦ The cottage belonged to State Senator Leroy Johnson, one of the key figures in Muhammad Ali's return to the ring. He had donated it to the Ali contingent for its training headquarters, and on this, the day of the Jerry Quarry fight, the interior was a shambles. The bedrooms, three of them, were crowded with unmade cots and half-filled suitcases. In the main room, where the curtains were drawn to provide a permanent gloom for TV and film watching, a mounted kingfish had fallen off the wall and lay with its tail in the fireplace. Beside it floated a half-deflated balloon with an inscription on it that read SOUL BROTHER. Scattered about

IN HIS IMAGE Out of the ring for more than three years, Ali had to remake himself as a fighter. **117** the floor were newspaper and boxing journals, along with strips of film, soiled socks, up-turned ashtrays and various items of athletic equipment, including a shuttlecock (there was a sagging badminton net out in the backyard), sweat pants and boots. Above an unmade cot a bedsheet was tacked to the wall to be used as a motion picture screen. A long sofa was set along one wall, with a television console opposite. In the corner of the dining alcove stood a big trunk marked MUHAMMAD ALI—THE KING. On it lay a yellow pad on which someone had written the words, "Joy to the whole wide wide world a champion was born at 1121 W. Oak Street Louisville Ky it was . . ." An unfinished document in the handwriting, it turned out, of Cassius Clay Sr.

By contrast, the kitchen was neat—a woman's touch provided by a cousin of the Senator who came in every day to provide meals for the camp. "I don't even dare look in those other rooms," she said.

OUTSIDE, MUHAMMAD ALI WAS JUST RETURNING FROM HIS weigh-in at the Regency Hyatt House in downtown Atlanta. The cottage began to fill with his entourage: his father; his brother, Rahaman; Angelo Dundee, his trainer-adviser; Bundini, his assistant trainer; his official biographer; his official photographer; sparring mates; his accountant and a number of business advisers; a couple of reporters; a man dressed entirely in green, including green shirt, tie and socks, who was a detective supplied by the police and who had a squat-nosed gun at this hip. Another armed man was posted outside. He was supposed to keep people away from the fighter, but his function seemed to be to show people to the cottage door.

At noontime Jim Jacobs, the former handball champion, arrived with a fight film he had recently completed on the career of the first black heavyweight champion, Jack Johnson, which he thought would particularly interest Muhammad Ali. The parallels between the two fighters are striking—both exiled from the sport, both in difficulty with legal authorities, both great showmen in and out of the ring. Ali lounged on the sofa, a telephone close at hand, and watched the film begin to flicker on the bedsheet. "Look at these advantages I have," he whispered. "Quarry—he don't have a machine and movies like this. He has nothing to look at but the walls."

To Jacobs's despair, Ali's attention was constantly interrupted by the phone at his side. Instinctively he picked it up when it rang, invariably to find the caller trying to cadge a few tickets for the fight. Ali would announce himself, often to a startled squawk from the other end, and he would go on to say that buses were scheduled to leave the Regency an hour before the fight, and he would arrange to see that those aboard got into the arena. Sometimes Ali knew the caller personally, and he would call out, "Sidney Poitier, you're my man" or "Whitney Young, my goodness."

Jacobs kept his film running throughout the interruptions. Ali paid as much attention as he could, lolling on the sofa, sucking on a blue plastic toothpick. Occasionally he rolled his shoulders to keep the muscles loose. "Jack Johnson," he said, reverently. He mentioned that the old fighter's facial features looked a little like Babe Ruth's. The phone rang, and he bent over the receiver, talking into it softly. He hung up the phone, and the sight of Johnson chasing a chicken caught his fancy; he wondered aloud if running after a particularly lively chicken wouldn't be a valuable training exercise for a fighter. He thought he might hire some for his next fight. At one point in the film the deep, simulated voice of Johnson announced, just prior to the Jim Jeffries fight, "If I felt any better, I'd be scared of myself . . ." and Ali laughed. One felt that he might have stored the line for future use. He was interested that Johnson always insisted on being the first fighter to climb into the ring, that this was so important to him that the procedure was a stipulation written into his contracts. But the Johnson antics in the ring were what made Ali lean forward out of the sofa; if he was talking to someone on the phone, his voice would trail off. When Johnson grinned and appeared to taunt Tommy Burns in the early rounds of their fight in Australia that won him the heavyweight championship, Ali commented, "He's something else." He watched Johnson make a derisive gesture with his glove, waving goodbye to Burns as he turned for his corner at the end of a round. "Look at that," Ali said. "He's signifying, 'See you later, partner.' I believe I'll do that with Quarry tonight."

Angelo Dundee stared uneasily across the room. "Just like him to pick up some crazy notion from that film," he said. "Why doesn't the phone keep ringing?"

On the bedsheet, scenes of the Johnson–Stanley Ketchel fight were beginning. Ketchel was a middleweight fighting far over his class (the publicity movies of the signing for the fight show him in a long camel's hair coat and extra-high cowboy boots to disguise his relative lack of stature), and at one stage of the bout Johnson bulled him to the canvas and then, almost apologetically, picked him up and set him on his feet as one would a child. Watching the film, one half expected Johnson to dust him off. Ali was delighted. "Tonight," he said, "just set Quarry down and pick him up." He rocked back and forth.

"Oh, my," said Dundee. "At the bell you never know what's going to happen with this fellow." (Before the second Liston fight, the one scheduled for Boston that was postponed when the champion suffered a hernia, Ali was toying with the idea of hiding a muleta in his boxing trunks. He planned to produce it in the first round and play Liston like a bull.)

WITH THE FIRST REEL OF THE FILM OVER, ALI SUDDENLY stood up, amid a flurry of phone calls, and announced that it was time for his lunch. He sat down in the dining alcove to a meal of beets, greens and lamb chops, which he announced were more digestible than other meats and thus just right for a fight day. He ate with considerable relish, and then announced he was going to "settle" his meal with a half-hour walk. He was accompanied on his stroll by reporters, a business adviser or two, the green-outfitted detective and Jim Jacobs, who in turn was accompanied by a camera crew. Ali led this contingent off into the woods carrying a seven-foot staff—a patriarchal figure with his flock capering about him.

The cottage seemed relatively quiet in his absence. Dundee said that he had not been surprised by the bedlam, the shouting, the phones going. "It's always been like this," he said. "Since the very beginning. The kid's big concern on the day of a fight is to look out for his friends. When he fought Doug Jones in Madison Square Garden he arrived at the back entrance with a whole mob of people, and he braced the door open and just passed these people though under his arm, one after the other. The matchmaker, who was Teddy Brenner, tried to stop him, and Clay said that if he couldn't get his friends in, well, that was that—he wasn't going to fight. Benner knew he wasn't fooling. So the mob got in."

WHEN ALI RETURNED HE TRIED TO TAKE AN AFTERNOON nap. That was on his own schedule—to rest for three hours in the afternoon and rise just an hour so before leaving for the fight. He could sleep quite soundly, he said, often with dreams that trailed off and changed so that he could never remember them, except that they were not about boxing. On this occasion he did not seem particularly anxious to sleep. Five or six people, most of them talking about his business affairs, followed him into his bedroom. Papers and folders were spread out on the bed for his inspection. He stripped himself naked and pulled a blue coverlet up to his waist. At one point he asked, "Does that mean I don't have to pay the taxes?"

A squabble started. Someone said, "It's a sub chapter S proposition. Nothing to it."

"Limousines," Ali said from the bed. "Can we make money buying into limousines?"

"The thing about the limousine business," someone said, "is that you got to keep the things filled."

Ali looked at him coldly.

A man recently appointed Ali's official business accountant kept spreading his hands and saying, "The time and the place, it is not here, please."

"Right," said Dundee from the door. "Let the man sleep."

The crowd finally filed out, to Ali's evident regret, and the door was closed.

During his rest, cars kept arriving and departing, ripping ruts in the wet grass out in back. People wandered in and out of the cottage, hushing each other loudly to let Ali sleep, some of them sitting out on the back porch to gossip and stare at the brown lake, as still as metal that lazy afternoon. From time to time Bundini tiptoed inside to the bedroom and squeaked the door open a crack to see if Ali was sleeping.

"Is he sleeping?"

"No. He was lookin' at me."

"Why don't you let him sleep?"

"He don't have to sleep. He's just restin'. You can get more tired sleepin' than restin'. You see, the champ don' need to rest for conditionin'. He's got that. He's got four winds. Most people got two winds, but the champ's got four. But that don' mean nothin' if your mind's tired. He's in there restin' up his mind."

Bundini's real name is Drew Brown—the other's a Hindi name he picked up in his seafaring days, which he sometimes says means "mystic," sometimes "good-luck man" and often, when the occasion rises, "lover." He has been an associate of Muhammad Ali since the early "bear-baitin' " Liston campaigns. His slogan is "Float like a butterfly, sting like a bee," and his particular function, besides his skill in the corner, is to keep Ali's mind keen

Even when resting, Ali thrived on a constant stream of callers and visitors.

and, as the time approaches, to pump him up for the bout, "fight-talkin'" him with a strong mixture of emotion and a kind of Baptist rhetoric. He looks enough like Ali to be mistaken for a close relative, and he has a similar exuberance of spirit—to a degree that one of his associates refers to him as "hysteria on a hoof."

Bundini stood in the kitchen and talked about the fight. "He win, and it's medicine for everyone. He's sellin' *pride*. Medicine. And he sellin' it down here in Klan lan'. The ol' Slave Master is lettin' him rumble. He do everyone some good if he win."

"What about Governor Maddox? He tried to proclaim a day of mourning."

"It do *him* good, too. The mornin' after the fight he gets the newspaper. He takes it into the bathroom. His wife is in there. They look at the paper. They whisper. 'He won.' 'He did?' 'He won in the second round.' 'Oh, my.' 'He come out, and after just six weeks trainin' he take the other boy.' 'My, he must be *somethin'*.' Well, when they whisper, man, you know they're human. The mission will get them."

"Does Muhammad Ali know he's on a mission?"

"Mission?" said Bundini scornfully. "Man, of course. What sort of man goes huntin' in the big jungle and doesn't know what he's shootin'? My goodness!"

There was a commotion outside on the lawn. The Rev. Jesse Jackson of SCLC and Operation Breadbasket strode into the house—a tall, impressive figure in a buckskin jacket, with a Martin Luther King medallion as big as a wine-taster's cup dangling from his neck. He was greeted by a number of admirers, but his face remained passive and solemn as he moved through the cottage.

"He's a young prophet," Bundini said. "Prophets recognize prophets. That's why he's here. This place is sort of a prophet place. The champ and me walk in the woods in the night, talkin' and thinkin' and throwin' stones, and you can look back and see the *glow* of the man, the shine of his eyes and his teeth."

ESSE JACKSON CAME INTO THE KITCHEN. HE LEANED AGAINST THE sink, and it was evident that for him the fight that night was a symbolic event of tremendous significance. "If Cassius loses tonight, Agnew could hold a news conference tomorrow," Jackson said. "Symbolically, it would suggest that the forces of blind patriotism are right, that dissent is wrong, that protest means you don't love the country. . . . They tried to railroad him. They wouldn't let him practice his profession. They tried to break his spirit and his body. Martin Luther King had a song: 'Truth crushed to the earth will rise again.' That's the black ethos. With Cassius Clay all we had was the hope, the psychological *longing* for his return. And it happened! In Georgia of all places, and against a white man."

"Ain't it *somethin'*," Bundini shouted. "The Master Painter from the Far Away Hills has arranged this. We're raisin' the flag!"

"So there are tremendous social implications," Jackson went on calmly. "It doesn't mean that Quarry is a villain. But the focus must be on Clay. He's a hero, and he carries the same mantle that Joe Louis did against Max Schmeling, or Jesse Owens when he ran in Hitler's Berlin. Injustice! In Atlanta, I have never sensed such electricity, such expectation in the streets. For the downtrodden, they need the high example—that their representatives, the symbol of their own difficulties, will win. Is that illogical?"

"What about the Frazier fight, if it ever happens?" someone asked.

Bundini said, "This fight is for the *people*. The night he fight Joe Frazier will be a different thing altogether. That fight will be for boxin' and for himself, a personal thing. He win that, and we won't have to jive no more."

Suddenly Ali called from his bedroom. He was stirring and he wanted Bundini to come in and give him a pep talk. "Let's talk spiritual," he said. Bundini joined him. Their voices rose from behind the door. Bundini's was much the louder. The two were arguing. Ali was saying that he wanted a pure knockout that night; he didn't want the fight stopped because of a cut. If that happened, if he cut his man, he would go for the kill rather than exploit his advantage carefully. It would be dangerous, but at least, if he were successful, there'd be no question mark left in anyone's mind.

Bundini raged at him. "What are you talkin' about? If you cut that eye you take that eye and you put it on the canvas if it's necessary, you hear? Think of the Quarry camp. Why, that man open a cut on *you*, and you think he say, 'Oh, my goodness, what a terrible thing! I cut him! I got to hurry up and knock him out.' Young man, you got to kick; you got to rumble. You got to get him in the first round. You got to stick him!"

Dundee opened the door, and a few people crowded in to look at Ali. He was sitting naked on the edge of the bed. He reached for his pants on the floor and, rocking his body back and then forward off the bed, he jumped into them with both feet going into the trouser legs simultaneously. He stood up in the same motion, hitched his trousers up and cinched the belt in. "Oh, my," Dundee said. He laughed. "And they've been telling themselves in Quarry's camp that he puts his pants on one leg at a time."

"I'm hungry," Ali was saying. "Tonight I'm going to eat me some ice cream and pie. But I dunno. It's so hard to run off that fat. Maybe I'll have some water and a cheeseburger."

He went into the main room and caught sight of Jesse Jackson. They jumped for each other and swung around the room shouting and hollering, Ali's face bright with excitement, Jackson's emotional and serious.

The phone rang. Ali broke away from Jackson and rushed for it. "This is Ali. How you doin'? Chile, you be at the Regency at nine o'clock. You'll be going to the fight. You and Mrs. Martin Luther King, I'm takin' you all."

Jim Jacobs had left the Jack Johnson film for him, and Ali set it going again. He wanted to see the early moments of it—the Burns fight, the Jeffries fight, and then a section in which Johnson intones, "I like Champagne corks, the smile of a pretty woman. I like life and I like it now. I'm Jack Johnson and I'm the champion of the world. I'm black. They never let me forget it. I'm black all right. I'll never let them forget it!"

Ali relaxed in his chair, his hands folded over his stomach. From the doorway Jesse Jackson watched him intently.

"Jack Johnson, he won the title when he was how old?" Ali asked.

"Thirty," he was told.

"It will be 10 or 15 years before I'm threatenin' to be whupped."

It was getting dark outside. The champion began to yawn. "He's beginnin' to get that feelin'. . . ." Bundini said. "Sort of a stage fright—all these people comin' to see him fight. It changes him. It's a different sensation. When I was at sea we used to call it the channel feelin'—the change, you know, and the feelin' of things goin' to happen when you're on the way out the river and you just begin to feel the motion of the sea."

At 7:30, a half hour before the scheduled departure for Atlanta, Ali ran the Johnson film for the third time. As the reel began to spool down, Ali clicked it off and stood.

"Let's go to war," Bundini said, and they walked out to the entourage of cars and buses waiting in the darkness on the front lawn. Jesse Jackson rode with Ali in the first car. The caravan reached the Regency and Ali stepped out and organized the loading of the buses. Mrs. Martin Luther King was late. She is well known for being late. Ali waited for 20 minutes, until he began to fidget and pace around, and finally he left a message for her. He was very sorry, he asked to have her told, but he couldn't stay and wait. . . . He had to go to a fight.

Ali's dressing room at the arena was small, not much wider than the length of the rub-

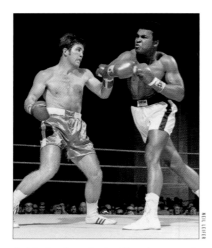

In his first bout back, Ali took on tough contender Jerry Quarry in Atlanta.

bing table set at one end, and only three or four paces long, hardly enough room, as Bundini said when he saw it, for Ali to exercise up some sweat. Dressing tables were set against opposite walls, their mirrors outlined with light bulbs. The first member of the contingent to use the dressing room had been Rahaman, Ali's brother. He had fought in a preliminary and stopped his opponent in the third round. He came bouncing into the dressing room, smiling broadly under a black mustache. "I feel good—sharp," he said. He is swarthy and heavy compared to his brother, with a ponderous but effective punch. Out of boxing for two years longer than his brother, though a year younger, he had come out of retirement this past summer to see how he would fare. His trainer, Sam Logan, a stoutish, mild though nervous man who teaches French on the side, rushed in and the two of them bulled each other around, kicking over a chair and yelling in delight. When he had calmed down Rahaman said, "Now it's time for Ali to cook." He seemed faintly put out that his brother had not seen his fight.

Rahaman was gone when his brother arrived, fresh from getting the two busloads of friends and hangers-on out onto the street and into the arena. He barely nodded when told of Rahaman's victory. He arrived with an hour to go to the fight. Even before he got out of his street clothes he was moving around the room, snapping out the jabs and staring at himself in the mirrors. "This room's too crowded," he said. "I want room to rest."

The room was cleared except for the group he would take to the ring, plus two interns assigned to the fight and the Rev. Jesse Jackson. Ali stripped quickly. He pulled on a pair of white boxing trunks and turned slowly in front of the mirror. "I am the champ," he said softly. "He must fall." He tried out the Ali shuffle, his white boxing shoes snapping against the floor.

"Angelo," he said, "I'm not wearin' the foul protector tonight."

Angelo looked up. He and Bundini were having words in the corner. In the days immediately before the fight there had been considerable argument about the regulation foulproof belt. Ali wanted to wear a small metal cup rather than the leather device, which bulked out his boxing trunks and made him look, at least to his eyes, fat. But Dundee had insisted on the belt. He warned Ali that Quarry was not only a body-puncher, but had nothing to lose; he had been known to hit "south of the border," and it was crazy to take chances.

Bundini had packed the equipment suitcase two days before and checked it out twice to see if everything was there, especially the foulproof belt, which was red and had Ali's name on it. To his astonishment, the belt was missing when he opened the suitcase in the dressing room. He and Dundee, who thought Bundini had simply forgotten it back at the cottage, had a low but harsh exchange. Ali, shadowboxing in the rear, gave no indication that he was aware of what was going on. Perhaps there was no need, since the belt was found under his bed the next morning.

Dundee opened Rahaman's suitcase and produced his protector, a black model marked "Standard." Ali looked at it warily. He turned to the mirrors and began some light shadowboxing, exhaling sharply with each punch thrown—a hard, distinctive, explosive snuffle. He does this in the ring as well, a habit common to many fighters and one which Ali has practiced from his earliest days. He compares it to the sharp exhalation that karate fighters make as they chop at their opponents.

Bundini was asked if Sugar Ray Robinson, always Ali's great idol, had the same habit. Bundini was out of sorts. He was angry about the protector and worried that Ali would refuse to wear his brother's. "Nah," he said, "he didn't make no noise like that. He made faces. Every punch, he made a face."

Ali, still exercising very easily, stopped and left the dressing room, for the lavatory. There were 40 minutes to go.

O N THE WAY BACK HE PASSED HIS OPPONENT'S DRESSING ROOM, just a step down the corridor from his own. It had a hand-lettered notice—QUARRY—tacked to the door. Ali could not resist the temptation. He pushed the door open and peered in. Quarry was sitting facing him, his knees jiggling, and he looked up. ✦ "Fellow," Ali said in a sepulchral voice, "you best be in good shape, because if you whup me, you've whupped the greatest fighter in the whole wide world."

He clicked the door shut before Quarry could come up with a reply, and back in his own dressing room he described what he had done with impish pleasure. It had been a ploy of a type that delights him—the unexpected materialization. On one occasion last year, driving through Queens with a reporter, he had stopped the car and tiptoed up behind a truck driver changing a tire. "I hear you're talking around town that you can whup me," Ali said. "Well, here I is."

The truck driver's ears had turned a quick red, and he spun on his haunches to stand up. Then, seeing Ali and recognizing him, he jaw dropped and he froze in a curious half stoop, the tire iron clattering from his hand. Ali grinned at him and stepped back into his car. It was the speculation of what had happened afterward that caught Ali's fancy, how the truck driver would come home that evening and look across the kitchen table at his wife and say, "Hey, Martha, I was changing a tire today. . . . I know you're not going to believe this, but I was changing this *tire. . . .*"

At five minutes to 10, with 35 minutes to go, Ali was lying on the table getting a rubdown from Luis Sarria, a melancholy Cuban who has been in Dundee's employ for 10 years and does not speak a word of English. "Tell him to rub harder," Ali told Angelo.

WITH A HALF HOUR TO GO A REPRESENTATIVE FROM Quarry's camp—Willie Ketchum—turned up in the dressing room to oversee the taping of Ali's hands. Ketchum had a towel over one shoulder of his Quarry jacket, and his jaws worked evenly on a piece of gum. Ali's eyes sparkled. "Well, look who's here," he said. "You all in trouble tonight."

"Who's in trouble?" Ketchum said. He knew he was in for some badgering.

"Your man's in for a new experience." Ali said. "He's up against the fastest heavyweight alive, quick and trim. Look at that." He slapped his belly. "Look how pretty and slim."

"You won't be when Jerry finishes," Ketchum said. "I know he's going to hit you."

"How's he going to do that?" Ali looked genuinely surprised. "Angelo, how can he get away from the jab? How will he ever see it?"

Dundee shrugged. He motioned Ali to the table and began the taping of his hands.

Ketchum challenged Ali: "And if Jerry moves in on you, throwing the big ones? Ho ho."

"He going to get hit right in the banana, "Ali said. "He never seen a right like that."

"If you beat Quarry tonight, you are the greatest heavyweight who ever lived," Ketchum said, and he added with attempted sarcasm, "Yeah, and if that happens I'll come in here and kiss you."

"Oh, my, no," said Ali. He looked at the taped hand Dundee had finished. "Hey," he said. "We will give you guys $500,000, *cash*, if you let me put a horseshoe in my gloves."

Ketchum blinked. "Aw," he said.

Dundee finished the taping, and Ketchum leaned over and crisscrossed the tape with pen strokes. When he stepped back, Ali stood up and moved close to stare into Ketchum's eyes. Ketchum is a tall man; standing, they braced each other, like fighters getting instructions from the referee. "Look into my eyes," Ali said. "I'm the real heavyweight. I am the fastest heavyweight that ever lived."

Ketchum did not back down. His jaw kept moving as he chewed the gum.

"I won some money on you once," he said. "I bet $50 at 7 to 1 that you'd whip Liston."

Ali began to turn away. "We'll give them a good show tonight," he said. "I couldn't pick no better contender."

"O.K., pal," Ketchum said. He cuffed Ali affectionately on the head and turned to go.

"Man, you had to get in one lick, didn't you," Ali called after him.

He turned back to the room. "How much time?"

"Twenty minutes."

Bundini said, "You stick him fast, you hear?"

"Who goes into the ring first?" Ali asked.

"Quarry," he was told.

He lay down on the rubbing table, his head to the wall. One of the young interns leaned forward and brashly asked what he was thinking at that instant.

Ali began his litany. He said he was thinking about the people in Japan and Turkey and Russia, all over the world, how they were beginning to think about the fight, and about him, and the television sets being clicked on, and the traffic jams in front of the closed-circuit theaters, and how the big TV trucks out in back of the Atlanta arena, just by the stage door, were getting their machinery warmed up to send his image by satellite to all those people, and how he was going to dance for them—"I got to dance," he said—all this in the soft, silky voice he uses when he does this sort of thing, almost the voice of a mother soothing her child to sleep with nursery rhymes.

"How about a verse?" the intern asked.

"Quarry/sorry," Ali said.

The intern was delighted. "Hey, that's pretty short," he said. "How about another?"

"I don't have time/to find a rhyme," Ali replied gently, and he went on with his thoughts, how finally he was thinking most of all of Allah, his God, the Almighty Allah, who had given him so many gifts. He began to enumerate them in his singsong voice— a long, free-verse ode to carrot juice, to honey, to the things that grew in the garden and that he ate, never anything man-made that came in cans, none of that stuff, but only what came fresh from the gardens, and then the woods in which he would run before the "cars were up" and their "poison," and he talked about how he would face East and thank the Creator for all of this, which had given him the strength to live right and to pray right. And he said that thinking of all that the Creator had done made it simple for him to look at Quarry and see how little he was, and how easy he could be whupped.

It was an odd sensation to watch this—Ali pumping himself up, the final instants of fueling a vehicle that within minutes would touch off—like watching an Antaeus derive his strength from the ground.

H IS MONOLOGUE CONCLUDED, ALI SWUNG HIS FEET TO THE floor and stood up. Fifteen minutes were left. Sarria applied a smear of Vaseline to the fighter's shoulders and started rubbing it into his torso. His body began to shine. A policeman stuck his head in, and the crowd noise, roaring at the entrance of some celebrity, swept in for an instant and made the blood pound before it was shut off by the door closing.

"They're waiting for me to dance," Ali said. His feet were shuffling. Jesse Jackson put up a hand as a target and Ali popped a few jabs, snorting his sharp exhalations, and then he stopped and looked at himself in the mirror. "The Temptations are out there," he said. "The Supremes are out there. Sidney Poitier's out there."

He peered at himself closely.

"A hair comb, somebody," he said. He held out his hand behind him, blindly, as he continued looking into the mirror, and someone slapped a comb into his palm as one might supply a busy surgeon.

He moved the comb through his short brush, flicking at some wayward tuft, until Dundee approached with the foul protector and the boxing gloves, new and gum-red from their packing cases.

Ali balked at the protector. "I'm not wearing that thing," he said. A chorus of dismay rose from around the room. "Just try it on and see," someone urged. Sulkily, Ali skinned out of his trunks and shimmied the protector up over his thighs. He pulled the trunks back over them. A babble of voices rose.

"It looks just fine."

"Trim, man. Beautiful. Trim."

Ali began some knee bends, hands out, and every time he came up above the level of the dressing tables he turned to look at himself in the mirrors. Then he stood up and slapped at his trunks disgustedly.

"Where are my brother's trunks?"

"Champ, those trunks look just *boss*."

"Slim and trim, champ, slim and trim."

A pleading chorus rose from those around the room, concerned that Ali's main intention was to get rid of the offending foul belt. Ali skinned off the trunks. Dundee reached into Rahaman's suitcase and produced a pair of white trunks. Ali took them, put them on over the protector and turned slowly in front of the mirror. Everybody stared at him.

"This is better," he said after a while. A quick chorus of approbation came from around the room.

"Right on, man."

"That's real trim."

"It brings your butt down just right."

Everyone was sweating.

"How much time?" someone asked.

"Ten minutes."

Ali began to shadowbox in earnest, throwing quick long jabs, flurries of combinations and big hooks that seemed to shudder the air in that tiny room. The onlookers flattened themselves back against the wall to give him room.

He stopped to tape his shoelace against the top of his shoes so that they wouldn't flop. "Too loose," he said. "In late rounds they can get soggy and, man, I want to dance."

The gloves were put on and he began another flurry of punches. Murmurs rose from those standing along the wall. "Hmmm, cook," called Bundini.

Hearing that, Ali stopped suddenly and turned to Bundini. "Now I don't want you to be hollerin' in the corner, Bundini," he said, "and start to get all excited and shout things like 'cook' and all that. It takes my mind off things."

Bundini was furious. "You expect me to keep my mouth shut when the cake is put in the oven?" he shouted. "When all the preparation and the mixin' is done and it's time for the fire, you expect me to stand around with my hands on my hips? Iffen you expect me to keep my mouth shut, you better kick me out of your corner and keep me in *here*."

"All right then, you stay out of the corner," Ali said. "You stay in here."

The two stared at each other, the enormity of what Ali had said beginning to hit. Bundini pressed his lips together and seemed on the edge of tears. "Aw, come on," Ali said gently. "You can come on out."

He started up his shadowboxing, the episode quickly forgotten, once again concentrating on himself in the mirrors. Bundini wouldn't look at him for a while. "My goodness," he said. Sweat began to shine on Ali's body. "I'm warm now," he said, looking at Angelo.

THE DOOR BURST OPEN AND SIDNEY POITIER RUSHED IN. ALI jumped for him and the two spun around the room in an embrace. "Sidney's here! I'm really ready to rumble!" Ali shouted. He held the slim actor off at arm's length and looked at him, elegantly got up in a tight, form-fitting gray suit. "Man, you exercise?" he asked admiringly. "Hey," he said, "give me a rhyme to psyche Quarry—when we're getting' the referee's instructions." He held up an imaginary microphone. Poitier bent his head in thought; he had been caught be surprise. "You met your match, chump," he intoned in his soft voice, ". . . tonight you're falling in . . ." He cast around desperately for a rhyme for 'chump.' ". . . You're falling in *two*," he cried, giving up.

"That's terrible," Ali said. "Man, you stick to actin' and leave me the rhymin' and the psychin'."

Poitier wished him luck amid the laughter, and disappeared.

Ali reached for a towel and began to rub off the Vaseline. "Is the ring nice?" he asked.

"Perfect," Dundee said.

"Is the closed-circuit system O.K.?"

"They say it is."

Outside, the noise of the crowd, impatient now, began to beat at the door. A big roar went up. "Quarry," someone said. "Quarry's gone."

Seconds to go. Ali stood immobile, perhaps to pray, which is his habit, and Jesse Jackson hopped off the rubbing table and embraced him, almost trembling with emotion.

A knock sounded at the door. "It's time," a voice called. Muhammad Ali gave one last peek at himself in the mirrors, and he went out into the corridor, his people packed around him.   ✦

Return

SMOKE AND FIRE Ali's 1971 showdown with Joe Frazier produced a classic bout, and Ali's first loss.

" 'They're all waitin' for me. Fans call me up, write me letters, telling me they worry about me, like will I or won't I be able to beat Jerry Quarry. . . . People tell me it can't be done. You can't come back. I git letters from black brothers beggin' me to be careful. Like Quarry's too tough. . . . and Ali you've been away too long.' "

ALI TO MARK KRAM,
"He Moves Like Silk, Hits Like a Ton," SI, 10/26/70

As Ali set up his Deer Lake, Pa., training camp, the greatest of heavyweights met his match.

In 1971, as the first Ali-Frazier fight drew closer, the hoopla transcended the sports world.

CABIN FEVER Ali wasn't about to take the news that Frazier had called him "crazy" lying down.

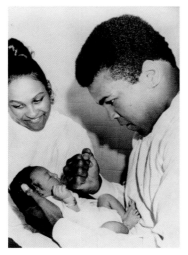

In 1972 Ali and Belinda greeted Muhammad Eban Ali, who weighed in at 7 pounds, 4 ounces.

A 1971 bout between Ali and hoops star Wilt Chamberlain was in reach until Wilt backed out.

"Nothing is the same anymore, not even the king of the world himself ... or, as Bundini Brown calls him: the Blessing of the Planet. 'Everything changes,' says Muhammad Ali. 'Governments change, kings fall, people change. I've changed.' He sits in the back room of the Fifth Street Gym in Miami Beach, back where he began 10 years before.... 'It's been so long,' he says, beginning to dress. 'I never thought I'd be back again, here again. Back in my old life again. All those years.' "

MARK KRAM,
"He Moves Like Silk, Hits Like a Ton," SI, 10/26/70

LOWDOWN In the unbeaten Joe Frazier, Ali faced an opponent who refused to be intimidated.

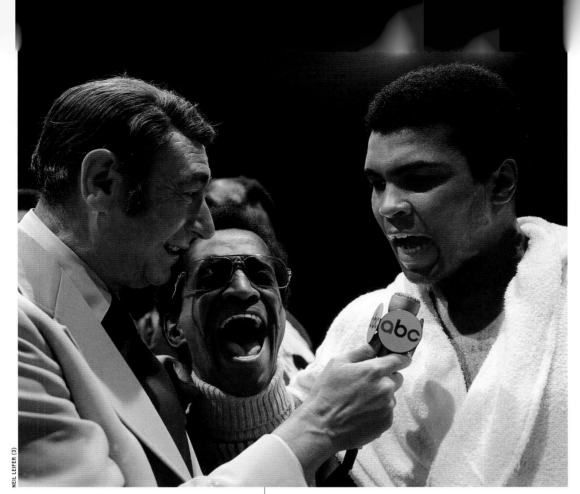

After beating Joe Bugner in 1973,
Ali mixed it up with Howard
Cosell (left) and Sammy Davis Jr.

At ringside on assignment for
LIFE magazine, Frank Sinatra
shot the Ali-Frazier fight his way.

FIT FROM A KING It was a star-spangled night in Las Vegas when Ali entered the ring for his first fight against Bugner wearing a robe given to him by Elvis Presley.

TABLE STAKES Fans watched in comfort as Ali dismantled light heavyweight king Bob Foster in Stateline, Nev., in 1972.

" 'But that ol' Clay is crazy. . . . He goes around the country, preaching that so-called black talk. He's a phony. You know what I mean. He calls people ugly. Now what do that have to do with anything? We didn't make ourselves—God made us.' "

<small>JOE FRAZIER TO MORTON SHANIK,
"I Got a Surprise for Clay," SI, 2/22/71</small>

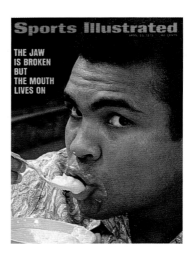

In 1973 Ali enjoyed a close brush with his boyhood idol, all-time great Sugar Ray Robinson.

His jaw may have been broken by Ken Norton in 1973, but there was no shutting Ali up.

Former light heavyweight champ José Torres's 1971 book gave a fighter's take on Ali.

BY GEORGE Before his second fight with Jerry Quarry, in 1972, Ali eyed young contender George Foreman.

AT THE BELL...

BY MARK KRAM

*We held our breath when Ali and Joe Frazier
finally came together to settle who deserved the
title that only one could have*
SI, MARCH 8, 1971

H E WILL BE THE FIRST IN THE RING, SO look at him with honest eyes because you probably will never see such impeccable talent again. Assessed by the familiar standards—punch, size, speed, intelligence, command and imagination—he is without peer and there is nothing he cannot or will not do in a ring. In the aesthetics of boxing, Muhammad Ali transcends the fighter. He is a Balanchine, a Dali, the ultimate action poet who has lifted so primordial an act to eloquent, sometimes weird, beauty. But for all his gifts, it is his fear of failure, of the moment, that is his real strength. All fighters have it, but few shape it into such a positive force. It seems to be the catalyst, the thing that detonates his intense public displays, his psychological war dance that opens the floodgates for his talent. ✦ Move across now to the other corner and there you will see the finest gladiator—in the purest sense of the word—in heavyweight history. To picture Joe Frazier one must recall what happened to Jerry Quarry when he elected to work within Frazier's perimeter. It was like the Wehrmacht crossing into Russia—and the end was the same. Even the most cynical of boxing people

NEIL LEIFER

SHOWDOWN Over 15 rounds, Ali and Frazier waged one of the fiercest of all heavyweight battles. **143** look at Frazier and rhapsodize about his drilling aggression, his volume of threshing-blade punches that make you forget his short arms. He does not have the single, crumpling punch of Marciano, or the sudden ferocity of Dempsey, but he is more mobile than either, and much better to watch. It is that animal joy that he exudes; one has the feeling that he has watched a man bring honesty, a nobility of spirit to his work.

Like deadly weaponry projected from opposite ends of the earth, Muhammad Ali and Joe Frazier collide Monday night at Madison Square Garden for the final sorting out of the heavyweight championship of the world. In itself, that is enough, but there is much more here than a title. This is *the* sporting event of our age, one of the great dramas of our time created by a unique permutation of factors: Ali's unjust exile, his sudden pyrotechnic presence and the political climate that demanded that return; the $2.5 million for each fighter, a bold, brilliant promotional gamble; the beautiful evolution of Joe Frazier; and the reality that both Ali and Frazier might retire no matter what happens.

THE THRUST OF THIS FIGHT ON THE PUBLIC CONSCIOUSNESS IS incalculable. It has been a ceaseless whir that seems to have grown in decibel with each new soliloquy by Ali, with each dead calm promise by Frazier. It has magnetized the imagination of ring theorists, and flushed out polemicists of every persuasion. It has cut deep into the thicket of our national attitudes, and it is a conversational imperative everywhere—from the gabble of big-city salons and factory lunch breaks rife with unreasoning labels, to ghetto saloons with their own false labels.

Americans are curious in their reaction to a heavyweight title bout, especially one of this scope. To some, the styles and personalities of the fighters seem to provide the paraphernalia of a forum; the issues becomes a sieve through which they feel compelled to pour all of the fears and prejudices. Still others find it a convenient opportunity to dispense instant good and evil, right and wrong. The process is as old as boxing: the repelling bluff and bluster of John L. against the suavity and decorum of Gentleman Jim; the insidious malevolence of Johnson vs. the stolidity of Jeffries; the evil incarnate Liston against the vulnerable Patterson. It is a fluid script, crossing over religion, war, politics, race and much of what is so terribly human in all of us.

The fight—mainly an athletic spectacular for many, though it provokes almost unbearable anticipation—also appears to have released manic emotion. The disputation of the New Left comes at Frazier with its spongy thinking and pushbutton passion and seeks to color him white, to denounce him as a capitalist dupe and a Fifth Columnist to the black cause. Those on the other fringe, just as blindly rancorous, see in Ali all that is unhealthy in this country, which in essence means all they will not accept from a black man. For still others, numbed by the shock of a sharply evolving society, he means confusion; he was one of the first to start pouring their lemonade world down the drain.

Among the blacks there is only a whisper of feeling for Frazier, who is deeply cut by their reaction. He is pinned under the most powerful influence on black thought in the country. The militants view Ali as the Mahdi, the one man who has circumvented what they believe to be an international white conspiracy. To the young he is an identity, an incomparable hero of almost mythological dimension. They all need him badly, and they will not part with him easily. They know that if ever a fighter lived who could smash their symbol into fragments it is Joe Frazier. Out of anxiety, a sense of dread, they respond with the most synthetic of accusations: Frazier is the white man's champion, contrived and manipulated to destroy what is once again so close to the black man's heart and soul.

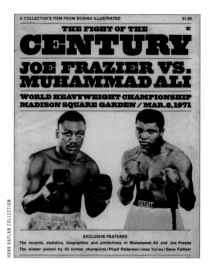

For fans and nonfans alike, Frazier and Ali offered the ultimate clash of styles.

"When he gets to ringside," says Ali, "Frazier will feel like a traitor, though he's not. When he sees those women and those men aren't for him he'll feel a little weakening. He'll have a funny feeling, an angry feeling. Fear is going to come over him. He will realize that Muhammad Ali is the real champ. And he'll feel he's the underdog with the people. And he'll lose a little pride. The pressure will be so great that he'll feel it. Just gettin' in the ring alone with thousands of eyes lookin' at you in those big arenas, and those hot lights comin' down that long aisle. It's going to be real frightful when he goes to his corner. He don't have nothing. But me . . . I have a cause."

It is one thing, however silly it may be, for the black man to impugn Frazier, but it is the worst sort of presumption for whites to denigrate him. Contrasted to Ali's past, Frazier's much more expresses the hard reality—other than politics—of what the black man's life has been and is. Quality of life to Frazier meant a plow, hours and days in the subtropical heat, calluses as big as hen eggs on his hands, and just enough to eat from a table crowded by a huge family. He was raised in South Carolina's Beaufort County—where the government first gave black people "forty acres and a mule," where a recent survey found abysmal poverty and a high percentage of parasites in the blood of black children, more than 50% of whom are infected. "Was I a Tom there . . . then?" asks Frazier.

Ali's early days in Louisville were those of a gifted prodigy rather than those of a ghetto kid. He was from a small family, and he lived and ate well. Work was foreign to him; he spent the summers on the baronial manor of William J. Reynolds, where he concentrated on boxing, playing and occasionally removing the leaves from the Reynolds swimming pool. He was paid $7 a day and, according to a policeman named Joe Martin who shaped his early training, "He drank a gallon of milk a day. They had this milk machine out there where you just pulled the spigot." Ali seems to have been cut off from the harshness of black life. He talked big, dreamed great scenarios, and then found a way to translate them into reality—thanks to the sizable lift given to him by the same kind of white syndicate that has helped Frazier.

What the two reflect seems lamentably lost amid ideologies, emotions, and a cross section of idiocy. Out of the ring, the true character of the fight is that Frazier and Ali encompass much of the best that sometimes is, and more often should be, in all of us—white and black. First, there is the courage of Ali, his obstinacy in the face of rank injustice and rejection. One may question his early motivation (which he himself did not fully understand) and, even now, ponder the argument that is so often posed about Thomas à Becket: Is a man less a saint because he tries to be a saint? After a while it was obvious that Ali was seeking political martyrdom. He got it, and he grew steadily and genuinely with his deed. His vision came high. He lost a fortune in his exile, all for a cause that has been neutralized by the slide of events and the vise of opinion.

If Ali, as some admirers think, is a man of the future, a man whose wiring is so special that he reacts unlike any other yet seen, then Joe Frazier is a rare copy of the old, revered, indomitable man. He came north out of Beaufort, pointed himself in a direction, survived the corruptive influences of North Philadelphia and, with radar accuracy, reached his target. The country, the blacks, need an Ali, and so also is there much room for a Frazier. He feels just as deeply about his people, but he does not know the levers of political action, does not have the imagination for social combat. He understands only the right of the individual to be an individual, to survive and grow and be free of unfair pressures.

THEY HAVE BROKEN CAMP NOW, ALI IN MIAMI, WHERE CRITICS blinked at his usual desultory gym work; Frazier in Philadelphia, where he was just as industrious as ever. But camps seldom reveal what will happen in a fight, and this one defies speculation. Certain points, however, may be made. Frazier must be extremely careful in the early rounds, especially in the first two, when he usually has not quite achieved the pulsating rhythm that is so vital to his style. One can expect Frazier to crowd Ali, to cut his punching radius and to deal with Ali's height by trying to beat him to the body and arms in the hope of bringing the head down to a more workable level. It is unlikely that Frazier will gamble with many right hands to the head, for this would expose him to Ali's wicked flash of a left hook. He will have to absorb some pain from Ali's jab, but he must slip it quickly or he will never be able to put his fight together.

The possibility of a Frazier decision is not as absurd as it may seem—aggressiveness means points, and Joe will definitely take the fight to Ali. In the end, though, the question, which Ali alone can answer, is: How much does he have left? He gave us no real evidence in the Quarry fight. He did what he had to do, but he did not labor long enough for any studied appraisal. He did get a lot of work against Oscar Bonavena, and what was seen was hardly vintage Ali. "The Bonavena fight saved him," says his trainer, Angelo Dundee. "He needed a tough, long fight and he got it. He's never been better. He will be something to watch." Even if he is, Ali will still be in for a hard night against the stark fact of Frazier—cut off from the insulation of his fantasy world in which there is seldom any fact.

It behooves him to listen to the wise counsel of his mother, who stopped off to kiss him goodbye before leaving for the Bahamas.

"Baby," she said, "don't underestimate this Frazier. Work hard. I'm too nervous."

"Don't worry, Mom," Ali said. "I'll be in top shape. He's a bum."

"Sonny . . . he's no bum," she said, then kissed him again.

Whatever the result, there is ample precedent to support the possible occurrence of the unexpected, the ludicrous, the bizarre, especially in an Ali fight. Going all the way back to Johnson-Willard, which many still believe Johnson threw, heavyweight title bouts have often been shrouded in controversy. It remained for Ali, with some help, to make the improbable familiar: the two Liston spectacles; the Chuvalo bout in which he allowed himself to be beaten to the body; the welter of claims of foul tactics when he was in with Terrell; and the night Patterson gimped about the ring because of a back injury and Ali cruelly taunted him. Critics and spectators are usually confused by these moments, and the reaction is often the growl of fix, for the most part an obsolete word in boxing today and certainly unrealistic in this fight.

Still, the prospect of an odd incident, even a close decision for Frazier, offers the potential for trouble, and one can already sense sinister vibrations. So the fight cannot afford the slightest murkiness: no breaches of rules and no confused interpretation of the rules. The referee, who should be black and not allowed to score, must be in absolute control; for him, scoring is diverting. Any bungling, any laxity in supervision is beyond consideration.

So now, with only the hallucinatory ranting of Ali to amuse us and whip the passions of his legions, we can only wait for the climax of the ring's strangest era. Wait and wonder if Ali will fulfill what he calls his divine destiny and deliver as romantic a moment as sport has ever known. Wait and feel the loneliness of Joe Frazier's position, sense his quiet desperation to remove the last obstacle in his life. Wait . . . as the drama tightens like a knotted rope in water.

Ali and Frazier came together in the ring on March 8, 1971, at Madison Square Garden in New York City. Mark Kram was at ringside to chronicle one of the hardest-fought, most compelling bouts in heavyweight history
SI, MARCH 15, 1971

H E HAS ALWAYS WANTED THE WORLD AS HIS AUDIENCE, wanted the kind of attention that few men in history ever receive. So on Monday night it was his, all of it, the intense hate and love of his own nation, the singular concentration and concern of multitudes in every corner of the earth, all of it suddenly blowing across a squared patch of light like a relentless wind. It was his moment, one of the great stages of our time, and it is a matter of supreme irony that after all the years that went into constructing this truly special night Muhammad Ali was in fact carefully securing the details for his own funereal end—in front of the millions he moved deeply.

The people, he said, would be in the streets of Africa and Asia waiting for word of what happened, and what they have heard—by now—is what they never will really believe. The sudden evil of Joe Frazier's left hook, Ali's bold effort to steal time by theatrics, his wicked early pace that left him later without any guns and his insistence on hooking with a hooker (a bad bit of business)—all of this combined to provide the push for his long, long fall from invincibility.

The first dramatic damage to Ali came in the 11th round when Frazier hooked him to the head and followed with a cruel left to the body that sent Ali rolling back to a neutral corner, a man who seemed caught in an immense, violent wave. He hung on, but his eyes took on a terrible softness and they were never the same again. At the bell, water was thrown in his face before he could reach his corner. There, with his medicine man, Bundini, desperately trying to inflame him, and his trainer, Angelo Dundee, shaking a finger frantically in his face, he was pasted back to a semblance of one piece. As he came out for the 12th, one could see that something was wrong with the right side of his face; it was swelling rapidly and his jaw seemed broken.

He spent almost the entire 13th round in a neutral corner, but he was not active and appeared in a trance, oblivious to the hoarse scream of Bundini: "You got God in your corner, Champ!" Ali responded in the 14th, but not convincingly, even though he did win the round; by now both fighters, their bodies graphically spent, were continually draped over each other, looking like big fish who had wallowed onto a beach. Then, in the 15th, Frazier exploded the last shells from that big left gun. It was near the middle of the round, and the left boomed into Ali's face, sending him to the canvas with his head ricocheting frightfully off the floor, his feet waving in the air. He got up and finished the round, but he had lost.

The work of Frazier—his glinting animalism, his intensity of purpose—cannot be minimized or in any way discredited. This was not a negative victory; his smothering pressure contributed much to Ali's weird behavior, the options Ali took in strategy and the exhaustion that began to devour him about the sixth round.

The bout was exciting, theatrical and bizarre—and a mild disappointment to some. "Neither fighter did well what he does best," said Cus D'Amato, boxing's mad scientist. "Frazier, the body puncher, went more effectively to the head, and Clay, the dancer, was flat-footed. But either because of this, or despite it, it was drama of the highest order."

It was obvious what Ali had in mind from the opening bell, and perhaps knowing what he had left in him, he followed the only course open: attack this machine early, shake his confidence. It was a sound tactic; early is when Frazier is most accessible. From the start Ali used flamboyance in an attempt to deflate Frazier's spirit. When both arrived in the ring, he danced across with a smile on his face, brushing abrasively close to Frazier, almost up against him, but the ploy appeared fruitless. In the first moments Ali began doing what he would repeat throughout the early rounds of the fight: every time Frazier's left hook caught him he would shake his head vigorously, telling his audience that the punch did not bother him, telling Frazier that he was wasting his time.

Ali was effective for a while, and there was a clean line to his work. The jab probed and distributed pain and perplexed Frazier. Joe seemed to be trying to stay low, but more and more he began to raise himself into the range of Ali's firepower. Soon, however, it was clear that he was not doing this out of confusion but by design. He was going to take what Ali had to give, and in so doing—he undoubtedly thought—he could intimidate Ali. Frazier took it all—the hard jabs by Ali and that flashing right that traveled instantly behind it. In the third round Joe came out smiling, as he often does at this point in his fights, and he beckoned for Ali to come out and meet him.

A long night was still ahead for Frazier, because this was an Ali determined to put a muzzle on all the mouths that have questioned his courage, his will, his ability to handle pain. "That man," Frazier said later, his own face covered with pyramids of hurt, "can sure take some punches. I went to the country, back home, for some of the shots I hit him with." And Ali's jab faded like a sick flower. His once remarkable legs gone, his arms heavy, he hung on the ropes and spent long and dangerous periods in the corners; it was astonishing that he escaped serious damage. "The way they were hitting," said referee Arthur Mercante, "I was surprised that it went 15. They threw some of the best punches I've ever seen."

"Everyone will remember what happened here," Ali had said before the fight. "What I want them to remember is my art and my science."

They will remember. Though not as he intended.

149

Kings

{ 1973 - 1974 }

CRAFTY WIN FOR MUHAMMAD

BY MARK KRAM

There were no bombs in his fists, but with artfulness ripened through the years, Ali took all that Joe Frazier could offer and easily won their rematch

SI, FEBRUARY 4, 1974

IT IS THE SAME WAY WITH A MAN WITH A HORN; WHEN the lip goes bad, so does the trumpet and the music that he alone made special. He is never the same again, but he can rise to a moment, catch a riff and carry it enough to make the world feel special for having heard him do it. So it was Monday night as Muhammad Ali suddenly erased all the doubts that had accompanied his self-created fantasies. The universe does indeed hold its breath for Ali, and then he gives it air. ✦ He was an artist in search of an art against Joe Frazier before a crowd of 20,788 at Madison Square Garden and millions of others who are moved by him in incomprehensible ways. He did not find what he was looking for, the touch that few men ever have to begin with—age, exile and his playful nature have taken that—but what he did find over 12 steaming rounds was what no man can give another, an understanding of his craft. It is one thing that separates the ring from absolute bestiality, this mostly invisible side of a fighter who takes it—the last thing he learns and the

ROUND TWO In the rematch against Frazier, Ali danced and grabbed his way to a 12-round decision. **153**

HERB SCHARFMAN

last thing that leaves him—and makes it a trenchant, if not dramatic, weapon. That is what Ali did against Frazier, his most persistent adversary over the years, a glorious laborer who came with both pick and shovel, but neither at the same time.

In the end, it was a unanimous decision for Ali: ring generalship over a one-man army fighting a war of attrition. If the fight ever seemed close, it was only because of Frazier's incessant pursuit, which cannot fail to impress even those who may consider it plug ugly, and the occasional bursts—spaced too far apart—of his left hook. For Ali knew what he was about on this night, recalling all the little things that make one a survivor: tying an opponent up, volleying when it would count most, skirting sure trouble like a bank robber.

From the opening bell, Ali took command, much in the way he did in their first fight, except that this time his firepower was lower in volume. Yet there was an economy to his moves, a smooth fluidity to his dancing. He was making every move count. His offense was busy, built on flash attacks of hooks and uppercuts. When he did not work, he made sure Frazer did not either, tying him up time and time again. In the second round Ali stopped Joe with a right hand. Frazer winced, momentarily reflected that he was still on his feet and continued his assault. The first four rounds were clearly Ali's, leaving Frazier only eight in which to salvage a fight that would turn out to be a severe blow to his career.

Joe never did find all his weapons. He appeared frustrated, unable to sustain an attack. He groped, floundering as Ali slipped most of his best shots. Then in the seventh and eighth rounds he appeared to generate something striking. Ali was slapping. His arms appeared heavy, like tree limbs weighted with Spanish moss. He was even reverting to his old habit of straying aimlessly into corners, a sign of a tired fighter. In the ninth, it looked as if Ali would lose another round, until suddenly he retrieved it with some solid work.

After that moment of Ali's command, the affair seemed hopeless for Frazier. Points would not win the match; Frazier would need a knockout. It never did come, and soon Ali was sitting on a platform in a chair in the interview room eating ice cream on a stick—the eternal child. His eyes bounced along the faces of the press and television, and they seemed to be saying that this can go on forever. "Answer me," he prodded. "Do I look like I'm 32 years old? Did I fight like a 32-year-old?" The answer is yes and no—depending on what was expected from the fight.

EVEN ALI'S OLDEST ENEMY, THE WHITE WORKING MAN, WHO could never abide his mouth, let alone his beliefs, seemed to ignore him as something not worthy of any squabbling. Frazier was not terribly meaningful to them, either—losers never are. As for Ali's hard core of brethren, those with the Borsalino hats and peacock flounces who hang on his every word and draw fire from him, none of them seemed beside themselves with anticipation as they had been for Fight I.

Yet they knew that the show, the bombast, the theatrical tempest that only Ali can provide would come—and it did. No one has changed prefight atmosphere more than Ali. It used to be a static thing: contrived news from training camps, all of it enough to gag a goat, if not the columnists who were paid by the promoters. Ali changed the script with his souffléd hysterias that time and again left his vast audience, detractors as well as supporters, in genuine awe.

Ali probably never had, nor will ever again have, a more perfect foil before a fight than Joe Frazier. Everything about Frazier is a source of material to Ali: his style as a fighter, suggesting a wild beast tangled in a thicket; that head that catches so many punches, leaving Ali to conclude that he is an utter fool; Frazier's simplicity as a man, his belief of live and let live. These are aspects of Frazier that Ali cannot abide, even if he does not despise them, for they are alien, abrasive to a man in desperate pursuit of immortality.

Ali finally got to Frazier, thus igniting the flame that gave Fight II a character of its own: pure enmity. Even days before the fight, it promised to be a match that would provide nothing more than a wistful reminder of the past, a bout between two men with bankrupt talents. Then, as Frazier and Ali met in a television studio to review films of their first bout, the lid came off, and beneath it was the raw torment of Frazier. Joe seemed to be handling the racial slurs well enough. "You went to the hospital," he said to Ali.

"I went to the hospital for 10 minutes and you went to the hospital for 10 months," Ali countered.

"Just for a rest," said Joe. "In and out."

"That shows how dumb you are," said Ali. The exchange went on, and Ali said again, "That shows how ignorant. . . ."

With that, Frazier got up and reached down to pull Ali out of his chair. Ali got a headlock on him, and the two tumbled off the stage. It is true that Ali, as always, had an eye on the closed-circuit receipts, or needed a psychological stimulant, but no doubt can exist about the intent of Frazier. They both were fined $5,000 for behavior "demeaning the sport of boxing," and that has to be one of the superb lines of our time.

In the ring, neither Frazier nor Ali could or did insult their business. For they are a special pair, and even with what they have left they were able to light up the night. Ali's critics wanted a crucifixion, but what they saw was a big man enter the ring and a bigger man leave it. Frazier's detractors wanted to see him beaten with bloody conviction, humiliated because he had so rudely throttled the myth of Ali the first time. Instead, they saw a wonderful foot soldier who has simply climbed out of too many trenches.

"How old those two fellas?" a lady in a gold fur asked, leaving the Garden.

"Thirty-two and 30," said a man next to her. "Frazier's 30."

"My, myyyyy, he looks sooooo old."

So he does. And there is a French phrase that tells a lot about what many thought after seeing him: "To say goodbye is to die a little."

He was a singular man—and also a fighter.   ✦

Kings

NEW HORIZONS For Ali,
journeying to Africa was both
a homecoming and the start of
a new chapter in his career.

ODD COUPLE Part vaudeville, part social history, the ongoing Cosell-Ali banter became a pop-culture touchstone.

Heavyweight king meets a prince: In 1974 Ali took a shot from the 13-year-old John F. Kennedy Jr.

The Greatest vs. the Smallest: Mishu, at 33 inches the world's tiniest man, stood tall against Ali.

"Ali still addresses mankind, but something has gone out of him. There is a vulnerability about him now, and not because of his deeply stained talent. Looking at him, one gathers that there is a sense of imminent danger in him, that something is on his trail and he cannot shake it. Often, after one of his long and, by this time, dull monologues about the "blue-eyed, blond white devils" and the face of Joe Frazier—'ugly, so ugggly'—he seems to become strangely silent.

"Ask him what is on his mind, and he will try to take you on another tour of his camp, or he will rhapsodize about the 'strength of rocks,' the virtues of log-cabin life. Ask him again what he often thinks about these days and he replies quietly: 'Age. Things gone. People dyin'. People bein' born. Don't know what it all means.' "

MARK KRAM,
"Scenario of Pride—and Decline," SI, 1/21/1974

ROAD WARRIOR Shrouded in the mist of a Pennsylvania dawn, Ali put in the miles in preparation for facing George Foreman.

ABSOLUTE POWER Before the Foreman fight, Ali strolled with promoter Don King (in white) and Zairian dictator **Mobutu (center).**

DOPE FIEND Shocking even his own corner, Ali unveiled the rope-a-dope in Zaire, risking ruin as he let Foreman punch away and exhaust himself.

NEIL LEIFER (2)

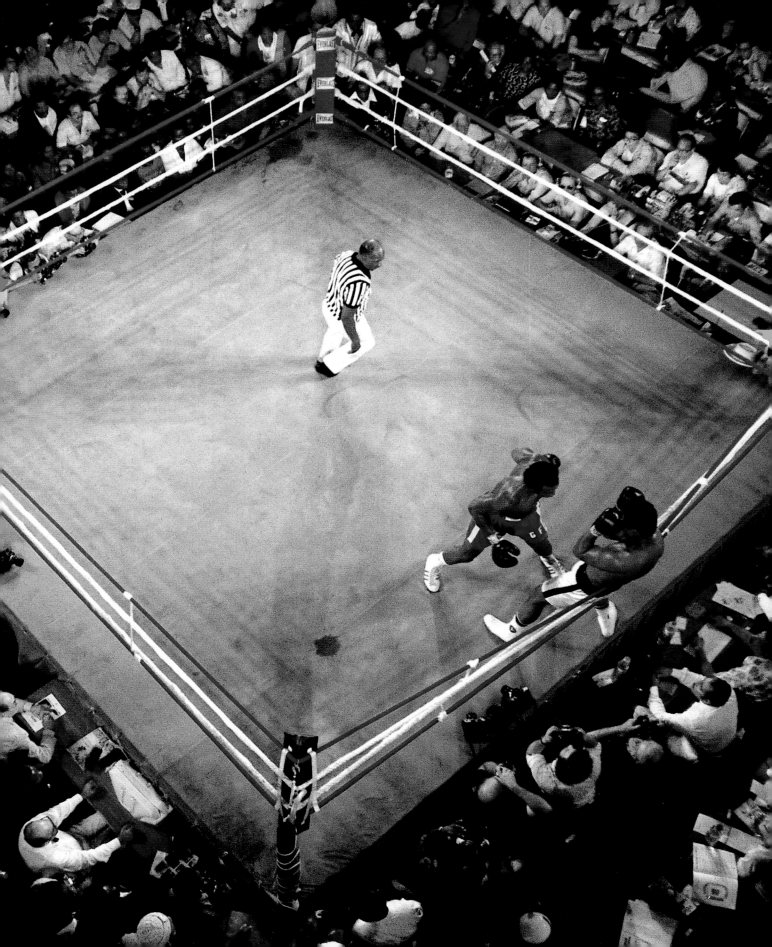

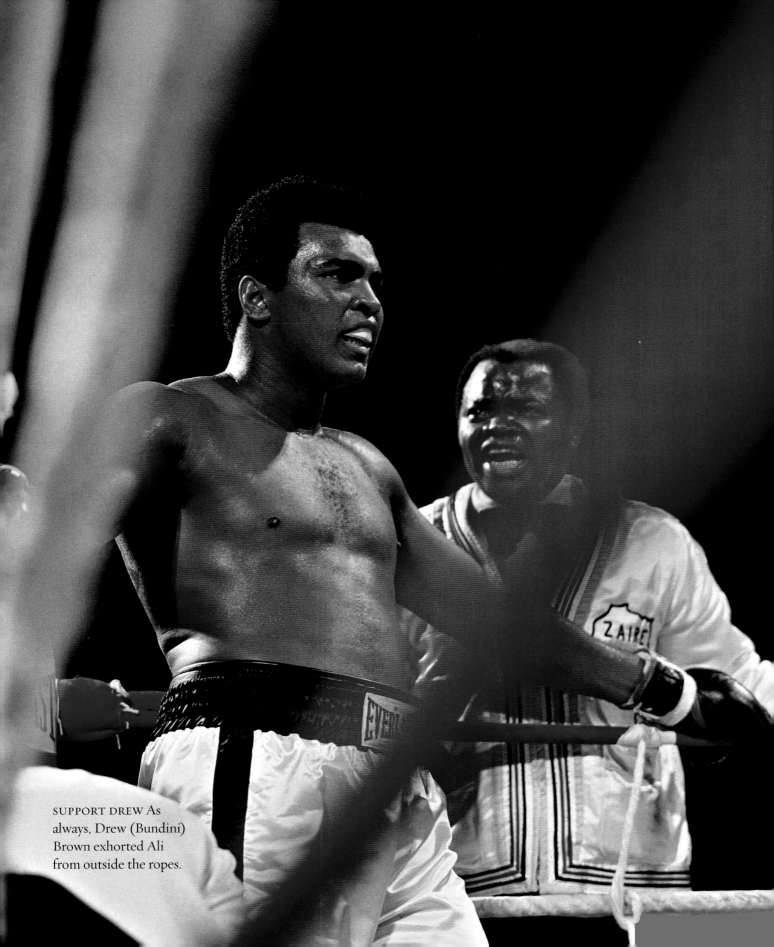

SUPPORT DREW As always, Drew (Bundini) Brown exhorted Ali from outside the ropes.

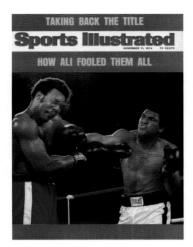

Ali's reclaiming of the title landed him on the cover of SI for the 18th time in his career.

No fighter had ever hit Foreman with the sort of cover-worthy shots Ali landed again and again.

"The intriguing irony of his career is that his two most inspired, memorable triumphs—his eight-round knockout of George Foreman in Kinshasa, Zaire, on Oct. 30, 1974, to regain the title stolen from him in 1967, and his 14-round war with Joe Frazier 11 months later in Manila—came years after he had lost his best stuff. Surely nothing else that Ali ever did inside the ropes was quite as spectacular as his dismemberment of Foreman, who had arrived in Africa with a menacing glower and a ring history that had Ali followers fearing for their man's life."

WILLIAM NACK, *"Forty for the Ages,"* SI, 9/19/1994

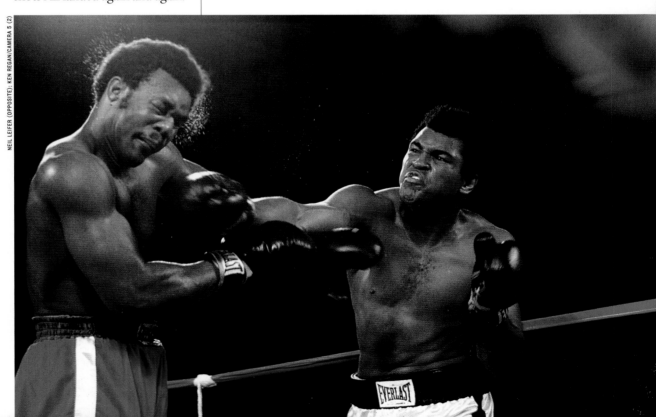

NEIL LEIFER (OPPOSITE); KEN REGAN/CAMERA 5 (2)

TEN AND OUT As referee
Zack Clayton tolled the count
over Foreman, Ali—and a
rapturous crowd—realized
he was champion again.

GEORGE
FOREMAN
MUHAMMAD
ALI
COMME EUX, AYEZ
MOBUTU
CE MATCH
CITOYEN

BREAKING A DATE
FOR THE DANCE

BY GEORGE PLIMPTON

Training to face George Foreman, Ali promised to overcome the champion's fearsome power with fancy footwork, but his secret plan was a stunner
SI, NOVEMBER 11, 1974

I T IS HARD TO IMAGINE WHAT THE EXTRAORDINARY events in the predawn hours under a pale African moon in Zaire are going to do to the future of boxing. Kids who for years in the backlots of the world have emulated the flamboyant and graceful style of their idol, Muhammad Ali, the butterfly who floats and stings like a bee, will now imagine themselves coming off their stools and standing stolidly and flat-footed in the corner of the ring, or, more extreme, lolling back against the ropes, their upper torsos out over the press-row typewriters at the angle of someone looking out his window to see if there's a cat on his roof. For such were the Ali tactics that surprised everyone—including the men in his own corner—and proved insoluble to George Foreman, the heavily favored heavyweight champion, leading him to destruction as surely as the big cartoon wolf, licking his chops, is tricked into some extravagantly ghastly trap laid by a sly mouse. ✦ The witnesses to all this, those lucky enough to see what will surely be considered one of the greatest

FIGHT CROWD The 1974 showdown between Ali and Foreman had all of Zaire jumping.   **171** fights in boxing history, began to fill the 60,000-capacity stadium at nightfall, hours before the main event scheduled for 4 a.m. They had come from all parts of a country that had thought of little else for a month. Both fighters had their strong partisans in Zaire, and many among the crowd were *féticheurs*, the witch doctors of Kinshasa who often turn up at sporting events on behalf of clients, handsomely paid to try to influence the outcome. Indeed, among many Zaireans the rumor was that Muhammad Ali himself had gone to one of the best féticheurs in town, perhaps even the Pygmy reputedly used by President Mobutu, and had paid a considerable sum for a spell to be cast against George Foreman. The odds were almost 3 to 1 against Ali and it seemed the sensible thing to do. The spell was supposed to manifest itself in the form of a beautiful girl "with slightly trembling hands" who would clasp Foreman's hand in some chance meeting— like Blind Pew passing the Black Spot—and the strength would slowly drain from him.

The féticheurs (often with their clients packed around them in adjacent seats) occasionally raise their voices in a loud humming incantation. They wear a slightly more ornate form of dress, and dangling from amulets or in leather pouches they carry the artifacts of their profession: bones, fingernail clippings, chicken claws, the tips of antelope horns and other such charms. And since proximity increases their effectiveness, it would be a sure bet that at fight time a number of these objects would have been planted under the boxing ring.

The ring also had been doctored, in a more prosaic fashion, by Angelo Dundee, Muhammad Ali's trainer. He turned up at the stadium on the morning of the fight to see that the floor was as fast as he could make it by coating rosin thickly on the baby-blue surface, and by hammering wedges under it to make the canvas drumhead hard, so that his fighter could get a toehold for his swift moves.

Dick Sadler, the champion's manager, had no objections to this. Since both fighters would use the same surface, it would serve Foreman just as well. "The best way to slow down a ring," Sadler said, "is with a hard left to the jaw, a right hand to the heart, and a left hook to the kidney. Though I'm not saying that my fighter's a kidney puncher."

Sadler was very confident. "When George hits a guy, he lifts them off their feet," he said. "To win, Ali must have some sort of a break, a fluke. There's too much against him—me, Sandy Saddler and Archie Moore—that's two Hall of Famers and over 300 knockouts between us. And then George Foreman . . . no, no, that's too many things."

Everything one heard about Foreman suggested someone indestructible and devastating. The conjecture everywhere, including Ali's camp, was that the answer lay in staying away from the champion's power, moving and hitting. "I can step in, pop-pop-pop, and then step out," Ali said. "I can't help tagging him. He don't want to be tagged. He cannot stand a beating." Ali produced a couplet:

> When all is said and did and done
> George Foreman will fall in one.

It was a joke. Everyone laughed. It was ludicrous. The emphasis with Ali so surely had to be on speed and dancing. On the last day of his sparring, Ali came to the ropes and looked out at the crowd. He rested his forearms on the top rope and, turning an arm, he opened one hand. A small sparrow flew out and rose quickly into the upper reaches of the gym. Bundini Brown, one of Ali's cornermen, had trapped it in the press bus and given it to him. "That's what I am," Ali said. "When I fight George Foreman, I'm going to fly like a bird."

ALI WAS UP AT 2 A.M. ON THE MORNING OF THE FIGHT. HE dressed in a black shirt, black trousers and the boots he considers the trademark of his profession. He and his party stood on the esplanade overlooking the River Zaire. The moon was directly above, and there was almost no conversation, the group looking out over the great river with the hyacinth drifting by in dark clumps, the mood that of men getting ready for a patrol.

But the long ride from N'sele to the great stadium in Kinshasa seemed to change Ali's spirits. The revolving overhead fans were going in his dressing room. Ali came in blinking, squinting his eyes open and shut like anyone getting up too early in the morning. He looked at some of the long faces around him and asked, "What's wrong around here? Everybody scared?"

He said that he had watched a horror film that evening called *Baron of Blood* and *that* had scared him, kept him right on the edge of his seat, but he wasn't frightened about what was coming. He scoffed at the thought. "This ain't nothing but another day in the dramatic life of Muhammad Ali. Scared? A little thing like this! Do I look scared?" He grinned and put on a mock face of fear, his eyes rolling. "Nothing much scares me. Horror films. I fear Allah and thunderstorms and bad plane rides. But this is like another day in the gym."

Someone reached for his hand and said, "Good luck."

"Luck?" he repeated in derision. "No man, *skill*!"

He undressed and put on a long white ceremonial robe with black trimmings for his ring appearance. "Look how long and beautiful it is. It's African and everybody can look at it and tell it's African." Usually Ali wears a robe designed by Bundini Brown, who now stood by, looking uncomfortable.

"Where's your robe, Bundini?" Ali asked.

Bundini brought his forward. It was trimmed with the Zairean colors and had a map of the country stitched above the heart. Bundini himself wore a matching jacket.

"Look how much better *this* one looks." Ali spun like a dress model in front of the mirror. "It's African. Look in the mirror."

Bundini refused. With his robe draped over his arm he stared fixedly at the fighter.

Ali slapped him, the sound quite sharp in the dressing room. "You look when I tell you!

Don't ever do a thing like that." He slapped him again. Bundini stood with his feet together, swaying slightly, still holding his robe and looking at Ali. He refused to look in the mirror.

No one took much notice. It was perhaps quieter, the hum of the fans turning, and then Ali shrugged and went over and sat on the edge of the training table. In a low singsong voice he began a soft litany of verses and musings, some of which stretched back 10 years to the night in Miami when he had won the championship from Sonny Liston: "Float like a butterfly, sting like a bee. . . . You can't hit what you can't see. . . . I been broke. . . . I been down. . . . but not knocked out. . . . it's strange getting stopped. . . ." He concluded the little review of his boxing career with a cry (very much discouraged by Zairean officials but one he cannot resist) which brought him clear up to the present: "Now! Let's rumble in the jungle!"

He hopped off the table and set about making Bundini feel better about the incident over the robe.

"Bundini, we gonna dance?" he called. Silence.

"Ain't we gonna dance, Bundini? You know I can't dance without you."

"You turned down my robe," Bundini said moodily.

Ali shrugged his shoulders. He said a champion ought to be able to make *some* decisions on his own—what to eat, when to sleep, what to wear—and he did it so beguilingly that finally Bundini had a smile working at his lips.

"Are we going to dance?"

"All night long," replied Bundini, back in form at last, and drawing it out like a response at a prayer meeting.

Someone called out, "Ten minutes."

Angelo Dundee began to tape Ali's hands. Doc Broadus, Foreman's representative, stood by to watch. Ali looked at him. "Tell your man to be ready for the dance," he said.

Broadus said, barely audibly, "He can't dance."

"What's he say?"

"George Foreman's man says he can't dance."

Ali feigned incredulity, and then he began to laugh. All around the room his people began to smile, most of them almost sheepishly, as if high spirits were not appropriate to what lay ahead.

Ferdie Pacheco, Ali's physician, came back from watching Foreman's hands being taped. "Man, is it tense in there," he said. "Not a sound. They got Foreman covered in towels so you can just see his eyes looking out."

"He's getting warmed up for the Big Dance," Ali said. "Are we going to dance with him?" he called out.

"All night long," replied Bundini.

The mental image of Ali dancing was what everyone carried out onto the field where the great crowd stood up to see him arrive. Not one person in Kinshasa or the watching world, except for Ali himself, had the slightest suspicion that in the first seconds of the fight, indeed at the sound of the opening bell, he would take a few flat-footed steps toward the center of the ring and then back himself into a corner—with Foreman, scarcely believing his eyes, coming swiftly in after him.

For one sickening moment it looked as if a fix were on, that since the challenger was to succumb in the first round it would be best if he went quickly and mutely to a corner so the champion could go to work on him. It was either that or Ali was going through the odd penitential rite he seems to insist on for each fight, letting himself suffer the best his opponent

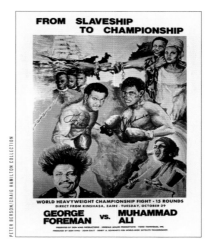

In his first major promotion King played heavily on the theme of black pride.

has to offer. In either case, the consequences were appalling to consider. Ali's cornermen rose as one and, in the shrieks reserved for warning someone walking blindly toward the edge of a cliff, they urged their man to stop what he was doing and start dancing.

Far from obliging, Ali moved from the corner to the *ropes*—traditionally a sort of halfway house to the canvas for the exhausted fighter who hopes perhaps the referee will take pity on him and stop things. Here was Ali in the same spot, his feet square to his opponent, leaning far back out over the seats, his eyes popping wide as if at the temerity of what he was doing, while Foreman stood in front of him and began to punch—huge heavy blows thrown from down around the hips, street-fighter style, telegraphed so that Ali was able to slip and block many of them. Then, with the bell coming up for the end of the round, Ali came off the ropes. While Foreman's arms were down in punching position Ali hit him with a series of quick, smart punches in the face, the best of them a right hand lead that knocked the sweat flying in a halo. The vast crowd roared, and perhaps there were a few who began to sense that they were not in for a night of lunacy after all. Angelo Dundee noticed that almost immediately Foreman's face began to puff up.

Still, when Ali came back to his corner his men stormed at him as he sat on his stool.

"What you doin'?"

"Why don't you dance?"

"You *got* to dance!"

"Stay off the ropes. . . ."

Ali, looking across the ring, told them to shut up. "Don't talk. I know what I'm doing," he said.

The second and third rounds were carbon copies of the first exciting round though, as Dick Sadler pointed out later, very few of the ingredients of scientific boxing were involved. No countering, no feinting, no moving; simply the hugely terrifying and unique process of seeing a man slowly drained of his energy and resources by an opponent swaying on the ropes, giving him—as Angelo Dundee was to say later—"a lot of nothing."

In the third round, in the midst of continued tremendous pressure from Foreman, Ali hit him some concussive shots, staggered him, and suddenly everybody except Foreman seemed to understand not only the plan but that it was working almost inevitably. Ali's cornermen looked at him as if they were a trio of Professor Higginses looking at their Eliza for the first time.

The notion of fighting Foreman out of a defensive position, blocking and making his opponent slug and miss to the point of weariness, was an idea Ali had only toyed with back in his Deer Lake, Pa., training period earlier in the summer. Then in Africa, spying on Foreman training sessions, he watched the doggedness with which the champion pursued his sparring partners, cutting the ring on them and perfecting this practice to such a degree that Ali realized far too great a percentage of his own strength and resources would have to be devoted to the simple process of escape. The Deer Lake tactics began to make more sense. Indeed, the only weakness attributed to Foreman was that he tended to get flustered and wild if things were not going exactly his way. Perhaps the surprise of Ali's defensive tactics would have this result. It seemed worth trying. If it did not work, if the Foreman punches seemed too devastating, Ali could always (if he survived) go back to the dancing techniques everyone expected.

Later, amidst the storm of excitement in his corner after the third round, he told Angelo Dundee that it seemed to be working, that Foreman's punches were acceptable ("They're not that bad"), and he told his astonished trainer that he was going out to continue to let Foreman pound at him.

In the fourth round Ali began to talk to Foreman. It is not easy to speak through a boxer's mouthpiece but Ali began doing a lot of it, more as the rounds progressed, as if it would quicken the matter of Foreman's destruction—"Is that the best you can do? You can't punch. Show me something. That's a sissy punch"—until he finally turned it around to what must have been a devastating thing for Foreman to hear: "Now it's my turn."

Still there was no change in Foreman's tactics. He kept it up, this useless exhaustion of energy, what Bundini Brown called the "emptying of the bank," the punches coming slower and more ponderously, until rising off his stool after the bell and coming across the ring at Ali, he seemed as pathetic in the single-mindedness of his attack plan as the mummies of Ali's beloved horror films, as programmed as the stiff-moving figure lurching through the mists after the life-giving draughts of tana leaves. Indeed, the Mummy had been Ali's name for Foreman, one of the inspired appellatives Ali finds for his opponents (the Washerwoman for George Chuvalo, the Bear for Liston), and nothing could have been more descriptive of Foreman's groping for him in the last rounds. "I am going to be the Mummy's Curse," Ali had said a few days before the fight.

BY THE EIGHTH ROUND NOTHING WAS LEFT. FOREMAN WAS helpless. But here was another ugly possibility, that Ali would choose to toy with his opponent and physically tease him as he had Floyd Patterson in Las Vegas. Herbert Muhammad, the son of the Black Muslim leader, sent up word from his ringside seat that his father would not want Ali to play around. Bundini passed it on in the corner, that Herbert did not want his daddy, Elijah, disgraced.

But Ali was not toying with Foreman any more than a circling mongoose fools with a prey exhausted from striking. In the sad business of dispatching a hulk, he did it quickly and crisply with a combination of lefts and rights that sent Foreman flying to the canvas on his back.

Archie Moore, his face round and benign under his wool cap, came up onto the ring apron; he moved along the ropes trying to attract Foreman's attention with arm motions, signaling him to turn onto his stomach and get a knee under him to push himself up. The count went to nine. Then Archie gave a small wince of despair as he saw referee Zack Clayton sweep his arms briskly back and forth over Foreman as if he were safe at home in a baseball game.

George Foreman could not remember the last seconds of the fight. He lay on the rubbing table in his red-walled dressing room, gold lamé towels draped over his shoulders, ice packs applied to his face. He asked Dick Sadler if he had been knocked out cold. Like a man flexing a leg that has gone to sleep, he began testing his senses, counting slowly backward from 100, and then calling out the names of everyone he could think of in his camp, a doleful roll call of more than 20 names. His first answers to reporters suggested a man trying to forget a somewhat hazy and uncomfortable dream, knowing that if he worked at remembering it, the bad scenes would come back. He said that he was not tired, that he felt truly that he had been in control of the fight and that he had felt "secure" until to his considerable surprise his cornermen had jumped into the ring. "He won the fight," Foreman said unsurely, "but I cannot admit that he beat me. It's never been said that I have been knocked out."

Over and over, as if in vindication of a program that could not have failed (it really hadn't, had it?), he repeated that he had followed Dick Sadler's directions "to the best of my ability." His only criticism was that "they had pumped my head up a little too much."

Then he repeated, at times so slowly that it seemed as if he were stumbling through a written text, what he had so often said in dressing-room statements following his victories: "There is never a loser. No fighter should be a winner. Both should be applauded."

The reporters stood around uncomfortably, knowing that it would finally sink in that for the first time in his pro career his generous words for a loser referred to himself.

The rest of Foreman's camp seemed just as bewildered. It was almost as if black magic were involved, that the girl from the féticheurs with her "slightly trembling hand" had indeed got to Foreman to drain the strength from him.

Dick Sadler threw his hands up in petulance. "Everything we planned to do—cutting the ring, overpowering Ali, going after him—was designed to put him on the ropes. And there he *was*. Just exactly where we wanted him." His voice was high-pitched with frustration. "The bird's nest was on the ground. It was time to sit down to eat the feast. But George didn't do it right. He wasn't doing what he was supposed to. Hard combinations. Getting in closer. He wasn't setting him up with the left hand. We *told* him. It didn't register."

Archie Moore had a more sanguine view. He pointed out that the champion did not really *have* Ali on the ropes. Ali had placed himself there, which was quite different, and thus he was in the tradition of the great "rope fighters" like Young Jack Thompson, a welterweight champion of the '20s who used the ropes with the skill of a spider on the strands of his web.

Moore cleared his throat. He is extravagant not only polysyllabically but in the use of metaphor, and he had one to offer. "Ali swayed so far back on the ropes that it was like he was sitting in an old convertible Cadillac. The '54 model," he added, being very accurate about such things. "Now, George tried to enter from the side doors. But they were *shut*. So George began to bang at them, hitting at Ali's arms that had the elbows protecting his hips, on up to the gloves protecting the lower mandible. On occasion George struck Ali some tremendous blows on the upper cranium, causing Ali no little discomfiture. But Ali weathered that, and he cunningly convinced George that he couldn't punch and other such nonsensical things, until George began to behave like he actually *believed* it, until this tremendous puncher lost his power from punching at that Cadillac's doors and turned from an atomic force into a firecracker. In short," said the great ex-fighter, "as they say in the idiom of Brooklyn, he blew his cool."

In the days after the fight, when his senses had fully returned, Foreman himself offered no excuses. "If you go out rabbit hunting," he said, "and you're a poor man, and all you got is a rifle, and a table, and a family at home . . . and out in the field there's a rabbit—Bam!—and you miss, it don't do no good to come with excuses to put on the table."

"But you had the rabbit dead in your rifle sights in the ring," someone said.

Foreman shrugged. "The tactics were mine. Every time I fought someone he eventually got it. Regardless of where he went or what he did in the ring, eventually he got it. I thought that was going to happen. One of the shots would get him. But this guy never really fought. He was like someone in a canoe. He rolled along with the tide, waiting for it to turn. He was clever."

The object of Foreman's admiration was trying out his new title. "Heavyweight champion of the world," Ali said, drawing out the words. "It's going to take about a week to sink in."

TEN YEARS BEFORE IN HIS SMALL TRAINING QUARTERS IN South Miami he had covered his mattress with a felt-tipped scrawl of those magic words next to his name (Cassius Clay then) to see how it would look if he won the title. Now a decade later, and after not having it for seven years, the title was his once more, and with it befitting adulation. It had been dawn when the new champion left the stadium on the night of his victory. Along the route out of town back to his training compound on the Zaire, at every village and crossing, the crowds that had heard the news were out along the road, often whole rows leaping in exultation, so that the passage of his small caravan—headed by a police car with an orange beacon twirling, then his Citroën and the two buses with his camp people—seemed like the return of a military column into liberated territory.

It was only when the convoy reached open country that the crowds began to dwindle. The first drops of rain began to fall. Heavy low clouds scudded on the hills ahead. It had rained furiously in Miami after Ali had won the championship from Liston. Now the rain drummed on the bus roof. For the last miles to the compound the convoy crept through the first driving downpour of the rainy season. In one of the quirks of good luck that finally graced the fight, the storm had held off just long enough; as it came down the river toward Kinshasa, it knocked out the huge signal-sending facilities to the satellites, so that the millions who watched the fight on closed circuit or on television sets would have seen their picture fade and then go blank if the storm had come through an hour or so earlier. When the storm reached the stadium in Kinshasa, the water drained down the seats onto the grass and toward the center of the field as if the ring stood above a gigantic sluice. Under the stadium stands, the water stood a foot deep in George Foreman's dressing room. In the city it thrashed the flame trees and sent the bright blossoms swirling down the boulevards.

Kinshasa is a city symbolically appropriate to the fall and shifts of dominance and power. Everywhere, usually at the end of a broad avenue, or in front of a government building, are great bare stone pedestals, now flat on top, with weeds growing in the cracks, on which once stood the imposing statues of Belgian colonial rule. On the promontory above the stretch of the Zaire which is still called Stanley's Pool, the famous statue of the explorer himself once stood, peering up the river under the palm of one hand like an Indian chief. It too has been pulled down and lies in a giant shed near the National Museum in a jumble of cast-iron horses and kings. The roof of the shed is tin. On the dawn of the day the heavyweight crown shifted hands, the sound of the rain on the roof must have been deafening. ✦

Thrilla

{ 1974 - 1976 }

MANILA—FOR BLOOD AND FOR MONEY

BY MARK KRAM

*The thrilla promised to be more a chilla
as Ali and Frazier expressed
bitter thoughts before the showdown*
SI, SEPTEMBER 29, 1975

HIS METAPHYSICAL BAGGAGE BY NOW lashed down to a handy place in his mind after a numbing 21-hour trip above a world that seems to have assigned him a regency never before known by a fighter, Muhammad Ali sits in the presidential suite looking out at the great ships of the world anchored in Manila Bay. The sun punches up slowly over the water, and the beauty of the scene is not lost on this man whose mind wanders forever and confusingly between the poles of simpleton and primitive genius. "Just look at those ships," he says, "think of all the monsoons they must have fought through to get here, all the mighty oceans that could have snapped them in half." ◆ "My, my," he says softly. "Ain't the world somethin'. Too beautiful for an ignorant and ugly man to be king of." ◆ A day later, with the wind and rain whipping against the windows of another hotel suite across town, Joe Frazier, the man who would be king, lies on his bed, trying to articulate the hurt that has burned through his

THREESOME King saw riches in a third Ali-Frazier bout, but for the fighters, far more was at stake.   **183** heart and mind for so long that the words come in spasms. And if words could consign a man to everlasting hell, Muhammad Ali would be damned right that very moment. Frazier tries to find control, tries futilely to reach back for equilibrium, leaning on country Baptist teachings and his own clear and gracious nature, which sticks out, oddly moving, like a common dark stone on a white mantelpiece. "I don't want to knock him out here in Manila," he finally says. "I want to hurt him. If I knock him down, I'll stand back, give him a chance to breathe, to get up. It's his heart I want."

So after a long five years that have seen two fights between them (the first a brilliant drama), that have seen Ali become an instrument of international politics and economics, have seen the proud foot soldier Frazier manhandled in the second fight, perhaps the rawest of sports feuds will come to a public end when Ali and Frazier meet for the third time next week in Manila. Listen to Ali about the fight, and the firmament is ablaze. Listen to Frazier, and you feel the sun on an open field that has to be worked, touch the blisters on his hands.

It is a proposition of the heart and blood for Frazier, an offering to Allah and another chance to light up the lives of the world's disenfranchised for Ali, but beyond all of this is that most unromantic of motives—money. If the bout goes 15 rounds, Ali will receive $4 million for 45 minutes' work, and Frazier will get $2 million. The revenue from closed-circuit television will surely break all existing records. As promoter Don King says, "This ain't just a sportin' event. This here is a dramatic contribution to the world's economy. Waiters will be waitin'. Bartenders will be tendin'. The brothers and sisters gonna be buyin' new clothes. Why, I got enough people on my payroll alone for this here happenin' to buy a jet plane, and go back and forth to New Orleans up until the year 2000. Jack, this is the ennnnnnd."

WHEN THE SUN COMES UP IN MANILA ON OCT. 1 (IN New York it will be 6 p.m. Sept. 30), thousands will have been camping overnight outside the Coliseum. The top ticket costs $300; the lowest price, for a bleacher seat, is $2. A crowd of 28,000, the largest for any athletic event in Philippine history, is expected, and what it will see at 10:30 a.m. will be a rare thing: two of the most luminous heavyweights in ring history in the kind of showdown that seldom comes once in a lifetime, not to mention thrice. There is nothing contrived here.

Even so, it is doubtful that Ali and Frazier will match their first fight, a masterpiece of courage and talent and high tension that left one damp with sweat and tingling hours later. Never before had two big men given so much so artfully and completely. And no one will ever forget the sight of Ali, finally crumbling under one of Frazier's cruel left hooks, his feet kicking high toward the ring lights. The knockdown hurt Ali's chances for a decision, and in the end Frazier, his face looking like a gargoyle's, was the champion. Frazier spent days in the hospital, and it was rumored that he would never be the same again. He did not do much to refute those rumors in his second meeting with Ali.

No title was at stake in January of 1974, but still the private limousines were parked two deep around Madison Square Garden, and the crowd came with the first fight exploding in its memory. No one cared that Ali had lost to Ken Norton once and barely beaten him another time, or that George Foreman had knocked down Frazier six times in two rounds. In this fight, Ali walked a thin line between ring generalship and slovenly style. Clinching whenever he could (he started 114 of them), Ali found a way to disrupt Frazier's attack. But there was not much of the old Joe visible. His thrilling aggression was gone, the ceaseless bob and weave almost nonexistent, and had the referee not blundered, thinking the bell had sounded, and prematurely separated them, Joe might have been knocked out in the second round. His lance had clearly dropped near to the ground. Was he through? Maybe not, but he was near the end.

Since then, Frazier has fought a total of 14 rounds in two fights, Ali 49 rounds in four fights. "He ain't in no shape for a man like me," says Ali. Yet Frazier looks very sharp in his daily workouts in the Folk Arts Theater, a beautiful structure that juts into Manila Bay. Every day about 2,000 people pay the equivalent of $1.25 to watch him snort and hammer his way through an assortment of sparring partners. The crowd always seems stunned by his animalism, by the toughness of his 217 pounds. Then Frazier goes to the ring apron and fields questions from the Filipinos before singing into the mike: *You tried to shake it off/ Ooh, but you just couldn't do it/'Cause there was a soul power in my punch/And like a good left hook I threw it/One minute you were standing so tall/The next second you began to fall.*

Ali hears that Frazier sings at his workouts and says, "Are you kiddin'? That man can't sing. He's the only nigger in the world ain't got rhythm." That kind of talk has finally and irrevocably eroded Frazier, but nothing has disturbed him more over the years than Ali's recent taunts. Over and over Ali shouts, "Joe Frazier is a gorilla, and he's gonna fall in Manila." The gorilla label, with all its inherent racism, stings. Frazier glances at a picture on his dresser. "Look at my beautiful kids," he says, plaintively. "Now, how can I be a gorilla? That's a dirty man. He's just like a kid when you play with him. He don't wanna stop, and then ya gots to whup him to make him behave. That's what this jerk Clay is like. Well, I guess he gonna talk. Ain't no way to stop him, but there will come that moment when he gonna be all alone, when he gonna hear that knock on the door, gonna hear it's time to go to the ring, and then he gonna remember what it's like to be in with me, how hard and long this night's gonna be."

The condemned man, Ali, is not hurrying through any last meal. Indeed, he seems to be preoccupied by his appeal to the masses. "My personality has attracted the world," he says. "My personality has gone so far till America can't afford me anymore. The American promoters can't have me no more 'cause they can't bid against so many countries. My personality and the power that Allah has given me has gone so far out that

America is cryin' and the Garden is dyin'. When I was a little boy, I used to say, 'Daddy, one day I'm gonna make $4,000 on the *Gillette Cavalcade of Sports*.' Can you imagine—$4,000! That's what I pay my cooks for a bonus. No nation can contain me anymore."

Or, if bored by his universal radiance, Ali will begin speechifying. The monologues are dead certain to clear a room. Especially when the subject is Allah. Through the years he has put together about 10 speeches, most of them written by the kitchen light of his fight camp. He listens to tapes that carry his messages: "He is beyond the reach of range and time. . . . He sees though He has no eyes. He created everything without a model, pattern or sample." Ali turns down the volume. "I get this in my mind," he interjects, "and I have real power over Joe Frazier. I can whup him. Allah knows if I will, I'll keep doin' His preachin' for Him. That's why I win all the time. I'm using my fame to talk about this man. The world's mystified by me. It likes to be mystified. You know, stuff like Batman and Robin, Dracula, the Wolfman, Mary had a child without a man.

"I train myself spiritually. Frazier's fightin' for money. I'm fightin' for free people. How many suits I got? One, two maybe. No watch, no ring, one pair of shoes. I've got Eldorados and Rolls-Royces, but I don't drive 'em anymore. Where's a man's wealth? His wealth is in his knowledge. If you don't think I'm wealthy, go talk to Joe Frazier and try to carry on a conversation. He's illiterate. I spoke at Harvard. They wanted me to be a professor of poetry at Oxford. I'm shockin' the world. But even I, Muhammad Ali, don't amount to nothin' more than a leaf in the wind. Ain't nothin' yours, either. You own nothin'. Not even your kids. You die, and they will be callin' somebody else Daddy when your wife remarries."

IT IS ENDLESS, THIS RELIGIOUS BACKWATER THROUGH WHICH ALL HIS listeners must wade. It is as if he believes that being the heavyweight champion is not enough and that the Filipinos want much more from him. The simple truth is that they want nothing more than to gaze upon him. Each day more than 8,000 of them shove their way into the theater to watch him work. Thousands more line the streets when he goes to an official function, and at five in the morning—an hour after the end of curfew but still pitch dark—bands of them accompany him on his roadwork, creating a charming scene of tenacious, small men trying to match the giant stride for stride along the boulevard by the bay. Once he stepped into a hole and he turned around and shouted, "Watch out for the hole." He ends his running on the steps of the Hilton, and there he sits in the dark in a gray sweat suit and black boots, tilting a large bottle of orange juice into his mouth. The sweat drops off him as he leans back on his elbows. He looks at the faces around him, listens to the heavy silence. "Look at their expressions," he whispers. "Ain't no man worthy of that kind of love."

At this time, he is likely to talk about boxing. He can feel his body, listen to its music as he ties once more to make it reach for the high note of condition. "You been watchin' my gym work?" he asks. "Don't pay any attention to it. I'm nothin' in a gym. I just use it to experiment, you know that. This fight is goin' to be won out here in the mawnin', and on that heavy bag. I hadn't worked on the heavy bag for a long time, until George Foreman in Africa. I kept hurtin' my hands all the time. They've never been in the best of shape, and the bag I had was brutal on 'em. Ya hit that old bag with a baseball bat and the bat breaks in two. This one is especially made in Mexico, and it's easy on the hands. It got me sharp for Foreman, seemed to give me strength. I never let it out of my sight now. I sleep with it in my room. My men carry it personally on and off planes. I am strong, and I kin feel it all hummin' inside me. That heavy bag has done a miracle. I got my punch back."

He sits there for a long time, and then retires to his room. He is alone now. He does not like to be alone. He needs his audience to abuse or charm. But now he is alone, except for his man, his mute body servant from Malaysia. Ali looks over at him, and says, as if he were an old sergeant major out of Kipling, "Look at him, he's so obedient. Always says 'yessir, yessir.' He'll go fetch anything for you. He'll even take your shoes off for you. He's civilized."

Ali arises and picks up a large book that has been written about him. "I haven't read 10 pages in all the books written about me. I can't read too good; a bad speller, too. I read one page and turn it and get tired. I just look at the pictures. I know that sounds dumb." He reads for a long minute, following each word with his little finger. "Oh, I wish I could read better." The frustration of a child is in his voice, and then it turns to anger as he is asked about the gorilla tag that he has pinned on Frazier. "The way I've been talkin' black power," he says, "nobody can get on me for bein' ignorant or racist. Why does he call me Clay? That's my nigger slave name. He's insultin' my name and my religion. He ain't nobody. I made him. Now he's just an old has-been. He envies me. When he was a kid, I was the champ. He's an old man now, long before his time, and I'm still the champ."

Frazier has avoided any personal collision with Ali. His trainer, Eddie Futch, does not want his man ruffled. Frazier and Futch refuse to be suckered into public exchanges with Ali. They think of nothing but the fight. Futch is particularly concerned about the choice of referee. It is sure to be a bitter issue. "It's the most vital aspect of the bout," says Eddie. "I want a referee who's goin' to let my man fight. I want one who's goin' to break Ali every time he starts leanin' in and holdin'. Give us this, and Joe Frazier will once more be heavyweight champion of the world."

Neither man will offer a prediction. Frazier never has and does not intend to start now: "I don't believe in predictin' I'm gonna knock a man out, because if you tell me you're gonna push me out the window at midnight, I'm gonna sit there and watch you along about 11:59." Ali says, "I'm too old for that stuff now. This is a serious fight. I'm goin' to be classical. None of this Russian-tank stuff, none of the rope-a-dope. I got too much at stake here. I got $16 million in fights waitin' for me."

Too many questions include a private choice. Can Ali once more orchestrate his body to his will against a man who has always tested both severely? Is he really in shape?

Has he maintained the form he showed against Joe Bugner in Malaysia last July? Some close to him say no, that the women and the problems that come with them have seriously disrupted his concentration.

What about Frazier? Is this gallant man finally at the end of the line? Can he summon up one last measure of his old self, the Frazier who made the heart pump wildly and the hands clammy? For both Frazier and Ali, a sense of finality creeps into their words as the bout nears. "This is a big gatherin'," says Frazier. "And I don't like big gatherin's. It's like when we were all back home in South Carolina, and all of us, all the relatives, would be havin' a fish fry in the backyard, and everybody would be laughin', but my momma would be sittin' there lookin' sadly out. She didn't like big gatherin's. Big gatherin's mean death."

Lost in a long silence, Ali comes out of it and suddenly says in a barely audible voice, "I'm goin' to have another test soon. It's time. Things have been goin' too good lately. Allah must make me pay for my fame and power. Somebody may shoot me, who knows? I might be kidnapped and told to renounce the Muslims publicly—or else. O.K., shoot me, I'll have to say. I feel somethin' out there. My little boy might die. He might get run over by a car the day before the fight. Allah's always testin' you. He don't let you get great for nothin'. It ain't no accident I'm the greatest man in the world." Then he looks at those ships in the bay, and who knows what wondrous and strange things are gliding through so unpredictable a mind. Only this is certain now: ahead lies the hatred of Joe Frazier, and Ali must journey through it. And it is a trip that few men should wish to make.

IT'S ALL IN WHERE THE FEAR FALLS
BY BUNDINI BROWN

SOME PEOPLE ASK ME EXACTLY WHAT IT IS I DO. I MEAN, YOU ALWAYS see me right there, in Ali's corner and all. They say that I have so many titles, but what I really am is the assistant to Angelo Dundee. Not an assistant—*the* assistant, the No. 1 man to him. I was *born* to do this; you might actually say that I got my job from God, if you know what I mean. Listen, if Muhammad Ali was a cake, I'd be the nutmeg in it. So much for what I do. Now what about the Ali-Frazier fight?

Ali is confident. He's been confident all along. But don't anybody try to predict or figure out just what he's gonna do when the fighting starts. I don't think anybody knows what Ali's gonna do, even himself. He has a built-in antenna that picks up moods. He's creative. He's not a boxing robot, you know. He is flesh and blood; I mean, one of the flesh-and-bloodest men I ever met.

First fight: We left Miami, and Ali was in superb condition. In New York all those people crushed around and you couldn't even walk the street, couldn't move in the Garden. So you're a young fellow and you feel all this confidence, plus you have ego and strength. So, with all that confidence, Ali played around with Frazier. Every time he has played around in a fight, he has got hurt. And I can't tell you what he'll do this time.

Remember, Ali has got all these personalities running around inside him. They come and go regularly. Sometimes he's a little boy, sometimes he's a fighter, and you can squeeze a father in there sometimes. Most of all, what you've got is a man who is magic, see, and because he's magic he knows he's got the whole world pulling for him, and that, plus his skill, is now making him cool down a little bit.

Second fight: We had Frazier out in the second round. I mean *out*! He was on Queer Street—only the referee thought he heard the bell. Listen, I ran right up there outside the ring, and I met Ali halfway down the outside of the ropes, and I reached right in and took out Ali's mouthpiece. I thought the fight was *over*; I had jumped up around Dundee and everybody. I wanted that mouthpiece out when they held up the champ's hand and all. But the referee called them back, and Ali went back fighting without a mouthpiece. And I had to get down out of there and pray for him and hope that Angelo hadn't seen all this and wouldn't get mad at me. Boy, I get nervous a lot, but I was never that nervous. I thought it was all my fault. And then, as the fight went on, I could slowly tell that Ali was born to do it. He got his job from God, too.

And now for the third fight. We are in better condition in every way and we've got a happy camp. Maybe I can't tell you just how Ali is gonna do it, but I can sure tell you why. No matter what you think of Frazier, remember this. Once you beat him, the confidence falls on *you* and the fear falls on *him*. It has to, because you've already beat him, see?

Ali just might beat him in the third round. I can't make the picks because I don't do the fighting. But doesn't it make sense? Second fight Ali had him beat in the second round. Third fight, in the third, the way I see it. Gotta be.

For one thing, I remember a little boy, and now I'm seeing a man in the ring. This time I'm going to sing my *Float Like a Butterfly* song right away. I always sing it sometime, but not right off. And folks ask me, can Ali hear me when he's there in the corner between rounds and I'm leaning over and all the fans are screaming and the place is a loud madhouse? Well, I'll tell you, Ali doesn't hear me so much as he gets a feeling in his head when I sing.

In a fight camp before a fight, it's the confidence. I'll tell you something that nobody else knows. In Zaire when Foreman cut his eye in training and they postponed the fight, that was the turning point. Understand now, if only Foreman had stood up and said, "Shoot, don't worry none about this little old cut, it's nothing. I'll fight him right now." If only he had done that, Foreman would have stole the whole show, the whole thing—and taken it away from Ali. But, no. The magic moment passed and all Foreman did was to walk his dog and not say anything, and he lost the confidence; he flat lost it. Even if they didn't let them fight—and they probably wouldn't have—Foreman would have stole it from us. But he gave it back. Then we were the stars. You play with a man's mind, and his body is gone.

Back to Frazier and Ali. If you understand about the confidence and about stealing the show, you'll understand how it's got to come out. How would you feel if you were Frazier? You know what you've got to do. But you remember the first fight. Can't forget it. You win it and you end up in the hospital. What? How many days—nine? Listen, a guy can get hit by a *car* and be out in three days.

Only thing everybody worries about is Ali playing around. Well, I don't know. But he's a man now, he knows he's the greatest. If he's the greatest, why play around?

'FLAMBOYANT EVENTS . . . HAVE THEIR PLACE'

Mark Kram interviewed Ferdinand Marcos

PRESIDENT FERDINAND MARCOS HAD GREETED MUHAMMAD ALI and Joe Frazier in his private study, a cool, dark place in the Malacañang Palace. After talking to the two fighters, the president consented to a private interview with SPORTS ILLUSTRATED. He sat behind a big desk, wearing a Barong Tagalog, the traditional long Philippine shirt made of banana and pineapple fibers. He said some people were waiting, but there was no need to hurry. It was two days short of the anniversary of the imposition of martial law in the Philippines. The fight—the use of sport to project the image of his country—was important to the President.

Do you have any critical thoughts about Ali vs. Frazier, Mr. President?

No, I intend to remain quiet about the two fighters. They look good, and Ali seems slimmer than I thought. I can't believe he is 229, as the reports say.

You look in fine shape yourself, sir.

Well, I exercise every day, and I have to. I was very active when I was in college, and then, too, the doctors insist that I exercise. I don't feel well if I don't exercise.

Have you done any boxing yourself?

Yes, as a flyweight and then as a bantamweight. I wrestled, too.

Are you especially fond of any one sport?

Well, I was a national champion in shooting. I won the championship when I was 16 and kept it for many years. My shooting got me in trouble. I was once charged with murder, but was acquitted.

What do you think of Ali? Do you think he transcends sports?

Yes, yes. My wife was watching television carrying the interviews with Ali. When I came into the room she said, "You know that Muhammad Ali, he doesn't act like a boxer or athlete. He is brilliant in his repartee. He would make a damned good politician."

Do you see Ali as a kind of symbol of the Third World?

Yes, no matter what he says, Ali symbolizes success in that part of the world which sees white men as colonial and the like. The old voices against colonialism are all over Asia again because of the Vietnam debacle, and Ali symbolizes a continuing protest against this racism and dominance because of color and birth. And while this may not be fascinating to the Western world, it is to Asians a highly charged matter.

Do you think the Philippines will benefit greatly from holding this fight?

We have benefited already. The fight publicizes our country. Many people do not know where the Philippines are and don't know what the situation is here. They think that the military runs the government, tanks are on the streets. Have you seen any tanks? They think people are arrested on any pretext. That there is oppression, tyranny and the civil government is nonexistent or inoperative. That there are no judges. But whatever you fellows say, you must see that the fight can be held here in peace and order.

In the hotel lobbies they used to shoot each other. The airport you came though, they tried to burn that down. They tried to burn down city hall. They kidnapped someone every day. Nobody, no visitors get hit over the head in Manila anymore. Under martial law we are very strict with criminals.

Do you have a scheme for a series of events, such as this one and the $5 million Fischer-Karpov world-championship match?

No, the fight just fell into place. Fischer is a friend, and we played chess long before he was champion. I learned to play in prison.

Will you be satisfied with what you get in return for your government's $4 million investment in the fight?

Actually, the investment will be recovered, and beyond that we will have this publicity, but it is not just the common crowd-getting type of publicity. It is the word of truth about the Philippines. Martial law connotes something oppressive, and therefore always meets with antagonism from people who don't understand that under our system, martial law has been utilized not as a weapon of the status quo, but a weapon of reform. Martial law here was proclaimed at the insistence of the people. I sought their advice.

Will you try to get more events like this?

Well, frankly, the economic technicians don't look with favor on flamboyant events like this. But I have always maintained that they have their place in the scheme of things in our development plans.

Thank you, Mr. President.

The people who had been kept waiting were seven cabinet ministers. Four were fired and three retired as soon as they entered the room, in a major move by President Marcos against corruption in the government.   ✦

Thrilla

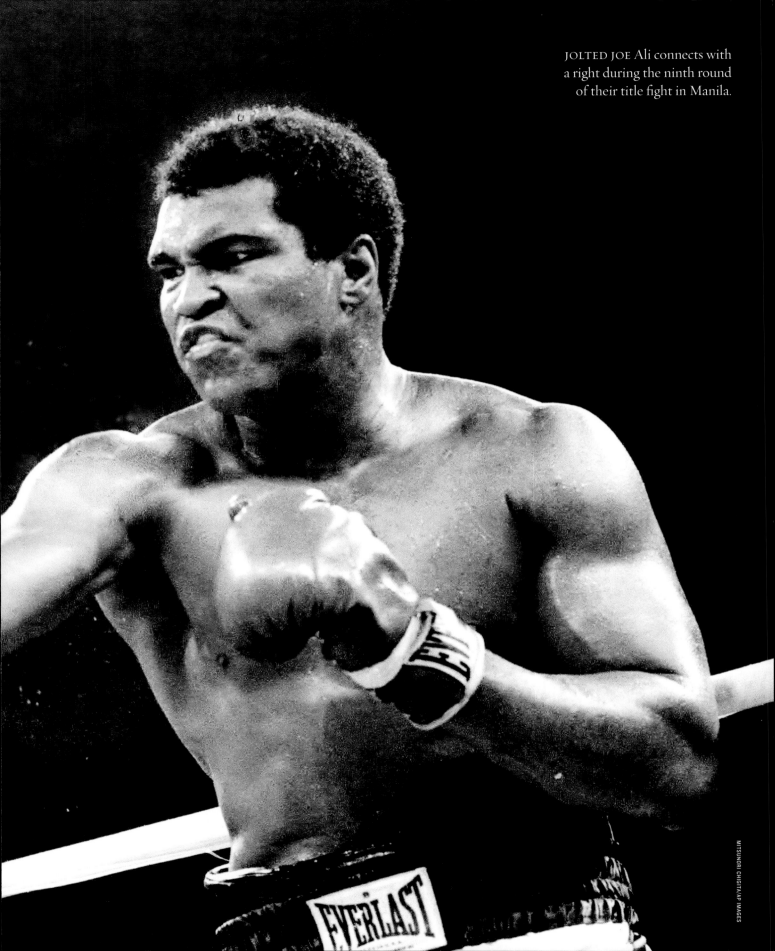

JOLTED JOE Ali connects with a right during the ninth round of their title fight in Manila.

MITSUNORI CHIGITA/AP IMAGES

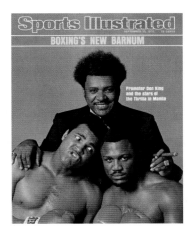

SI brought together the principals, King, Ali and Frazier, for this 1975 pre-Thrilla cover.

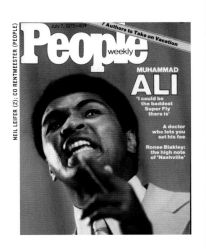

By 1975, not even PEOPLE magazine could resist a cover on the most famous man in the world.

" 'The power of the world,' says [Don] King, 'is slowly shifting, and you don't have to be no prophet like . . . who was the old dude? Yeah, Nostradeemusss. It's right in front of your nose, if you wanna look. But I don't care about politics. Just call me a promoter. Not the first black one. Not the first green one. But *theeee* promoter, Jack. There ain't no others, 'cause they've only had three in the history of the world: P.T. Barnum, Mike Todd, and you are lookin' at the third. Nobody kin deny it. They mock me at their peril.'

"Some do though—with passion. They look upon him as a blowhard, a mountebank—and look at the way he dresses, like an M.C. in a cheap nightclub. 'Just an uppity nigger, right?' says King. But the facts bit back in his defense: he has raised $35 million in less than a year for his boxing spectaculars; he has made more money for Muhammad Ali 'than Ali done in all his previous fights in his whole career.' "

MARK KRAM,
"There Ain't No Others Like Me," SI, 9/15/1975

CAMPAIGN TRAIL Always the populist, Ali took a break from roadwork to play with a baby.

Ali was feted like visiting royalty in Manila, including an audience with first lady Imelda Marcos.

Smokin' Joe stayed unbuttoned during the prefight walk-up, a look that won over local police.

"Soon Ali got down to real business, announcing a title defense against Joe Frazier on Oct. 1 in Manila. Frazier is a crusty barnacle that has stuck to him throughout his postexile career, the one man who can bring real drama back to the heavyweight division. Up to now the public faith has been severely used by Ali, by his manager Herbert Muhammad and by his promoter Don King. Before the sun set in steamy Malaysia, Ali was at work on Joe Frazier."

MARK KRAM, *"A Two-Ring Circus,"* SI, 7/14/75

THRILLA

LEANING TOWERS The Thrilla was a brutal war of attrition; both champ and challenger were worn down after 14 of history's most vicious rounds.

NEIL LEIFER (2)

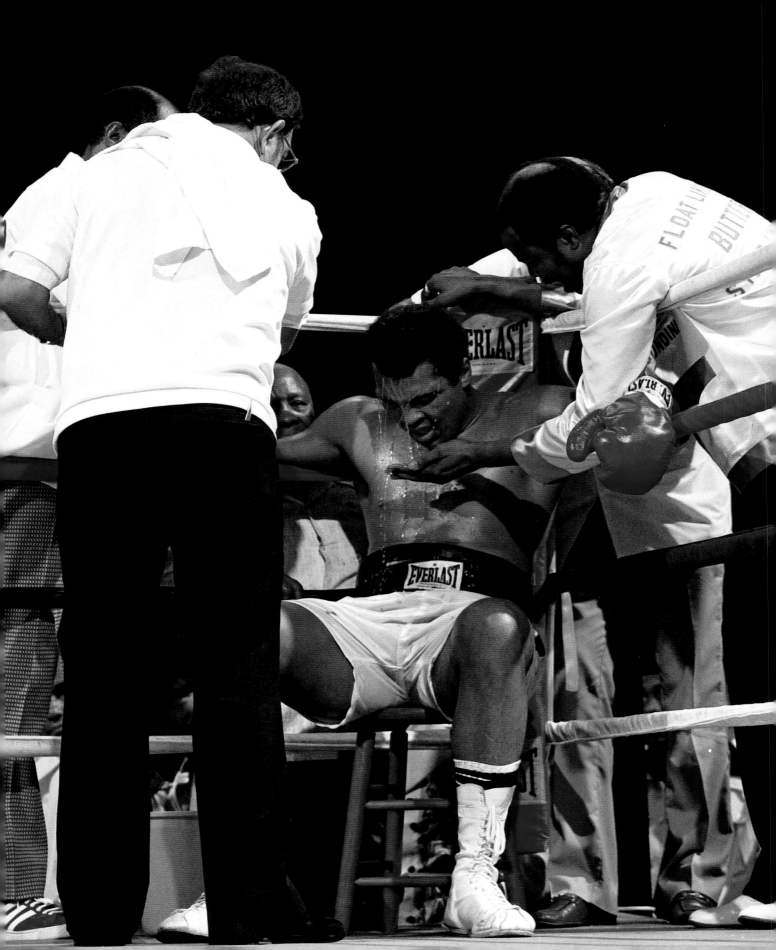

"I knew Ali would take a beating. Eddie Futch, Frazier's manager, he's a smart man. His fighter is a hooker, and Futch would see to it that those ropes were tight. I know what Joe Frazier is. He's a good fighter. I had to contend with him myself. Some people said Ali hurt Frazier so bad in their first fight that Joe didn't have nothing left for me, which is why I knocked him out so fast. That's ridiculous. Just some more foolishness. Look at what Joe has done to Ali since then."

GEORGE FOREMAN WITH EDWIN SHRAKE,
"Man, Big George Is Back," SI, 12/15/1975

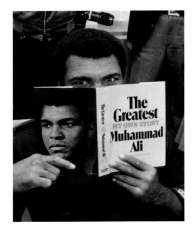

Ali's autobiography was a best-seller in 1975; there would eventually be over 100 biographies.

Ali had transformed from a dancer to a slugger by the time he met Frazier in Manila.

THE BELL TOLLS Ali
would later admit that
he almost didn't answer
the bell for the 15th.

THE SPOILS Ali, his father by his side, accepts a trophy from President Ferdinand Marcos.

Despite losing to Ali, Frazier mustered the energy to do his own shuffle at a postfight party.

The champ always had time for reporters; here he holds court the day after defeating Frazier.

"Remember, Ali has got all these personalities running around inside him. They come and go regularly. Sometimes he's a little boy, sometimes he's a fighter, and you can squeeze a father in there sometimes. Most of all, what you've got is a man who is magic, see, and because he's magic he knows he's got the whole world pulling for him, and that, plus his skill, is now making him cool down a little bit."

DREW (BUNDINI) BROWN,
"It's All in Where the Fear Falls," SI, 9/29/1975

"LAWDY, LAWDY, HE'S GREAT"

BY MARK KRAM

*Joe Frazier said that of Muhammad Ali, but so fierce
and unsparing was their 1975 confrontation in Manila
that the phrase could have applied to them both*

SI, OCTOBER 13, 1975

T WAS ONLY A MOMENT, SLIDING PAST THE EYES like the sudden shifting of light and shadow, but long years from now it will remain a pure and moving glimpse of hard reality, and if Muhammad Ali could have turned his eyes upon himself, what first and final truth would he have seen? He had been led up the winding, red-carpeted staircase by Imelda Marcos, the First Lady of the Philippines, as the guest of honor at the Malacañang Palace. Soft music drifted in from the terrace as the beautiful Imelda guided the massive and still heavyweight champion of the world to the long buffet ornamented by huge candelabra. The two whispered, and then she stopped and filled his plate, and as he waited the candles threw an eerie light across the face of a man who only a few hours before had survived the ultimate inquisition of himself and his art. ✦ The maddest of existentialists, one of the great surrealists of our time, the king of all he sees, Ali had never before appeared so vulnerable and fragile, so pitiably unmajestic, so far from the universe he claims as his alone. He could barely hold his fork, and he lifted the food slowly up to his bottom lip, which had been scraped pink. The skin on his face was dull and

NEIL LEIFER

BIG GUNS Though Ali repeatedly landed tremendous shots, Frazier kept coming, right till the end.   **205**

blotched, his eyes drained of that familiar childlike wonder. His right eye was a deep purple, beginning to close, a dark blind being drawn against a harsh light. He chewed his
food painfully, and then he suddenly moved away from the candles as if he had become
aware of the mask he was wearing, as if an inner voice were laughing at him. He
shrugged, and the moment was gone.

A couple of miles away in the bedroom of a villa, the man who has always demanded
answers of Ali, has trailed the champion like a timber wolf, lay in semidarkness. Only his
heavy breathing disturbed the quiet as an old friend walked to within two feet of him.
"Who is it?" asked Joe Frazier, lifting himself to look around. "Who is it? I can't see! I can't
see! Turn the lights on!" Another light was turned on, but Frazier still could not see.
The scene cannot be forgotten; this good and gallant man lying there, embodying the
remains of a will never before seen in a ring, a will that had carried him so far—and now
surely too far. His eyes were only slits, his face looked as if it had been painted by Goya.
"Man, I hit him with punches that'd bring down the walls of a city," said Frazier. "Lawdy,
Lawdy, he's a great champion." Then he put his head back down on the pillow, and soon
there was only the heavy breathing of deep sleep slapping like big waves against the
silence.

Time may well erode that long morning of drama in Manila, but for anyone who was
there those faces will return again and again to evoke what it was like when two of the
greatest heavyweights of any era met for a third time, and left millions limp around
the world. Muhammad Ali caught the way it was: "It was like death. Closest thing to dyin'
that I know of."

Ali's version of death began about 10:45 a.m. on Oct. 1 in Manila. Up to then his attitude had been almost frivolous. He would simply not accept Joe Frazier as a man or
as a fighter, despite the bitter lesson Frazier had given him in their first savage meeting.
Aesthetics govern all of Ali's actions and conclusions; the way a man looks, the way he
moves is what interests Ali. By Ali's standards, Frazier was not pretty as a man and
without semblance of style as a fighter. Frazier was an affront to beauty, to Ali's own
beauty as well as to his precious concept of how a good fighter should move. Ali did
not hate Frazier, but he viewed him with the contempt of a man who cannot bear anything short of physical and professional perfection.

Right up until the bell rang for Round 1, Ali was dead certain that Frazier was through,
was convinced that he was no more than a shell, that too many punches to the head
had left Frazier only one more solid shot removed from a tin cup and some pencils.
"What kind of man can take all those punches to the head?" he asked himself over and
over. He could never come up with an answer. Eventually, he dismissed Frazier as the
embodiment of animal stupidity. Before the bell Ali was subdued in his corner, often
looking down to his manager, Herbert Muhammad, and conversing aimlessly. Once,
seeing a bottle of mineral water in front of Herbert, he said, "Whatcha got there, Her-

bert? Gin! You don't need any of that. Just another day's work. I'm gonna put a whuppin' on this nigger's head."

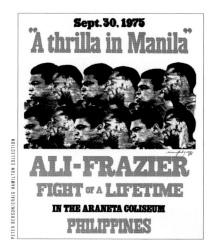

The reality exceeded the hype, as the fight proved to be a thriller for the ages.

Across the ring Joe Frazier was wearing trunks that seemed to have been cut from a farmer's overalls. He was darkly tense, bobbing up and down as if trying to start a cold motor inside himself. Hatred had never been a part of him, but words like "gorilla," "ugly," "ignorant"—all the cruelty of Ali's endless vilifications—had finally bitten deeply into his soul. He was there not seeking victory alone; he wanted to take Ali's heart out and then crush it slowly in his hands. One thought of the moment days before, when Ali and Frazier with their handlers between them were walking out of the Malacañang Palace, and Frazier said to Ali, leaning over and measuring each word, "I'm gonna whip your half-breed ass."

By packed and malodorous Jeepneys, by small and tinny taxis, by limousine and by worn-out bikes, 28,000 had made their way into the Philippine Coliseum. The morning sun beat down, and the South China Sea brought not a whisper of wind. The streets of the city emptied as the bout came on public television. At ringside, even though the arena was air-conditioned, the heat wrapped around the body like a heavy wet rope. By now, President Ferdinand Marcos, a small brown derringer of a man, and Imelda, beautiful and cool as if she were relaxed on a palace balcony taking tea, had been seated.

True to his plan, arrogant and contemptuous of an opponent's worth as never before, Ali opened the fight flat-footed in the center of the ring, his hands whipping out and back like the pistons of an enormous and magnificent engine. Much broader than he has ever been, the look of swift destruction defined by his every move, Ali seemed indestructible. Once, so long ago, he had been a splendidly plumed bird who wrote on the wind a singular kind of poetry of the body, but now he was down to earth, brought down by the changing shape of his body, by a sense of his own vulnerability, and by the years of excess. Dancing was for a ballroom; the ugly hunt was on. Head up and unprotected, Frazier stayed in the mouth of the cannon, and the big gun roared again and again.

Frazier's legs buckled two or three times in that first round, and in the second he took more lashing as Ali loaded on him all the meanness that he could find in himself. "He won't call you Clay no more," Bundini Brown, the spirit man, cried hoarsely from the corner. To Bundini, the fight would be a question of where fear first registered, but

207

there was no fear in Frazier. In the third round Frazier was shaken twice, and looked as if he might go at any second as his head jerked up toward the hot lights and the sweat flew off his face. Ali hit Frazier at will, and when he chose to do otherwise he stuck his long left arm in Frazier's face. Ali would not be holding in this bout as he had in the second. The referee, a brisk workman, was not going to tolerate clinching. If he needed to buy time, Ali would have to use his long left to disturb Frazier's balance.

A hint of shift came in the fourth. Frazier seemed to be picking up the beat, his threshing-blade punches started to come into range as he snorted and rolled closer. "Stay mean with him, champ!" Ali's corner screamed. Ali still had his man in his sights, and whipped at his head furiously. But at the end of the round, sensing a change and annoyed, he glared at Frazier and said, "You dumb chump, you!" Ali fought the whole fifth round in his own corner. Frazier worked his body, the whack of his gloves on Ali's kidneys sounding like heavy thunder. "Get out of the goddamn corner," shouted Angelo Dundee, Ali's trainer. "Stop playin'," squawked Herbert Muhammad, wringing his hands and wiping the mineral water nervously from his mouth. Did they know what was ahead?

Came the sixth, and here it was, that one special moment that you always look for when Joe Frazier is in a fight. Most of his fights have shown this: you can go so far into that desolate and dark place where the heart of Frazier pounds, you can waste his perimeters, you can see his head hanging in the public square, may even believe that you have him, but then suddenly you learn that you have not. Once more the pattern emerged as Frazier loosed all of the fury, all that has made him a brilliant heavyweight. He was in close now, fighting off Ali's chest, the place where he has to be. His old calling card—that sudden evil, his left hook—was working the head of Ali. Two hooks ripped with slaughterhouse finality at Ali's jaw, causing Imelda Marcos to look down at her feet, and the President to wince as if a knife had been stuck in his back. Ali's legs seemed to search for the floor. He was in serious trouble, and he knew that he was in no-man's-land.

Whatever else might one day be said about Muhammad Ali, it should never be said that he is without courage, that he cannot take a punch. He took those shots by Frazier, and then came out for the seventh, saying to him, "Old Joe Frazier, why I thought you were washed up." Joe replied, "Somebody told you all wrong, pretty boy."

Frazier's assault continued. By the end of the 10th round it was an even fight. Ali sat on his stool like a man ready to be staked out in the sun. His head was bowed, and when he raised it his eyes rolled from the agony of exhaustion. "Force yourself, champ!" his corner cried. "Go down to the well once more!" begged Bundini, tears streaming down his face. "The world needs ya, champ!" In the 11th, Ali got trapped in Frazier's corner, and blow after blow bit at his melting face, and flecks of spittle flew from his mouth. "Lawd have mercy!" Bundini shrieked.

The world held its breath. But then Ali dug deep down into whatever it is that he is about, and even his severest critics would have to admit that the man-boy had become finally a man. He began to catch Frazier with long right hands, and blood trickled from Frazier's mouth. Now, Frazier's face began to lose definition; like lost islands reemerging from the sea, massive bumps rose suddenly around each eye, especially the left. His punches seemed to be losing their strength. "My God," wailed Angelo Dundee. "Look at 'im. He ain't got no power, champ!" Ali threw the last ounces of resolve left in his body in the 13th and 14th. He sent Frazier's bloody mouthpiece flying into the press row in the 13th, and nearly floored him with a right in the center of the ring. Frazier was now no longer coiled. He was up high, his hands down, and as the bell for the 14th round sounded, Dundee pushed Ali out saying, "He's all yours!" And he was, as Ali raked him with nine straight right hands. Frazier was not picking up the punches, and as he returned to his corner at the round's end the Filipino referee guided his great hulk part of the way.

"Joe," said his manager, Eddie Futch, "I'm going to stop it."

"No, no, Eddie, ya can't do that to me," Frazier pleaded, his thick tongue barely getting the words out. He started to rise.

"You couldn't see the last two rounds," said Futch. "What makes ya think ya gonna see in the 15th?"

"I want him, boss," said Frazier.

"Sit down, son," said Futch, pressing his hand on Frazier's shoulder. "It's all over. No one will ever forget what you did here today."

And so it will be, for once more had Frazier taken the child of the gods to hell and back. After the fight Futch said: "Ali fought a smart fight. He conserved his energy, turning it off when he had to. He can afford to do it because of his style. It was mainly a question of anatomy, that is all that separates these two men. Ali is now too big, and when you add those long arms, well . . . Joe has to use constant pressure, and that takes its toll on a man's body and soul." Dundee said: "My guy sucked it up and called on everything he had. We'll never see another one like him." Ali took a long time before coming down to be interviewed by the press, and then he could only say, "I'm tired of bein' the whole game. Let other guys do the fightin'. You might never see Ali in the ring again."

I N HIS SUITE THE NEXT MORNING HE TALKED QUIETLY. "I HEARD somethin' once," he said. "When somebody asked a marathon runner what goes through his mind in the last mile or two, he said that you ask yourself why am I doin' this. You get so tired. It takes so much out of you mentally. It changes you. It makes you go a little insane. I was thinkin' that at the end. Why am I doin' this? What am I doin' here in against this beast of a man? It's so painful. I must be crazy. I always bring out the best in the men I fight, but Joe Frazier, I'll tell the world right now, brings out the best in me. I'm gonna tell ya, that's one helluva man, and God bless him." ◆

Greatest

{ 1976 - 1981 }

ONCE MORE TO THE MOUNTAIN

BY PAT PUTNAM

*Thirty-eight years old and way out of shape,
Ali succumbed to the lure of an $8 million
purse and returned to the ring*

SI, APRIL 14, 1980

THE VANGUARD OF MUHAMMAD ALI'S CLAN was gathering. Lana Shabazz, the camp cook, was seated at a long planked table preparing lunch. With her in the log house that serves as kitchen and dining room were Jimmy Ellis, the former WBA heavyweight champ who had been promoted from sparring partner to assistant trainer; Abdul Rahaman, the tough security chief once known as Captain Sam; and Howard Bingham, the photographer. Drew Brown, known as Bundini, had had a big night and was still sleeping in one of the camp's 14 log cabins. Those in the room all wanted to know one thing: Who was Ali going to fight, Larry Holmes, or Mike Weaver? ✦ That he would fight again was all too apparent. He was here, wasn't he, here in his $500,000 training complex high on Sculp Hill overlooking Deer Lake, Pa. The three-time heavyweight champion had arrived the night before, in the backwoods darkness, and he had just climbed from the Paul Bunyanesque bed in his private cabin.

NO TIME TO REST Unwilling to settle into retirement, Ali kept plotting for another title shot.   **215**

"Too late to run," Ali decided, a grin accentuating his new mustache. Then he yawned.

With her gleaming knife poised over a large carrot, Lana eyed the sleepy Ali. "Who you going to fight?" she demanded with finality.

Ali's answer was distorted by another yawn. "The Marine," she said.

Ellis' eyes widened. "Who?" he asked. "I thought you were going to fight Holmes."

Ali shook his head, the electric light picking up the gray advancing through his hair. "Naw. I'm going to fight the Marine. Then I'm going to beat up on Holmes."

Lana was still puzzled. "Which Marine?"

"The one that just knocked out John Tate," Ali said. "Mike Weaver. Weaver the Beaver."

The carrot was halved by a stroke from Lana's knife. "You got to whup him," she said.

Sighing, Ali lifted the front of his brown warm-up jacket. Thick coils of midsection spilled into view. Ali clutched fistfuls of offending flesh. "Ain't this disgusting? I can't hide it no more. I don't want to hide it no more. Going to get rid of it."

An hour later, Ali, idle these past 18 months, took the first step in what he knew would become three months of agony, self-imposed torture, as he pushed himself to sculpt his 38-year-old body into fight trim.

"So he's really gone back to the mountain," said Angelo Dundee, the little trainer Ali will soon beckon from Miami. "I never thought he'd do it. I really believed that before he fought again the mountain would have to come to him."

His trunks tugged high to cover the jiggling jelly roll, Ali came into the gym for his first workout at Deer Lake. He walked past the speed bag. The heavy bag remained unused. Instead he pointed toward Henry Clark, a journeyman, and climbed gracelessly into the ring, where, like beached whales, the two floundered through a couple of rounds.

"Just warming up," said Ali, panting as Ellis toweled his face. "You next," Ali growled, pointing toward a slender youth, who eagerly reached for a battered head guard.

As he had for his historic second fight with Leon Spinks, Ali has once more imported light and fast sparring partners from the amateur ranks. "He needs those little guys," Dundee explained. "He is going to look slow as hell, but they'll bring out all the speed and reflexes he's got left. He won't look like much for five weeks, but then watch him."

The youth Ali had beckoned was Charles Carter, a 21-year-old welterweight from Yakima, Wash., with an 84–14 record and cobras for hands. "I'm going to put a real whuppin' on you, boy," Ali threatened.

"What you're going to do is learn my name," the unawed Carter responded.

Even when he was young and trim, which was about three presidents ago, sparring was never one of Ali's more ardent pursuits. He can get in more loafing during 10 rounds of ring work than most people could manage in the same time while stretched across a bed.

Midway through the second round Carter began to challenge him: "Come on, old man, let's see you fight." Later Carter would explain, "I wasn't trying to be a wise guy. I was just trying to get him to work. He was loafing. I was trying to get him up on his toes."

As penalty for his rashness, Ali made Carter work six full rounds. "You know my name now?" Carter gasped when it was over.

"Get back in here, boy," Ali yelled at him. "You ain't done."

Carter flew across the ring, got in two quick licks and then darted between the ropes. Ali laughed. He worked two more rounds with Roosevelt Green, a young welterweight, before packing it in.

In the dressing room Ali fell backward onto a couch. His eyes closed. "God, 10 rounds and I'm exhausted," he moaned. "*Ten* rounds!"

"What you expect, you're just in off the street," Rahaman told him.

"No more sparring," Ali said.

Rahaman nodded his approval. "I hope not."

"Tomorrow I got to work."

"All you were doing today was telling your body it was time to go back to work," Rahaman said. "You was just getting rid of the laziness."

"I hope so," Ali said. He sounded semi-convinced.

EVEN AT THE ADVANCED AGE OF 38 AND CARRYING MORE SUET than sinew, Ali induced a wild scramble among promoters when he announced he was ready to put up his fists once more. The winner appears to be Murad Muhammad, an obscure peddler out of Newark whose chief claim to fame is that he promoted all of James Scott's light-heavyweight fights at Rahway State Prison.

Bob Arum, who holds the options for Weaver's next three fights, had offered Ali $4.5 million for his comeback in New Orleans against John Tate. That looked like the fight until March 31, when Weaver erased the Tennessee giant from the WBA's championship roster with one short left hook.

Don King, the orator who decides the ring fortunes of WBC champ Larry Holmes, had countered with an offer of $7 million. But that offer was set for self-destruct: King had offered Holmes only $3 million.

"To hell with that," stormed Richie Giachetti, Holmes's manager. "Don said we should give Ali the most money. Why? We've got what he wants. We should get as much and more, and Larry feels the same way. If Ali gets $7 million, then we get $7 million. And that's the way it is." By week's end King reportedly had withdrawn his offer to Ali.

Dr. Ferdie Pacheco, Ali's personal physician for many years, said, "I don't see any helter-skelter race to the bank to get the money out. I hear about all those million-dollar offers, but a lot of that talk is like Miami Beach mortgage money. It's all on paper."

But while Arum and King were out shaking the money trees, Murad Muhammad, 29, who was once an Ali bodyguard, set off on a six-day transcontinental trip that netted him $10 million in backing from a California firm called Prime Corp.—reportedly a mining business—and the apparent acceptance of Ali vs. Weaver. In giving Murad Muhammad the rights to Weaver's first defense, Arum will get a percentage of the TV revenue, whether it be network or closed circuit.

If the complex package doesn't unravel, Ali will be paid $8 million, while Weaver will get $2 million. Scheduled for July, the fight is to be held in the 165,000-seat Stadium Maracana in Rio de Janeiro. On April 3 in Chicago, Ali was given $250,000 by the Prime Corp. people, which he will keep even if the deal should die.

When Holmes received word that it apparently would be Weaver and not he who would be fighting Ali, he wasn't disappointed. "Ali's not crazy," Holmes said. "He doesn't want to fight me. I used to be his sparring partner and I had to hold back. I thought I could beat him then. Now I *know* I can beat him. But as a friend I have this advice for Ali. You don't need all those houses and cars. If you're broke, sell the houses and the cars. You can do other things. Don't swallow your pride just to make some money. Don't get into the ring.

"You can't beat nobody—well, you can beat Weaver, he's a plodder. I just hope you haven't sold your pride and sold yourself and your family out. Let your kids have their pride. They could be the proudest kids in America because their father was the greatest fighter who ever lived. Don't take that away from them."

Ali's decision to return to the ring actually was made five months ago, about 30 seconds after Tate beat Gerrie Coetzee in South Africa to claim the WBA title Ali had abdicated.

"When I realized what had happened," says Ali, who had watched the fight on television, "I yelled, 'I'm back!' I knew I could beat Tate."

His young wife Veronica wasn't all that ecstatic. "If you are going to do it, do it," she told her husband. "But I don't like it."

Ali was so excited at the prospect of winning the title for the fourth time that last fall he went to the Main Street Gym in Los Angeles and sparred with Eddie (The Animal) Lopez, a vicious gym fighter who had once knocked out Bernardo Mercado in a workout.

Ali went in looking like a balloon. Time and again Lopez berated him as a fat old man. As the round ended, Ali ripped off his headgear snarling, "You want to fight. Let's fight."

For the next two rounds it was the old Ali fighting inside a fat man's body. Firing dazzling combinations, he assaulted the stunned Lopez with controlled fury. And when he was done, Lopez told him, almost reverently, "Hey, man, I was only kidding."

Not until March did Ali return to the gym. He worked several days at the 5th Street Gym in Miami Beach. On the fourth day he got cut in a corner of his upper lip. It required six stitches outside, four inside, but Ali insists he didn't grow the mustache to hide them.

Dundee sees the split lip as a blessing: "After the cut he went to work. In just that short period he got down to 242 pounds."

At camp, Ali said he weighed 248. It may be the truth or he may have forgotten to weigh one of his legs. Dundee says it doesn't matter.

"The weight is no problem," says the man who has trained Ali since his third pro fight. "If he stays in camp, if he runs and eats properly and exercises, then he'll get into shape. But he won't want to run. You've got to push him. You say, 'O.K., go get knocked out.' Then he'll run. He's got to force himself to stay in camp. In the past he always found nine million excuses to go somewhere. That's bad. But if he stays in camp he can do it. Nobody else could at his age, but he can. But will he do it? That's the question."

P ACHECO FORECASTS ONLY DISASTER. IN 1977, AFTER 12 YEARS WITH Ali, he quit when Ali refused to retire. Nothing that has happened since has changed Pacheco's mind. ✦ "Eight million is hard for anybody to turn down," he says. "But his wife, his mother, me, even Don King, are telling him not to fight. He trained in Miami and didn't look good. That cut. Ali never cut. He's like us all; he's getting old. There is a loss of muscle tone, of elasticity of the skin. As happens to all of us, his face is falling. It's a time in life when plastic surgeons reap the benefits and old fighters begin to cut."

Floyd Patterson, the former heavyweight champion, who fought until 37, echoes Pacheco. "I've been hit when I was young and when I was old," he says, "and the punch that didn't leave a scratch when I was younger left a gash when I was older. He's taking a hell of a gamble at an age when the reflexes slow and the legs aren't what they used to be. But Ali is extraordinary. He brainwashes himself into believing he can do something, and it usually ends up that he does it. But you can't brainwash yourself into being young again."

For his part, Weaver isn't thinking of Ali's sagging facial features, or of his slowing reflexes, or of the legs that seem to have been robbed of their lightness. Ali is Weaver's idol. He has been ever since he first won the title in 1964, the year Weaver was 11.

"I like him and I love him," Weaver says. "I don't want to fight him, but I will if I have to. I won't like it before the fight and I'll hate it after the fight, but during the fight when I'm beating up on him I won't think about it."

If the fight comes off, Ali gives Weaver no chance.

"He got beat nine times by a bunch of bums," says Ali. "And he was losing big to Tate until he got lucky with one punch. I see him as my tune-up for Holmes. Weaver would give me my timing back. I want Holmes bad. He told me to stay in my rocking chair. Well, I'm going to get out of my rocking chair and beat his butt bad. Hell, Holmes is *30*. That's too old to be a serious threat to me."

Ali's eyes take on a dreamy quality. "I beat Weaver and win the title for the fourth time. Then say Holmes gets lucky and beats me. *Then* I come back and win the title for the *fifth* time. The five-time heavyweight champion. Tell me what ever happened in the world that was greater than that?"

"Well," says a friend, "this is Easter and . . ."

"I'm talking about sports," Ali said. ✦

SPINX JINXED Despite punches like this straight right, Ali lost his title to the young Leon Spinks in 1978.

Greatest

FEELING OLD At 36, Ali was
never busy enough to hold off
the raw but relentless Spinks.

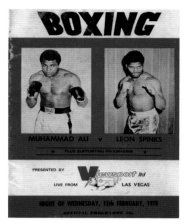

For closed-circuit viewers around the world, the untested Spinks seemed a long shot at best.

After their fight, the former champ, none the worse for wear, raised a smile from his successor.

"Old lines repeated over and over, familiar gestures of widening eyes and threatening fist being shaken at some opponent or planted heckler; mock fury that has to be restrained by handlers at weigh-ins. It is all so creakingly old. But peer closer and there is much more: his accessibility, the way he exposes himself to the crowds, his genuine humanity that is felt more than heard, his caring about what happens to us all."

MARK KRAM, *"One-Nighter in San Juan,"* SI, 3/1/1976

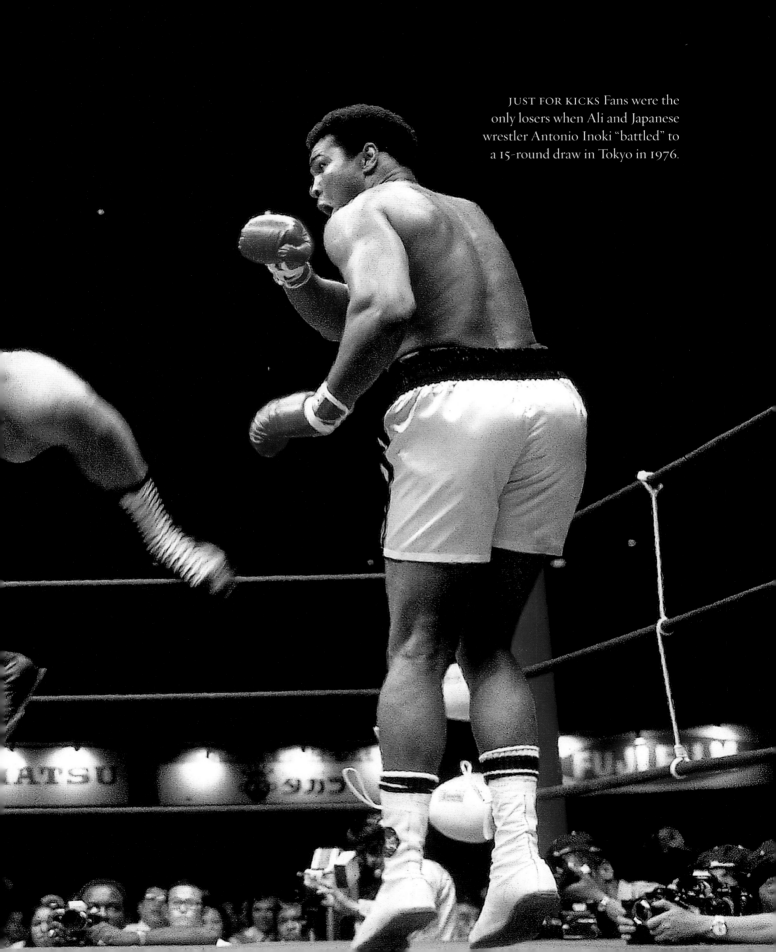

JUST FOR KICKS Fans were the only losers when Ali and Japanese wrestler Antonio Inoki "battled" to a 15-round draw in Tokyo in 1976.

IN YOUR FACE Ken Norton, a virtual unknown when he upset Ali in 1973, was never intimidated by the Greatest.

Comedian Dick Gregory helped Ali prepare for Norton with a customized concoction.

Before their rubber match, Norton tagged Ali with a right hand in the Yankee Stadium outfield.

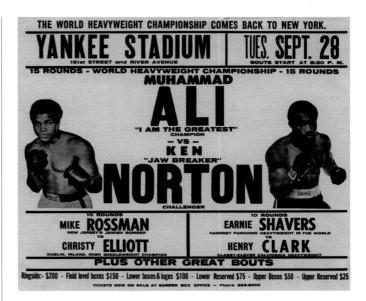

After trading wins in California in 1973, Ali and Norton brought their rivalry to New York in 1976.

"Just a few hours before his title defense against Ken Norton last week, Muhammad Ali sat shoeless, his feet up on a kitchen table in an apartment on the Upper West Side of Manhattan, isolated from all the chiselers and half-wits who snap at his peace and concentration before a big fight, away from some of those parasites around him who call themselves aides and had hastened his recent decline. After thinking about suitable endings for his strange and incomparable career Ali suddenly turned to his host and said, 'Maybe I should reach up and pull down the mike in the middle of the ring and announce . . . "Laaaaadies and gentlemen, you have seen the last of the eighth wonderrrr of the world. Muhammad retires." ' "

MARK KRAM,
"Not the Greatest Way to Go," SI, 10/11/1976

In 1977, Ali—who else?—starred in his own biopic. As an actor, critics said, he was no heavyweight.

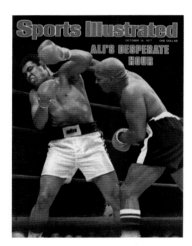

The fights got harder: In 1977 Ali won a 15-rounder against dangerous puncher Earnie Shavers.

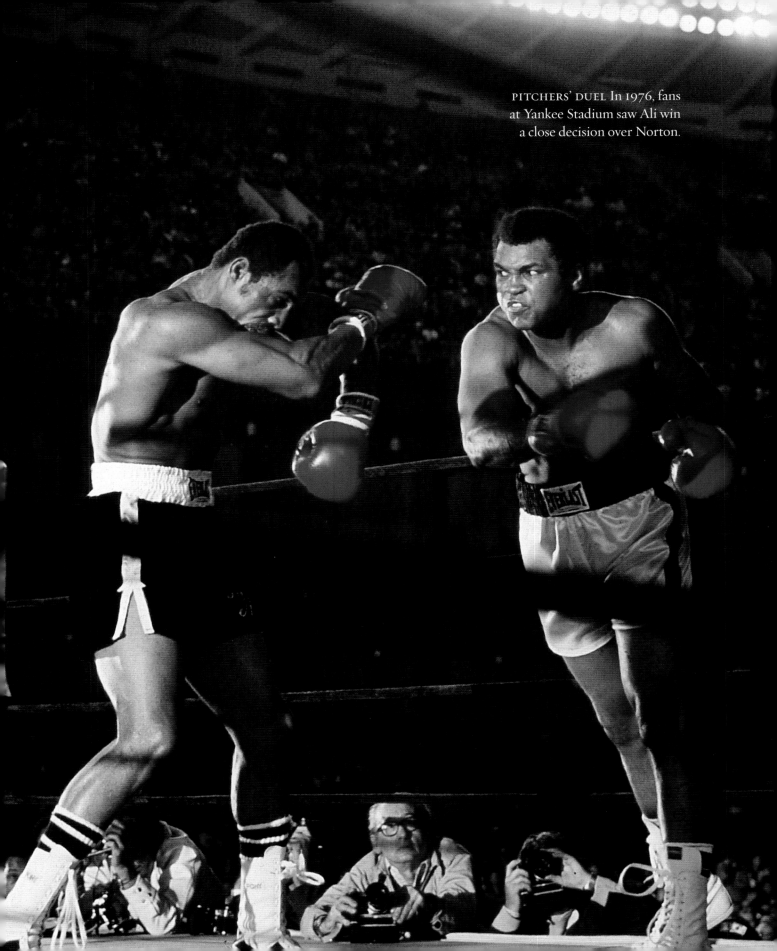

PITCHERS' DUEL In 1976, fans at Yankee Stadium saw Ali win a close decision over Norton.

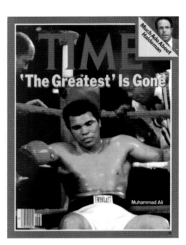

The image of Ali, battered into defeat by Holmes in 1980, struck a chord far beyond boxing.

Don King (center) orchestrated a showdown that kicked off in style, but ended sad and ugly.

When the bell rang to start round 11, the crowd in Las Vegas witnessed the close of an era.

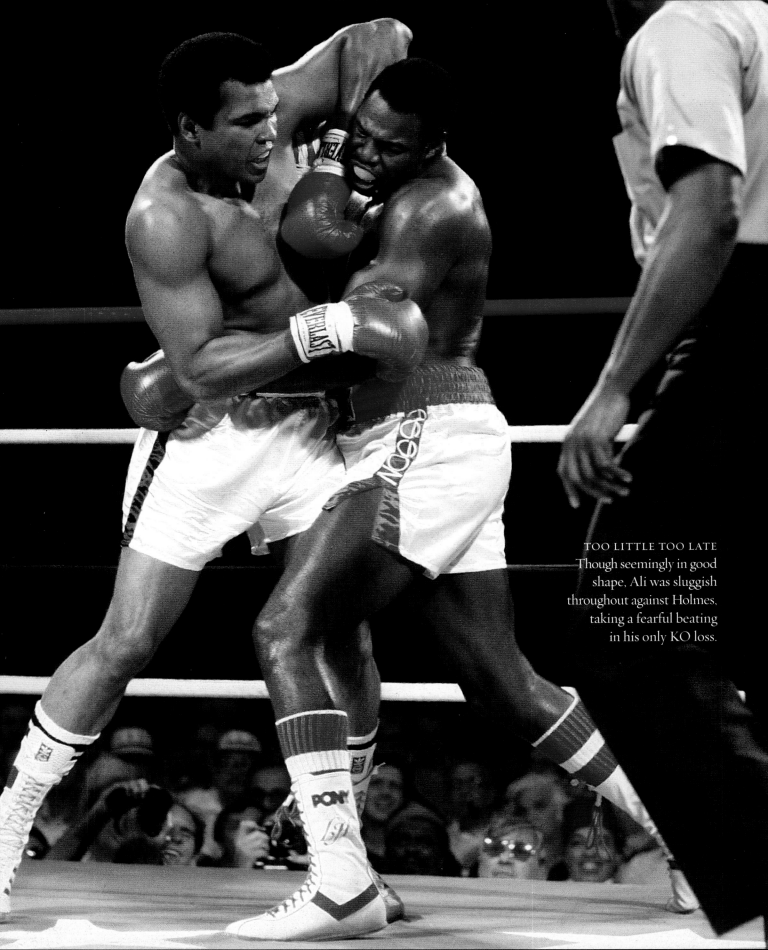

TOO LITTLE TOO LATE
Though seemingly in good
shape, Ali was sluggish
throughout against Holmes,
taking a fearful beating
in his only KO loss.

ONE MORE TIME TO THE TOP

BY PAT PUTNAM

*Circling around a confused Leon Spinks, old master
Ali jabbed a bit, grabbed a bit and won the world title
all over again in their Battle of New Orleans*

SI, SEPTEMBER 25, 1978

THIS WAS NOT THE OLD MUHAMMAD ALI, NOT by a half. But on September 15 in the New Orleans Superdome, driven by an ambition as vaulting as the structure, Ali dominated without letup a badly confused Leon Spinks. And after 15 perpetual-motion rounds, Ali had won the world heavyweight championship for an unprecedented third time. The decision was unanimous and indisputable. ✦ As a fight it was not so much a contest as it was a demonstration by an old master educating an inexperienced youngster in the fine points of the craft. But at 36, Ali teaches a better game than he plays. The result was that, as a whole, the fight was sloppy. ✦ "Sloppy?" howled a happy Angelo Dundee, the trainer who had plotted Ali's battle plan. "It was *beautifully* sloppy. It was gorgeous sloppy. And it was the only damn way we were going to beat Spinks." ✦ The plan was simple. Ali would jab, jab, throw a right and grab. When Spinks came flailing in, Ali would hook his left hand around the back of Spinks' head and pull him

THE RIGHT STUFF This time, a refocused Ali outworked and outmuscled the smaller Spinks.   **235** into an embrace, effectively limiting Spinks to one or two punches or pulling him off balance. And Ali would dance, baby, dance. He would tie up Spinks and then dance away from him on the break, circling to the right, circling to the left. And the fight went on as plotted. From the fifth round on, Dundee was shouting across the ring at Spinks, "Where did he go, Leon? Where did he go?"

Spinks was clearly asking himself the same question. Where Ali assuredly did not go was to the ropes, as he had done while losing his beloved championship to Leon in their fight in Las Vegas in February. Gone was the infamous rope-a-dope, by means of which Ali had coasted for long periods during his last few fights. This was the first time in recent memory that Ali stayed in the center of the ring, circling, jabbing and throwing occasional, if not very accurate, combinations, the first time in years he had not engaged in extraneous foolishness. And when in doubt, he would seize Spinks in a mighty bear hug. At 221 against 201, it was no contest.

Like many in the mammoth crowd, referee Lucien Joubert would have preferred something more pure in the way of boxing, and in the early rounds he warned Ali repeatedly as he unclasped Ali's hand from Spinks' head. Finally, at the end of the sixth round, he told Dundee that he had taken the fifth round away from Ali.

"For what?" Dundee said.

"For holding. I warned him about it."

"Now you tell me," Dundee yelled. "You take a round away from my guy and now you tell me? What the hell were you waiting for?"

But at this stage of the fight it didn't matter. Now, instead of throwing just one punch after the jab, Ali began unloading combinations, and if they weren't causing any particular pain, many of them were scoring points.

"Goodbye, Leon!" Dundee shouted.

Spinks looked across the ring at Dundee and smiled. And at the end of the seventh round, when Ali permitted himself the luxury of a little Ali shuffle on the way back to his corner, the outcome seemed clear.

All through the fight Spinks kept looking desperately to his corner for advice, but all was chaos. He had arrived at ringside with an entourage of 11, including a clutch of Marine Corps buddies, and every one of them was shouting instructions. Across the ring, Dundee watched the confusion, then turned and surveyed the usual two dozen or so members of Ali's team. "Well," he said, "their crazies can match our crazies, anyway."

Ali is used to such bedlam. For the 25-year-old Spinks, the situation was serious. It became more so when George Benton, the well-regarded trainer who had masterminded the upset victory over Ali seven months ago, quit in disgust. Overcome with frustration, he walked out on the fight at the end of the fifth round. "My God," he said, "it's a zoo."

Only minutes before the fight, Sam Solomon, Spinks' principal trainer, had told Benton his plan for instructing Spinks during the fight: Benton would be permitted to give advice only every third or fourth round. They would alternate. One round, Solomon would whisper in Spinks' ear; the next round, it would be Michael, the champion's younger brother. Unless, of course, Art Reddon, the gunnery sergeant who had coached Spinks in the Marines, had some counsel. And at one point Marshall Warren, Spinks' accountant, was shouting advice as loudly as any of them.

"Remember," Solomon told Benton, "if it's not your turn in the corner and you have something to say to Leon, just tell the guy whose turn it is and he'll relay the message."

The situation had been even more chaotic in the dressing room before the fight, when it was discovered that no one among the horde of friends, relatives and functionaries jammed

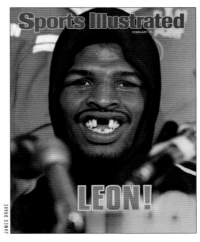

After his first bout with Ali, new champ Spinks flashed his distinctive smile.

into the room had remembered to bring Spinks' protective cup, his water bucket and water bottle. "Go get a cup," Solomon said to Chet Cummings, a public-relations man for Top Rank, the fight's copromoters. "For God's sake, get Leon a cup."

"A cup?" said Cummings, a knowledgeable fight man who never dreamed that anyone could be that dumb. Cummings turned to Vickie Blain, another Top Rank employee, and said, "Go get Leon a cup for ice."

"Not that kind of cup," Solomon yelled, "A *cup* cup, for God's sake. A *cup* cup!"

Finally they borrowed a protective cup, two water bottles and a bucket from Mike Rossman, who had won the WBA world light heavyweight championship earlier in the evening and was sharing the dressing room with Spinks.

"You couldn't believe the scene in there," Benton said later. "There's at least 30 outsiders hanging around getting in everybody's way. Then Sam tells me how every fourth round I might get to talk to Leon. I mean, I'm no freaking yo-yo. What am I supposed to do? Go in and say, 'Remember four rounds ago when I said to . . .' Then he tells me how we can relay instructions. Now it's rule by committee. It was amateur hour, and amateurs were running the show."

Benton had not wanted to be there at all. The first fight had been quite enough. But in July he had received a letter inviting him to New Orleans as a special guest. The letter was from Mitt Barnes, Spinks' manager in absentia. Benton had not replied and had decided not to go. He knew Solomon didn't want him there.

But then, two weeks before the fight, as Spinks' training sessions grew less and less productive, Michael Spinks and Butch Lewis, a Top Rank vice president who at one point was in charge of Spinks' career, had convinced Leon that he needed former middleweight contender Benton in his corner. After four phone calls Lewis finally persuaded Benton to come. He arrived nine days before the fight.

"When I got there, I saw that Leon was doing all the wrong things," Benton said. "He'd forgotten all the things I had him doing for the last fight. The boy could be a hell of a fighter, but he needs a teacher, and I can only do so much for him in a week or two. He'd lost his jab. He wasn't bobbing and weaving. I told him, 'Leon, it's time you got to work.'"

Benton went to work, but there was little he could do about what was going on inside Spinks' head. The young man has a deep love for his family and a great loyalty to old friends. He tries desperately to make them all happy, and when squabbles began during the weeks before the fight, Spinks was deeply disturbed.

Seven days before the fight, there was a shouting match with Michael. Later Michael said, "I laid something on him I couldn't get off my mind. I told him that I had to chase him to New Orleans, that he was trying to run away from the family and that he owed them more than that." After the argument Leon went out to train. As he began jumping rope, tears began to stream down his cheeks.

That night, as he had for many of the previous nights, and as he did for the rest of the nights leading up to the fight, Spinks fled alone to the many small and dangerous bars deep inside the New Orleans ghetto. There he tried to drink away the pain.

"He was drunk every night he was here," said Top Rank president Bob Arum. "Leon went to places our people didn't dare go. I'm surprised he didn't wind up with a knife in him."

At one point Spinks moved out of the fight headquarters at the Hilton Hotel and disappeared. No one, not even Solomon, knew where he had gone. "He had left the hotel and moved into a house and didn't tell anybody where it was," Butch Lewis said. "Nobody knew how to reach him. We almost went crazy. Finally we had to get a policeman to beat on a policeman who was part of Leon's security guard to find out where he was."

WHILE SPINKS TRAINED AND DRANK HIS WAY THROUGH the disharmony, Ali was maintaining his strenuous training pace. He rented a yellow brick home near Lake Pontchartrain, north of town, and there he ran each morning and there he suffered on the green rubbing table set up in the living room.

Every morning at seven, after running between three and five miles, Ali stretched out on the table while trainer Luis Sarria held his ankles with powerful hands, and he went through 12 groups of varying sit-ups, doing 30 or so in each group. The last 40 days before the fight he did 8,014 sit-ups, a number logged by one of his many aides.

On the fourth day before the fight, after Ali had complained of unnatural weariness after a workout, a local doctor discovered that his blood was low in salt, iron and potassium. After that, each morning with his breakfast of two trout, scrambled eggs and two slices of unbuttered whole-wheat toast, Ali swallowed 11 pills to make up the deficiencies.

"God, I have suffered and suffered and suffered. It really hurts," Ali said one morning from the table. He lay face down staring at a green flowered rug, his arms dangling almost to the floor as Sarria's fingers worked on his body. "The last fight. It's time for a new life. I'm going to put on a three-piece suit, carry a briefcase and fly around the world working for human rights and dignity. I'm going to form my own United Nations with a headquarters in Washington and the flags of the world flying from the top. I'm going to have a big warehouse in Cleveland filled with food and clothes, and when there is a disaster anywhere in the world I'm going to fly there in my Learjet and help the people. I don't want to fight no more. I've been doing it for 25 years and you can only do so much wear to the body. It changes a man. It has changed me. I can see it. I can feel it."

"I think this time he's ready," said Dundee. "He has been cruel to himself. The bricks are all there, but he is 36 and they can tilt and fall. Nobody knows what's inside. What I'm counting on is how badly he wants to win it for the third time, to be the only man ever to do it. He has a sense of history. And, let's face it, Ali is not like other men."

A day later Benton was saying pretty much the same thing. Despite his nocturnal adventures, Spinks had trained hard. He was in excellent shape. Benton could see no way he could lose. Yet . . . ?

"Forget all the nonsense that has been going on around him," Benton said. "This kid has no business losing this fight. No business at all. I can't see anything the other guy can do to beat him. Ali can't win this fight. The only way he can win is if Leon falls on his face. Or if he lets what is inside his head beat him. But I've said that so many times about Ali before. Liston. Foreman. Frazier. The draft thing. Ali always comes up on his feet. It's like there is a mystical force guiding his life, making him not like other men. When I think of that—and when I think of the fight—it's scary."

Then came the fight, and Benton's scary feeling turned to outrage. After leaving the corner, he watched a few more rounds on a TV monitor in the dressing room. After the 12th round he picked up his equipment bag and left.

Back in the ring, Spinks was looking to his corner again.

"Wiggle," Michael shouted at him. "Wiggle."

"Give him the old gusto," Solomon yelled.

Equally cogent advice was shouted by the others. In the 13th, so far behind that he could win only by a knockout, Spinks was advised by one of his cornermen to start jabbing to the body. Why not? It was as good as telling him to wiggle or to give him the old gusto.

And then it was over, with Ali still dancing, and Spinks doggedly chasing him, still trying to find him, still trying to hit him.

The decision was announced: 10-4-1, 10-4-1, 11–4. And Spinks was there in the middle of the ring, one of the first to raise his idol's right arm in victory. Score one more for the venerable master. And shed a tear for the kid from the ghetto who never really had a chance.   ◆

Statesman

"THE FIGHT'S OVER, JOE"

BY WILLIAM NACK

I

*More than two decades after they last met in the ring,
Joe Frazier was still taking shots at Muhammad Ali,
but this time it was a war of words*

SI, SEPTEMBER 30, 1996

T IS ALWAYS THE PUNCH A FIGHTER DOES NOT SEE
that hurts the most, and the little girl was so sweet and innocent-looking,
standing shyly at her mother's side, that there was no way Joe Frazier
could have seen it coming. ✦ The former heavyweight champion of the world was
sitting under a tent on the bank of the Delaware River in Philadelphia, at a
place called Penn's Landing, where his touring autograph show had set up shop
at an outdoor festival. With his son Marvis, Joe trains and manages fighters out
of his Broad Street gym in Philly, but he also spends an inordinate amount of
time signing his name in that long, sweeping script on photographs of himself
and on merchandise from his portable store. On this languid September afternoon, under a sign that announced MEET YOUR PHILLY SPORTS HEROES,
flanked by stacks of SMOKIN' JOE hats ($10) and T-shirts ($23), Frazier was
signing everything put in front of him, gratis, schmoozing with parents as he
posed for pictures with their children and hamming it up for the cameras. He
was all grins and merriment for the scores of people who had waited in the sun
for an audience. ✦ At about 2:30 p.m., Frazier looked up and saw a petite and

GEORGE KALINSKY

MATCHES MADE IN HEAVEN The three Ali-Frazier bouts may be boxing's greatest trilogy. **243** demure 10-year-old, Ginnysue Kowalick, her head slightly bowed, standing across the table. "My daughter doesn't know you too well, Joe," said the girl's mother, Marilyn Kowalick. "She has a question, but she's too shy to ask."

Frazier nodded. "O.K.," he said.

"She wants to know if you ever beat Muhammad Ali," Marilyn said.

A scowl passed like a shadow down Frazier's face, and for a long moment he sat reeling in his chair, leaning back as his eyes rolled wildly from side to side, and he groaned, groping for words: "Agghh. . . . Ohhh. . . . Agghh. . . ."

Alarmed at Frazier's reaction, Marilyn leaned forward and said, "I'm sorry."

At last reassembling his scattered faculties, Frazier looked at Ginnysue and said, "We locked up three times. He won two, and I won one. *But look at him now.* I think I won all three."

TWO DAYS EARLIER, AT THE ESSEX HOUSE IN NEW YORK CITY, THE object of Frazier's turbulent emotions sat folded on a couch in a suite of rooms overlooking Central Park. He lay back and fumbled with his third package of shortbread cookies. White crumbs speckled his black shirt— the remains of his day, the emblematic story of his life. Ali had just spent most of an afternoon signing a limited edition of large photographs that showed him, dressed in luminous white, holding the Olympic torch during the opening ceremonies of the 1996 Games in Atlanta. He was in New York for the screening of yet another documentary celebrating his life, this one a TNT production with the unlikely title *Muhammad Ali: The Whole Story*.

Ali speaks in barely a whisper now, unless he has an audience, and then his voice rises raspingly, just enough to carry a room. Surrounded by a small group of fans and followers at the Essex House earlier that day, he could not resist the chance to perform. He raised his right fist in the air and said, "This is the piston that got to Liston!" He also asked the gathering, "Know what Lincoln said when he woke up from a two-day drunk?"

A dozen heads craned forward. Ali's eye's widened in shock. " 'I freed the *whooo*?' " he blurted to the nearly all-white audience. High, nervous laughter filled the room.

"I saw Joe Frazier in Philly last week," a voice nearby said quietly.

Ali's eyes grew wide again. "Joe Fraysha?" he whispered.

He has known for years of Frazier's anger and bitterness toward him, but he knows nothing of the venom that coursed through Frazier's recent autobiography, *Smokin' Joe*. Of Ali, Frazier wrote, "Truth is, I'd like to rumble with that sucker again—beat him up piece by piece and mail him back to Jesus. . . . Now people ask me if I feel bad for him, now that things aren't going so well for him. Nope. I don't. Fact is, I don't give a damn. They want me to love him, but I'll open up the graveyard and bury his ass when the Lord chooses to take him."

Nor does Ali know what Frazier said while watching him, with his trembling arm, light the Olympic flame: "It would have been a good thing if he would have lit the torch and fallen in. If I had the chance, I would have pushed him in."

Nor does Ali know of Frazier's rambling diatribe against him at a July 30 press conference in Atlanta, where Frazier attacked the choice of Ali, the Olympic light heavyweight gold medalist in 1960 and a three-time heavyweight champion of the world, as the final bearer of the torch. He called Ali a "dodge drafter," implied that Ali was a racist ("He didn't like his white brothers," said Frazier) and suggested that he himself—also an Olympic champion, as a heavyweight, in 1964—would have made a better choice to light the flame: "Why not? I'm a good American. . . . A champion is more than making noise. I could have run up there. I'm in shape."

And while Frazier asserts at one turn that he sees "the hand of the Lord" in Ali's Parkinson's syndrome (a set of symptoms that include tremors and a masklike face), he also takes an eerily mean-spirited pride in the role he believes he played in causing Ali's condition. Indeed, the Parkinson's most likely traces to the repeated blows Ali took to the head as a boxer—traumas that ravaged the colony of dopamine-producing cells in his brain—and no man struck Ali's head harder and more repeatedly than Frazier.

"He's got Joe Frazier-itis," Frazier said of Ali one day recently, flexing his left arm. "He's got left-hook-itis."

Ali's wife, Lonnie, shields him from such loutish and hateful pronouncements. "I don't want him hearing negative things," Lonnie says. "It's trash."

ALI HAS BEEN LIVING RENT-FREE IN FRAZIER'S HEAD FOR MORE than 25 years, ever since Ali—after being stripped of his heavyweight championship in 1967 for refusing induction into the U.S. Army, and then serving a 3½-year suspension from boxing—emerged from his banishment and immediately set about regaining his title, which by then was held by Smokin' Joe. At Ali's urgent pleading, Frazier backed him in his fight to regain his boxing license, but no sooner had that been accomplished than Ali began cruelly berating his benefactor, a man who had grown up mule-poor in Beaufort, S.C., the son of a struggling farmer and bootlegger. The young Frazier had migrated to Philly, taken up boxing and become the precursor of Rocky Balboa, training by tenderizing sides of beef in a kosher slaughterhouse with his sibilant left hook.

Over the next five years, from their first fight in New York City, on March 8, 1971, until their third and last in Manila on Oct. 1, 1975, Ali humiliated and enraged and ultimately isolated Frazier, casting him as a shuffling and mumbling Uncle Tom, an ugly and ignorant errand boy for white America. But the most lasting characterization of all was the one Ali coined on their way to the Philippines in '75, the one that came near the end of the singsong rhyme he would deliver with that mischievous smirk on his moon-bright face: "It will be a killa and a chilla and a thrilla when I get the gorilla in Manila!"

Of all the names joined forever in and annals of boxing—from Dempsey-Tunney to Louis-Schmeling, from Zale-Graziano to Leonard-Hearns—none are more fiercely bound by a hyphen than Ali-Frazier. Not Palmer-Nicklaus in golf nor Borg-McEnroe in tennis, as ardently competitive as these rivalries were, conjure up anything remotely close to the epic theater of Ali-Frazier. Their first fight, snagged in the most turbulent political currents of our time, is widely viewed as the greatest single sporting event of this half century. And the third fight—for its savagery, its shifting momentum and its climactic moment, in which the two men sat battered on their stools—is regarded, by consensus, as the most surpassing prizefight in history.

So here it is, 25 years after Ali-Frazier I, and Frazier is burning like the flame that Ali set off with his Olympic torch. Feeling that history had treated him unfairly, Frazier is haunted and overshadowed by his old tormentor, the very figure he did most to help create. Frazier was one of the greatest of all gladiators, but today he finds himself cast as just another player in the far larger drama of Ali's life. He is trapped and wriggling in the Ali mystique, embedded in the amber of Ali's life and times.

For Ali is as near to a cultural saint as any man of our era. His appearance on the Atlanta stage was a window, thrown suddenly open, on the long journey he has taken through the lights and shadows of our unresolved past—America's past. As his left arm shook, he lit the flame and choked the breath of a nation. His life has become an extended public appearance: He swims among crowds wherever he goes, leading with the most recognizable chin on the planet. He tells old knock-knock jokes, receives visitors like a Middle East potentate and signs off on the next book about his life. And now and again, just for old times' sake, he leans over to whisper in Joe Frazier's ear.

As he did when his eyes widened in that suite at the Essex House. And then he gave the impish grin. "Joe Fraysha?" Ali said. "You seen the gorilla? From Manila?"

The geometry of the lives of Ali and Frazier is forever fixed in history. The line between them, once as curved and sweeping as a left hook and as long as a flicking jab, is today as irreducibly short as the one that joins their names. The two men left each other scarred in different ways. Ali's wounds are visible on the surface; you can see them on his face. Frazier's wounds lie deeper within; you can hear them in the pain in his voice.

THERE HAD NEVER BEEN A NIGHT LIKE THIS ONE IN NEW YORK CITY. By 10:30 on the evening of March 8, 1971, when the two fighters climbed into the ring at Madison Square Garden, Ali in red trunks and Frazier in green-and-gold brocade, there was a feral scent and a crackle to the place. The Garden was a giant bell jar into which more than 20,000 people had drifted, having passed through police barricades that rimmed the surrounding streets. They came in orange and mint-green and purple velvet hot pants, in black leather knickers and mink and leopard capes, in cartridge belts and feathered chapeaux and pearl-gray fedoras. Some sported hats with nine-inch brims and leaned jauntily on diamond-studded walking sticks. Manhattan listed toward Babylon.

"I looked down from the ring, and it was a sea of glitter," recalls Eddie Futch, who was then Frazier's assistant trainer. "I have never seen any boxing event that had so many celebrities."

Angelo Dundee, Ali's trainer, was making his way through the tumult to the ring when he heard someone call his name: "Hey, Ange!" Dundee looked up. Frank Sinatra snapped his picture; the singer was working for LIFE magazine. Burt Lancaster was doing radio commentary. Ringside seats had sold for $150, but scalpers were getting $1,000. "Plumage, pimps and hustlers," says Bobby Goodman, the fight publicist. The fighters were each getting a record $2.5 million, an astronomical sum in those days, and the worldwide television audience was 300 million. The Garden ring was the wrist on which America was checking its pulse.

The boxer-dancer with the beautiful legs had arrived to do battle against the puncher-plodder with the thick thighs. Of course, the fans had come to see more than a classic clash of styles. The match was billed as the Fight of the Century, and the sporting world had been waiting for it for more than three years, ever since Frazier knocked out Buster Mathis in 11 rounds on March 4, 1968, to win the vacant New York heavyweight title and begin laying claim to being the toughest man on earth—the toughest, at least, with a passport. The previous year Ali had been stripped of his world championship and his freedom to travel abroad, and during his ensuing 43-month absence from the ring, Frazier buried his implacable hook into every heavyweight who stood in his way, finally winning the vacant world title on Feb. 16, 1970, by knocking out Jimmy Ellis in the fifth round.

During his exile Ali, who had to earn his money on the college lecture circuit, began to knock at Frazier's door, seeking help to get back his license to fight, saying that an Ali-Frazier match would make them both rich. "He'd come to the gym and call me on the telephone," says Frazier. "He just wanted to work with me for the publicity so he could get his license back. One time, after the Ellis fight, I drove him from Philadelphia to New York City in my car. Me and him. We talked about how much we were going to make out of our fight. We were laughin' and havin' fun. We were friends, we were great friends. I said, 'Why not? Come on, man, let's do it!' He was a brother. He called me Joe: 'Hey, Smokin' Joe!' In New York we were gonna put on this commotion."

For Ali, the most gifted carnival barker in the history of sports, the commotion was father to the promotion. So when Frazier stopped his car in midtown Manhattan and walked into a store to buy a pair of shoes, Ali leaped out, his eyes bulging, and cried, "It's Joe Frazier, ladies and gentlemen! Smokin' Joe! There he is! He's got my title! I want my title! He ain't the champ, he's the chump. I'm the people's champ!"

Frazier, a proud and soft-spoken rural Southerner, had never witnessed anything like this. It rattled him at first. Butch Lewis, a companion of Frazier's and later a promoter himself, explained to him what Ali was doing: "He'd not disrespecting you. This is Ali! This is what will make the payday. *This is not personal.*"

Lewis says the men shared more than anyone knows. Frazier knew that Ali was in need of money. On at least two occasions, Lewis says, Frazier slipped Ali cash when he needed it, once giving him $2,000 to pay an overdue bill at the City Squire Motor Inn in New York City. But now Ali was dabbing curare on the tip of his rhetoric.

All through Ali's youth in Louisville and his early years as a champion, he had been a blend of his chesty, arrogant, yakety-yak father, Cassius Clay Sr., and his gentle, uncommonly sweet mother, Odessa. "Ali is softhearted and generous to a fault," says his former fight doctor, Ferdie Pacheco. "Essentially a sweet guy whose whole demeanor aims to amuse, to entertain and be liked." Yet there was a period in Ali's life, after he revealed that he had joined the separatist Black Muslims in 1964, when that side of his personality disappeared—"when he was not particularly pleasant to anyone," says Pacheco, recalling the two years before Ali's exile, when he fought Floyd Patterson and Ernie Terrell. "He was a hateful guy."

Neither Patterson nor Terrell would call him Ali—they used what he called his "slave name," Cassius Clay—and so in the ring he played with each of them as a cat would with a wounded mouse, keeping them alive to torture them. "What's my name?" he demanded of them as he landed his punches at will. Goodman, who was Terrell's publicist then, says, "He gave Ernie a merciless beating around the eyes. Ernie had double vision for a long time."

If Ali emerged from his exile years a softer man, as many contend, he had not forgotten how to sting and wound an opponent. "There was an awful mean streak in Ali," says Dave Wolf, then one of Frazier's confidants. "He did to Joe verbally what he did to Terrell physically."

The Ali who had laughed and bantered with Frazier, who had raised all that good-natured commotion in Manhattan, now appeared to be a man transformed—stripped of his disguise. "Joe Frazier is too ugly to be champ," Ali said. "Joe Frazier is too dumb to be champ. The heavyweight champion should be smart and pretty, like me. Ask Joe Frazier, 'How do you feel, champ?' He'll say, 'Duh, duh, duh.' " That played to the most insidious racial stereotype, the dumb and ugly black man, but Ali reached further: "Joe Frazier is an Uncle Tom." And further: "Ninety-eight percent of my people are for me. They identify with my struggle. . . . If I win, they win. If I lose, they lose. Anybody black who thinks Frazier can whup me is an Uncle Tom."

In fact, because of Ali's work for racial justice and because of the sacrifices he made in his stand against the Vietnam War, the vast majority of blacks—as well as an increasing number of whites—saw his battles as theirs and were drawn to him as a force for social change. The most prominent voices of the 1960s, a decade torn by conflict and rebellion, had been silenced. Dr. Martin Luther King Jr. was dead. Bobby Kennedy was dead. Senator Eugene McCarthy had drifted like a blip off the screen. Ali alone remained alive in the ruins—the most commanding voice for and symbol of the decade's causes.

In the month leading up to the fight, he brought to bear all the horsepower of his eloquence. His demeaning of Frazier, Ali now says, had but one purpose: "To sell tickets." Of course, Frazier says there was no need to sell anything, because their purses were guaranteed, but this argument ignores the fact that Ali was always selling more than tickets. The consummate performer, he was selling himself. And there are those who say that Ali's rhetoric was merely a part of his act, the tappety-tap-tap of his every-day walking shtick. But whatever compelled him to violate all the canons of fairness and decency in his portrayal of Frazier—whether it was meanness, bravado or a calculated plan to enrage and rattle his opponent—he succeeded in isolating Frazier from the black community.

And Frazier? He felt manipulated, humiliated and betrayed. "He had me stunned," Frazier says. "This guy was a buddy. I remember looking at him and thinkin', What's wrong with this guy? Has he gone crazy? He called me an Uncle Tom. For a guy who did as much for him as I did, that was cruel. I grew up like the black man—he didn't. I cooked the liquor. I cut the wood. I worked the farm. I lived in the ghetto. Yes, I tommed; when he asked me to help him get a license, I tommed for him. For him! He betrayed my friendship. He called me stupid. He said I was so ugly that my mother ran and hid when she gave birth to me. I was shocked. I sat down and said to myself, I'm gonna kill him. O.K.? Simple as that. I'm gonna kill him!"

So by the time they climbed through the ropes that night in the Garden, the lure of the fight went far beyond the exquisitely contrasting styles of the two men. For many viewers Ali was still the mouth that poured, the renegade traitor and rabble-rouser whose uppity black ass needed dusting. For many others, of course, he symbolized all successful men of color who did not conform in a white man's world—and the hope that one, at least *one*, would overcome. Frazier had done nothing to earn the caricature of Uncle Tom, but Ali had lashed him to that stake as if to define their war in black and white. Frazier knew the scope of Ali's appeal. A Bible-raised man, he saw himself as David to Ali's Goliath.

"David had a slingshot," Frazier says. "I had a left hook."

FOR 14 ROUNDS, ALMOST A FULL HOUR IN WHICH THE GARDEN never stopped rocking, Frazier pursued and pounded the former champion like a man simultaneously pushing a plow and chopping wood. Ali won the first two rounds, dancing and landing jabs and stinging rights, but by the third, under a remorseless body attack climaxed by a searing hook to the ribs, his feet had begun to flatten, and soon he was fighting toe-to-toe, his back pushed against the ropes.

249

It was a fight with two paces, fast and faster, and among its abiding images is that of Frazier, head down and body low, bobbing and weaving incessantly, taking lashing lefts and rights from Ali, then unloading that sweeping hook to the jaw, and Ali waving his head defiantly—*No, no, that didn't hurt*—and coming back, firing jabs and hooks and straight rights to Frazier's head. It was soon clear that this was not the Ali of old, the butterfly who had floated through his championship years, and that the long absence from the ring had stolen his legs and left him vulnerable. He had always been a technically unsound fighter: He threw punches going backward, fought with his arms too low and avoided sweeping punches by leaning back instead of ducking. He could get away with that when he had the speed and reflexes of his youth, but he no longer had them, and Frazier was punishing him.

Frazier quickened the tempo in the third and fourth, whaling Ali with lefts and rights. Ali moved as he fired jabs and landed rights and shouted at Frazier, "Do you know I'm God?"

"God, you're in the wrong place tonight," Frazier shot back. "I'm takin' names and kickin' ass!"

The Garden crowd was on its feet. Frazier mimicked Ali in the fifth, dropping his hands and laughing as Ali struck him with a left and a right. Frazier's ferocious head and body attacks began to slow Ali down, but the former champion scored repeatedly as Frazier moved in, and by the start of the eighth the crowd was chanting, "Ali! Ali! Ali!" Looking inspired, Frazier bore in, crashing a hook on Ali's head and following it up with two rights. After Ali mockingly tapped him on the head, Frazier drove a fiery hook into the ex-champ's jaw, and after the bell that ended the round members of the crowd were chanting, "Joe! Joe! Joe!"

Starting the 11th Frazier was winning on two of the three cards, and it was here that he took possession of the fight. As Ali stood in a neutral corner, Frazier stepped inside and let fly a thunderous hook to the jaw that snapped Ali's neck and buckled his legs. Ali looked gone. A hard right sent him sagging on the ropes. Another wobbled him again. At the bell he was still on his feet, but he moved shakily back to his corner.

If Ali-Frazier I was the most memorable athletic event of our time, surely it was the 15th round that made it so. About twenty seconds after the opening bell, Frazier threw the most famous left hook in boxing history and raised the evening to the realm of myth. The punch began south of his brocade trunks, somewhere down in Beaufort, and rose in a whistling arc that ended on the right side of Ali's jaw, just above the point of the chin. Ali sprawled on his back, the tassels on his shoes flying in the air. "I looked up," Ali says today, "and I was on the floor."

Frazier turned and walked away. Earlier in the fight, after pounding Ali with hooks to the head, he had asked his cornermen, "What is keeping this guy up?" Now he asked it again as he turned and saw Ali climb to his feet at the count of four. Frazier won a unanimous decision—"I kicked your ass!" he would yell at Ali as the final bell sounded—but among the enduring moments of that night was the one in which a battered Ali rose off that deck.

The two fighters sent each other to the hospital. Ali went briefly for a swollen right jaw, which made him appear to need a tooth extraction, and a lumpy-faced Frazier was in and out for two weeks for treatment of exhaustion, high blood pressure and kidney problems. The two men also left each other irreversibly diminished. They would never be the same fighters again.

T HIRTY-FIVE MONTHS WOULD PASS BEFORE THEY WOULD MEET FOR Ali-Frazier II, on Jan. 28, 1974, at the Garden. But by then the context in which they had fought had changed so dramatically that there is no comparing the two bouts. On Jan. 22, 1973, Frazier had lost his title when George Foreman hit him a few times with his wrecking-ball right and knocked him senseless in the second round in Kingston, Jamaica. So there was no championship at stake in Ali-Frazier II. By then, too, the social causes of the '60s were no longer ardent issues. But the Vietnam War had become such a national plague that Ali's popularity had climbed at roughly the same rate that the war's had declined.

The only thing that remained the same was Frazier's incandescent animus toward Ali, unappeased by his victory in '71. Five days before the second fight, sitting together before a national TV audience on ABC, they were discussing the first bout when Frazier referred to Ali's visit to the hospital. "I went to the hospital for 10 minutes," Ali shot back. "You went for a month."

"I was resting," Frazier says.

"That shows how dumb you are," Ali said. "People don't go to a hospital to rest. See how ignorant you are?"

Frazier had not had much formal schooling, and Ali had touched his hottest button. "I'm tired of you calling me ignorant all the time," snapped Frazier. "I'm not ignorant!" With that, he rose and towered over Ali, tightening his fists, his eyes afire. When Ali's brother, Rahaman, rushed to the stage, Frazier turned to him and said, "You in this too?" Here Ali jumped to his feet and grabbed Frazier in a bear hug. They rolled off the stage and onto the studio floor, and Goodman remembers Frazier holding one of Ali's feet and twisting it, like the head of a chicken, while Futch screamed, "Joe! Joe! Don't twist off his foot! There won't be a fight!"

Ali was bug-eyed as Frazier left in a fury. "Did you see how wide Clay's eyes opened up?" Frazier said. "Now I really got him scared!"

Frazier got nothing. Ali won an easy 12-round decision, nearly knocking Frazier out in the second round and then clinching and smothering whatever attack Frazier tried to mount inside. Indeed, Ali put on a boxing clinic, fighting at his range instead of Frazier's, and many of Frazier's sweeping hooks appeared to lack the snap they'd had three years before. The Ali-Frazier rivalry might have ended right there, in fact, if Ali had not taken events into his hands so magnificently nine months later in Kinshasa, Zaire, knocking out Foreman—the baddest man on the planet—in an upset that staggered the memory and fired the imagination.

Ali's victory in Africa eventually led to Ali-Frazier III, the final combat, in the Philippines. Here the two fighters got guaranteed purses, $4.5 million for Ali and $2 million for Frazier, plus a percentage of the gross. Once again Ali had become the largest draw in sports, and once again he went at Frazier with a vengeance, correcting his diction and carrying around, in his shirt pocket, a small rubber gorilla. At a press conference before the fight, Ali pulled out the doll in front of Frazier and began beating it, saying, "All night long, this is what you'll see. Come on, gorilla! We're in Manila! Come on, gorilla, this is a thrilla!" Black people cringed, but not a few whites laughed, and Frazier felt again the heat of his own anger.

No one knew what to expect when these two aging fighters came together that morning in Manila. Several major U.S. newspapers didn't bother sending a writer to cover the fight. But those who were there witnessed prizefighting in its grandest manner, the final epic in a running blood feud between two men, each fighting to own the heart of the other. The fight called upon all of their will and courage as they pitched from one ring post to another emitting fearful grunts and squeals.

By the end of the 10th round Ali looked like a half-drowned man who had just been pulled from Manila Bay. His aching body slumped, glistening with sweat. He had won the early rounds, snapping his whiplike jab on Frazier's face, but as in '71 Frazier had found his rolling rhythm after a few rounds, and by the fifth he had driven Ali into his corner and was thumping his body like a blacksmith. Ali's trainer was frantic. "Get outta the goddam corner!" screamed Dundee. It was too late. The fight had shifted from Ali to Frazier.

For the next five rounds it was as if Frazier had reached into the darkest bat cave of his psyche and freed all his pent-up rage. In the sixth he pressed and attacked, winging three savage hooks to Ali's head, the last of which sent his mouthpiece flying. For the first time in the fight, Ali sat down between rounds. Frazier resumed the attack in the seventh, at one point landing four straight shots to the body, at another point landing five. In the ninth, as Ali wilted, their fighting went deeper into the trenches, down where Frazier whistles while he works, as he landed blow upon blow he could hear Ali grunting in pain. In his corner after the 10th, Ali said to Pacheco, "This must be what dyin' is like."

Frazier owned the fight. He was sure to regain his title. And then came the 11th. Drew (Bundini) Brown, Ali's witch doctor, pleaded with him, "Go down to the well once more!" From wherever it is that such men draw the best and noblest of themselves, Ali emerged reborn. During the next four rounds he fought with a precision and fury that made a bloody Frazier weave and wobble. In the 12th Ali landed six consecutive punches to Frazier's head, and moments later he slammed home eight more. By the end of the round an archipelago of lumps had surfaced around the challenger's eyes and brow.

Futch could see Frazier's left eye closing. Before the 13th, he told his boxer, "Move back and stand up a little, so you can see the target better." That was just what Ali needed, more room and a taller man to fire at. "Boy, did he take advantage of that," says Futch. Ali threw punches in flurries, so many blows that Frazier reeled helplessly. A right cross sent Frazier's white mouthpiece twirling four rows into the seats. Futch kept thinking, *Ali has to slow down. He cannot keep this pace. Not into the 14th round!* By then Frazier's face was a misshapen moonscape, both eyes closing, and in the 14th Ali fired barrages and raked a nearly blind Frazier with rights and lefts. Futch stared at Ali and thought, *Incredible!* When the bell tolled, it tolled for Joe.

"The fight's over, Joe," Futch told him before the beginning of the 15th.

Frazier jumped up from his stool. He said, "Eddie—"

"Just sit down, Joe."

A BENUMBED AND EXHAUSTED ALI, HIS LIPS SCRAPED RAW, LAY ON a cot in his locker room in Manila and summoned Marvis Frazier, Joe's 15-year-old son, to his side. "Tell your dad the things I said I really didn't mean," Ali said. ✦ Marvis reported back to his father. "He should come to me, son," Joe told him. "He should say it to my face."

Back in the States, Ali called Lewis and asked him for Frazier's private number. Ali told Lewis that he wanted to apologize to Frazier for some of the things he has said. Lewis called Frazier, but, he says, Frazier told him, "Don't give it to him."

In the 21 years since then, Ali and Frazier have seen each other at numerous affairs, and Frazier has barely disguised the loathing he feels toward his old antagonist. In 1988, for the taping of a film called *Champions Forever*, five former heavyweight title holders—Ali, Frazier, Foreman, Larry Holmes and Ken Norton—gathered in Las Vegas. A crowd of people were at Johnny Tocco's Gym for a morning shoot when Frazier started in on Ali, who was already debilitated by Parkinson's. "Look at Ali," Frazier said. "Look what's happened to him. All your talkin', man. I'm faster than you are now. You're damaged goods."

"I'm faster than you are, Joe," Ali slurred. Pointing to a heavy bag, Ali suggested a contest: "Let's see who hits the bag the fastest."

Frazier grinned, not knowing he was back in the slaughterhouse. He stripped of his coat, strode to the bag and buried a dozen rapid-fire hooks in it, punctuating each rip with a loud grunt: "Huh! Huh! Huh!" Without removing his coat, Ali went to the bag, assumed the ready stance and mimicked one Frazier grunt: "Huh!" He had not thrown a punch. He turned slowly to Frazier and said, "Wanna see it again, Joe?" In the uproar of hilarity that ensued, only Frazier did not laugh. Ali had humiliated him again.

After the shoot, at a luncheon for the fighters, Frazier had too much to drink, and afterward, as people milled around the room and talked, he started walking toward Ali. Thomas Hauser, Ali's chronicler, watched the scene that unfolded over the next 20 minutes. Holmes quietly positioned himself between Ali and Frazier. "Joe was trying to get to Ali," Hauser said, "but where Joe went, left or right, Holmes would step between him and Ali. Physically shielding him. Joe was frustrated. After about 10 minutes of this, Foreman walked up to Larry and said, 'I'll take over.' " So for the next 10 minutes Frazier quietly tried to get around 290 pounds of assimilated Big Macs. At one point Frazier leaned into Foreman, but Foreman only leaned back. "Keep it cool, Joe," Foreman whispered. "Be calm."

Ali had no idea this was going on. "He was walking around like Mr. Magoo," says Hauser. "He was oblivious."

While Frazier's hostility toward Ali was well known to the fight crowd, it was not until his book came out last spring that he took his venom public. When Phil Berger, who wrote the book, began interviewing Frazier last fall and heard what he wanted to say about Ali, he warned Frazier of the damning impact it would have. "Ali's become like a saintly figure," Berger said.

Too bad, the fighter replied. "That's the way I feel."

With his book and his unseemly harangue against Ali at the Olympics, which had the strong whiff of envy, Frazier may have done himself irreparable damage among the legions who have admired him steadfastly. What he wants from Ali is an apology for those long years of vilification—the apology he did not want to hear when Lewis called him on Ali's behalf after Manila.

Ali has expressed contrition more than once for the things he said. In Hauser's 1991 oral history *Muhammad Ali: His Life and Times*, Ali says, "I'm sorry Joe Frazier is mad at me. I'm sorry I hurt him. Joe Frazier is a good man. I couldn't have done what I did without him, and he couldn't have done what he did without me."

Wolf understands Frazier's rage, but he sees Ali today and does not see the man behind the cruel jibes of the past. "I'm not sure that part exists anymore," Wolf says. "Whether it is the Parkinson's or just maturing, that part of him is gone." So that leaves Frazier, imprisoned in the past, raging against a ghost.

Lewis, still a close friend of Frazier's, has pleaded with him to cut Ali loose. At the real root of Frazier's discontent, says Lewis, is his sense that history has not dealt with him fairly—that his Olympic triumph and his heavyweight championship years have been forgotten, and that time has turned him into just another stitch in the embroidery of Ali's legend. "You have your place in history, and Ali has his," Lewis tells Frazier. "You can't reflect back in bitterness. Let it go."

Futch's gentle voice still rings the clearest. His words in Manila, after 14 savage rounds that left Frazier's eyes nearly as blind as his heart is now, still echo faint but true. "The fight's over, Joe. . . . The fight's over, Joe. . . . The fight's over, Joe." ✦

STILL FIT Ali and Frazier—Joe in his original robe—pose 22 years after their 1971 title bout.

Statesman

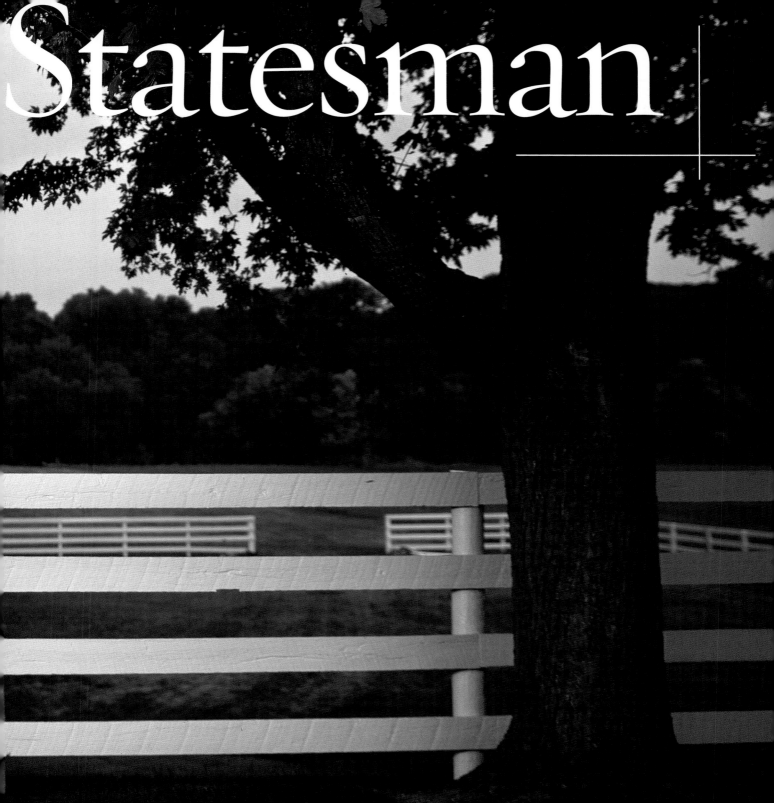

LION IN WINTER The champ takes a ride along a fence on his Michigan estate.

Superstars Peyton Manning and Tiger Woods looked to Ali for inspiration, and some fun.

"The world sees the trembling and the awful new Ali Shuffle, and feels sorry for the champ. Don't be. His mind is still bright. He still composes poetry nearly every day. He still studies the Koran and the Bible. *Ali* isn't alive only at your local Odoplex 24. He's still here, in the whispers."

RICK REILLY,
"Better Than the Movie," SI, 12/24–12/31/2001

Ali said that he was more afraid when his daughter Laila fought than when he was in the ring.

MAGIC MOMENT Ali
shook up the world all over
again when he opened the
1996 Olympics in Atlanta.

His longtime reputation as a peace-loving man cemented good relations with the Dalai Lama.

Two beloved, and controversial, senior statesmen: Ali and Clinton at a black-tie affair.

"Moment of the Year, 1996? Ali, of course. Ali emerging from the darkness, from the past, from the recesses of our imagination. Ali, a ghost in white, materializing after midnight to accept the flaming torch high on a ledge in Olympic Stadium during the opening ceremonies of the Atlanta Games. The massive crowd rising, straining to see who would have the honor of lighting the cauldron, and then crying 'Whooooaaa' in astonishment, the 'Whooooaaa' washing into a 'Whoop,' a hands-to-the-sky celebration.

"How much finer than the other fine moments? . . . First because of the surprise, the most known face on the planet showing up at the most unexpected instant. But more so because it was loaded, this simple moment, loaded with so much more meaning than anything a man could do in any game or race.

"Moment of the Year, 1996? You take the sudden and the swift, the whooshes and the swooshes. I'll take the trembling still life."

GARY SMITH, *"All Too Human,"* SI, 12/30/1996

DEVOTION As a devout Muslim, Ali prayed toward Mecca five times daily; here, in 1984, he kneels on a prayer rug.

ALI AND HIS ENTOURAGE

BY GARY SMITH

PHOTOGRAPHS BY GREGORY HEISLER/CPI

For two decades, the champ and his followers were the greatest show on earth, and then the show ended. But life went on
SI, APRIL 25, 1988

ROUND MUHAMMAD ALI, ALL WAS DECAY. Mildewed tongues of insulation poked through gaps in the ceiling; flaking cankers pocked the painted walls. On the floor lay rotting scraps of carpet. ✦ He was cloaked in black. Black street shoes, black socks, black pants, black short-sleeved shirt. He threw a punch, and in the small town's abandoned boxing gym, the rusting chain between the heavy bag and the ceiling rocked and creaked. ✦ Slowly, at first, his feet began to dance around the bag. His left hand flicked a pair of jabs, and then a right cross and a left hook, too, recalled the ritual of butterfly and bee. The dance quickened. Black sunglasses flew from his pocket as he gathered speed, black shirttail flapped free, black heavy bag rocked and creaked. Black street shoes scuffed faster and faster across black moldering tiles: *Yeah, Lawd, champ can still float, champ can still sting!* He whirled, jabbed, feinted, let his feet fly into a shuffle. "How's that for a sick man?" he shouted. ✦ He did it for a second three-minute round, then a third. "Time!" I shouted at the end of each one as the second hand swept past the 12 on the wristwatch he had handed to me.

LATE ROUNDS His entourage scattered, Ali retired to his Berrien Springs estate. **265**

And then, gradually, his shoulder began to slump, his hands to drop. The tap and thud of leather soles and leather gloves began to miss a quarter-beat . . . half-beat . . . whole. Ali stopped and sucked air. The dance was over.

He undid the gloves, tucked in the black shirt, reached reflexively for the black comb. On stiff legs he walked toward the door. Outside, under the sun, the afternoon stopped. Every movement he made now was infinitely patient and slow. Feeling . . . in . . . his . . . pocket . . . for . . . his . . . key. . . . Slipping . . . it . . . into . . . the . . . car . . . lock. . . . Bending . . . and . . . sliding . . . behind . . . the . . . wheel. . . . Turning . . . on . . . the . . . ignition . . . and . . . shifting . . . into . . . gear. . . . Three months had passed, he said, since he had last taken the medicine the doctor told him to take four times a day.

One hand lightly touched the bottom of the wheel as he drove; his clouded eyes narrowed to squint. His head tilted back, and the warm sunlight trickled down his puffy cheeks. Ahead, trees smudged against sky and farmland; the glinting asphalt dipped and curved, a black ribbon of molasses.

He entered the long driveway of his farm, parked and left the car. He led me into a barn. On the floor, leaning against the walls, were paintings and photographs of him in his prime, eyes keen, arms thrust up in triumph, surrounded by the cluster of people he took around the world with him.

He looked closer and noticed it. Across his face in every picture, streaks of bird dung. He glanced up toward the pigeons in the rafters. No malice, no emotion at all flickered in his eyes. Silently, one by one, he turned the pictures to the wall.

Outside, he stood motionless and moved his eyes across his farm. He spoke from his throat, without moving his lips. I had to ask him to repeat it. "I had the world," he said, "and it wasn't nothin'." He paused and pointed. "Look now. . . ."

Black blobs of cows slumbering in the pasture, trees swishing slowly, as if under water rather than sky. Merry-go-rounds, sliding boards and swings near the house, but no giggles, no squeals, no children.

"What happened to the circus?" I asked.

He was staring at the slowly swishing trees, listening to the breeze sift leaves and make a lulling sound like water running over the rocks of a distant stream. He didn't seem to hear.

And I said again, "What happened to the circus?"

The Doctor

A man of infinite variety. Medical doctor, jazz connoisseur, sports figure, confidant of the great. —Excerpt from Ferdie Pacheco's publicity brochure

"This is a painting of myself when I was 30 and living alone and messing around with a German woman who loved when there was sweat and paint all over me . . . and this

FIGHT DOCTOR In the mid-'70s a worried Ferdie Pacheco urged his patient to quit boxing.

is a screenplay that I've just cut down from 185 to 135 . . . and this one here is a 750-page epic novel, a very serious look at the immigrant experience in Tampa . . . and this is a painting I did of Sherman's March—that stream of blue is the Union soldiers . . . and that one is a screenplay I just finished about two Cubans who steal a Russian torpedo boat, and a crazy Jewish lawyer—Jerry Lewis is going to play the part and direct it—picks them up in a boat. . . ."

In one way, Ferdie Pacheco was just like his former patient Muhammad Ali: He needed laughter and applause. He led people to each of his paintings, lithographs, cartoons and manuscripts the way Ali once led them to continents to watch him talk and fight. Both worked on canvas: Ali, when his was not near to dance on, used parlor magic tricks to make eyes to bright and wide; Pacheco, when his was not near to dab on, told long tales and jokes, dominating a dinner party, from escargots to espresso, with his worldliness and wit.

In another way, they were not alike at all. Ali lived for the moment and acted as he felt, with disregard for the cord between action and consequence. This allured the doctor, whose mind teemed with consequence before he chose his action. "In an overcomplicated society," he says, "Ali was a simple, happy man."

Twenty-five years ago Pacheco was a ghetto doctor in Miami. Today he can be found in his home, white shorts and paint-smeared white smock covering his torso, blue Civil War infantryman's cap atop his head, stereo blaring Big Band jazz, telephone ringing calls from agents, reporters and TV executives as he barefoots back and forth, brushing blue on three different canvasses and discoursing, for anyone who will listen, upon the plot twist he has just hatched for Chapter 16 of his latest novel. He receives a six-figure salary from NBC for commenting on fights, has quit medicine, has become a painter whose works sell for as much as $40,000, and has completed 600 pen-and-ink drawings converted into lithographs (17,000 of which sold on the first mail-out order), six books (two of which have been published, including *Fight Doctor*), eight screenplays (four of which have sold), and a play that may soon be performed in London. He has also formed a Florida-based film production company and appeared across the country as a speaker. "But on my tombstone," he says, "it will say 'Muhammad Ali's doctor.' It's like being gynecologist to the queen."

In our time, will we see another comet that burns so long and streaks so fast, and whose tail has room for so many riders? "The entourage," some called the unusual collection of passengers who took the ride; the traveling circus, the hangers-on, others called it. "These people are like a little town for Ali," his manager, Herbert Muhammad, once said. "He is the sheriff, the judge, the mayor and the treasurer." Most were street people, thrown together on a lonely mountaintop in Pennsylvania where Ali built his training camp, until they burst upon the big cities for his fights. They bickered with each other over who would do what task for Ali, fist-fought with each other at his instigation—two of them once even drew guns. And they hugged and danced with each other, sat for hours talking around the long wooden dinner table, played cards and made midnight raids on the refrigerator together. "That's right," said Herbert Muhammad. "A family."

Because they were there for Ali, he never had to worry about dirty underwear or water bills or grocery shopping; he could remain an innocent. Because Ali was there for them, they could be mothers and fathers to the earth's most extraordinary child.

For a decade and a half he held them together, took them to the Philippines, Malaysia, Zaire, Europe, and the Orient, their lives accelerating as his did, slowing when his did, too. But among them one was different, the one who obeyed the law of consequence. Ferdie Pacheco ejected while the comet still had momentum, and made a missile of himself.

"I had an overwhelming urge to create," he says. And an ego that kept telling him there was nothing he couldn't do. "On napkins, tablecloths, anywhere, he'd draw," says his wife, Luisita. "I shouted 'Help me!' when I was delivering our child. He said, 'Not now'—he was busy drawing me in stirrups."

Few knew him in the early Ali days: What reason was there to consult the doctor when Ali was young, physically unflawed and all-but-unhittable? Pacheco was the son of Spanish immigrants, a first-generation American, who had established a general practice in Miami's black Overtown district and become a regular at Miami Beach boxing matches, where he met cornerman Angelo Dundee and began to treat Dundee's boxers for free. One day, a patient named Cassius Clay came to him. And Pacheco became part of the entourage.

"It satisfied my Iberian sense of tragedy and drama," he says, "my need to be in the middle of a situation where life and death are in the balance, and part of it is in your hands. Most people go out of their way to explain that they don't need the spotlight. I see nothing wrong with it.

"Medicine—you do it so long, it's not a high-wire act without a net anymore. At big Ali fights, you got the feeling you had on a first date with a beauty queen. I'd scream like a banshee. It was like taking a vacation from life."

The first signal of decline was in Ali's hands. Pacheco began injecting them with novocaine before fights, and the ride went on. Then the reflexes slowed, the beatings began, the media started to question the doctor. And the world began to learn how much the doctor loved to talk. Style, poise and communication skills had become the weaponry in the land that Ali conquered: A member of the king's court who could verbalize—not in street verse, as several members could, but in the tongue the mass markets cried for—and foresee consequence as well, could share Ali's opportunities without sharing his fate. The slower Ali spoke, the more frequently spoke the doctor.

Ali reached his mid-30s stealing decisions but taking more and more punishment; Pacheco and his patient reached a juncture. The doctor looked ahead and listened, heard the crowd's roar fading, the espresso conversation sobering. His recommendation that Ali quit met deaf ears. The same trait that drew him to Ali began to push him away.

He mulled his dilemma. Leave and risk being called a traitor? Or stay and chance partial responsibility for lifelong damage to a patient who ignored his advice?

Pacheco followed his logic. He wrote Ali a letter explaining that cells in Ali's kidneys were disintegrating, then parted ways with him and created laughter and applause on his own. Ali followed his feelings and went down a different path.

Today the ex-fighter turns dung-streaked canvases to the wall, the ex-doctor covers his wall with new canvases. In his studio, Pacheco shakes his head. "I feel sorry for Ali," he says, "but I'm fatalistic. If he hadn't had a chance to get out, I'd feel incredibly sad. But he had his chance. He chose to go on. When I see him at fights now, there's no grudge. He says, 'Doc, I made you famous.' And I say, 'Muhammad, you're absolutely right.' "

The Facilitator

What if a demon crept after you one day or night in your loneliest solitude and said to you: "This life, as you live it now and have lived it, you will have to live again and again, times without number; and there will be nothing new in it, but every pain and every joy and every thought and sigh and all the unspeakable small and great in your life must return to you. . . . The eternal hourglass of existence will be turned again and again—and you with it, you dust of dust!" Would you not throw yourself down and gnash your teeth and curse the demon who thus spoke?
—FRIEDRICH NIETZSCHE

Warm Vegas night air washed through the '76 Cadillac convertible. "We had fun, mister," said the driver. "We *lived*, mister. Every day was history. Millionaires would've paid to do what I did. To be near *him*."

He fell silent for a few blocks. The lunacy of lightbulbs glinted off his glasses and his diamond-studded heavyweight championship ring. "When I was a little boy, I used to watch airplanes in the sky until they became a dot, and then until you couldn't even see the dot. I wanted to go everywhere, do everything. Well, I *did*. Europe, the Far East, I saw it all. He was pilot, I was navigating. Hell, yes. The most exciting days of my life. Every day, I think about them. We were kids together, having fun. He was my best friend. I think I might have been his."

The car stopped at an intersection. A woman, thick in the thighs and heavy with makeup, walked across the beam of his lights. His eyes didn't flicker. Frantically, hopelessly, the blinking lightbulbs chased one another around and around the borders of the casino marquees.

"You could feel it all around you, the energy flow," he said. His foot pressed the accelerator, his shoulders rested back against the seat. "When you're with someone dynamic, goddam, it reflects on you. You felt: Let's go *do* it. I met presidents and emperors and kings and queens and killers, traveling with him. Super Bowls, World Series, hockey, basketball championships I saw. I was big in the discos, Xenon, Studio 54. There was myself, Wilt Chamberlain and Joe Namath: the major league of bachelors."

Quiet again. The traffic light pooled red upon the long white hood. Dead of summer, down season in Vegas. The click of the turn signal filled the car. Then the click-click-click of a cocktail waitress, high-heeled and late for work. He peered into the neon-shattered night. "What could I find out there tonight?" he asked. "A girl more beautiful than I've been with? A girl more caring than I've been with? What would she tell me I haven't heard before? What's left that could impress me? What's left I haven't done or seen? It burnt me out, I tell you. It burnt me out for life. . . ."

Gene Kilroy had no title. Everyone just knew: He was the Facilitator. When Ali wanted a new Rolls-Royce, Kilroy facilitated it. When he wanted to buy land to build a training camp, Kilroy facilitated it. When a pipe burst in the training camp or a hose burst in the Rolls, when Marlon Brando or Liza Minnelli wanted to meet Ali, or Ali wanted to donate $100,000 to save an old-folks' home, Kilroy facilitated it.

At hotels he usually stayed in a bedroom that was part of Ali's suite. As soon as they entered a city, he collected a list of the best doctors, in case of an emergency. He reached for the ever-ringing phone, decided who was worthy of a visit to the throne room. He worried himself into a 10-Maalox-a-day habit, facilitating. "Ulcer," he said. "You love someone, you worry. Watching him get hit during the Holmes fight, I bled like a pig—I was throwing up in the dressing room. And all the problems before a fight. It was like having a show horse you had to protect, and all the people wanted to hitch him to a buggy for a ride through Central Park."

The trouble with facilitating was that it left no mark, no KILROY WAS HERE. He has covered the walls of his rec room with 50 Ali photos. He reminisces every day. He watched videos of old Ali interviews he helped facilitate, and sometimes tears fill his eyes. "I wish I had a kid I could tell," he said. And then, his voice going from soft to gruff: "I'll get married when I find a woman who greets me at the door the way my dogs do."

The Vegas casinos, they knew what Kilroy might be worth. All those contacts around the world, all those celebrities who had slipped into the dressing room on a nod from the Facilitator: perfect qualifications for a casino host. First the Dunes hired him, then the Tropicana and now the Golden Nugget.

Each day he weaves between blackjack tables and roulette wheels, past slot machines and craps tables, nodding to dealers, smiling at bouncers, slapping regulars on the back, dispensing complimentary dinners and rooms to high rollers and "How are ya, hon?" to cocktail waitresses. He no longer gambles: All the lust for action is gone. All that remains is the love arranging a favor, of helping other members of Ali's old "family" when they hit hard times, of facilitating someone else's wants now that his are gone.

"As you know, I was all over the world with Ali," he said, leading a multimillionaire into one of the Golden Nugget's suites. "I got the royal gold-carpet treatment everywhere. But this"—he swept his arm across the room—"solidifies the epitome of luxury. *Look*. Your Jacuzzi. Your sauna." Again and again his beeper would sound, and he would be connected with another wealthy client. "Sure, I'll have our limo pick you up at the airport. . . . Your line of credit is all set, $100,000."

Whenever Ali comes to Vegas to see a fight, he will mix with high rollers at Kilroy's request or sign a couple of dozen boxing gloves, a stack of a hundred photographs, mementos Kilroy passes out to favored clients. In his world, Ali souvenirs are currency. "One man was so proud of the things I'd given him," he said, "that when he died, he was buried with his Ali picture and boxing gloves. I can give people their dreams."

When Ali is near, Kilroy looks at him and remembers what the two of them once were. Sometimes he feels helpless. How can he facilitate away Ali's great fatigue with life—when he too, feels sated and weary? "I remember one day not long ago when he was signing autographs, and I was standing next to him. We heard someone say, 'Look at Ali, he's a junkie.' Muhammad's eyes get kind of glassy sometimes now, you know. I wanted to choke the guy. But Ali nudged me and kind of smiled. God, I hope he wins this last fight. . . ."

On an impulse he picked up the phone and dialed Ali's number. "Hello, it's Gene. . . . You've been out walking, huh? I wish I could walk with you. . . . I can barely hear you. . . . I *said*, I wish I could walk with you. . . . It's good you're walking; you'll feel a lot better. . . . Hey, wouldn't it be nice to have a reunion at Deer Lake? Get everybody together—Sarria, you, me, Bundini, Pat, Lana. Get Lana to cook a roast, potatoes, gravy, everything. Wouldn't it be? . . . No, not bring back *old* memories. Bring back *great* memories. . . . Yeah. . . . O.K., well, get some rest. See you, champ. . . ."

He hung up the phone and stared at the wall. He glanced at his watch. Another day was nearly finished, a day of facilitating rooms and meals and money for men who still had the appetite, and he knew what he would do that night. "I could call and have three girls if I wanted," he said. Instead he would drive past the riot of blinking lights, past the ads for bare-legged showgirls and sequined singers, through the warm night air of Vegas to his home in the suburbs. His three dogs, all boxers, would jump up and lick him, and he would let them, and he would call his 80-year-old mother, eat dinner and settle back for an evening of TV amid the Ali photos. "The foxhole," he said. "I'm going back to the foxhole."

The Cook

"Next! How many? Two? O.K., let's move it, please! Next! You getting' big, honey! How come you don't stop by more to see me? Soup! Chicken noodle soup, anybody? Next! Hey, Eskimo, what you doin'? Ain't you beautiful? You want two? Gonna kill yo'self, storin' up all them fat cells. Next!"

She stood in a food-splotched apron in the basement cafeteria of a private school on East 70th Street in Manhattan, stuffing pita pockets with barbecue and rolling her hips to the music from the radio. Her hips, her soul and her name—Lana Shabazz—are those of a jazz singer, but the gaze she gave the children was that of a mother.

Hardly none of 'em down here know. That's nothin' off my teeth, no need for 'em to. I got my own life, I don't need 'em fussin' over me. Get up at five every mornin', draw me a bath, get dressed in my whites for work. Still live out of suitcases—that's from being with him. Then I go drink coffee in a deli or a restaurant. Nice to sip and socialize with folks. By seven, I'm down here workin' myself tired to the bone runnin' this kitchen, the kind of tired you got to soak out in another big hot bath at night. Ain't easy, but I'm happy, course I am.

"Lana," the headmaster called, "do you have some tea?"

"Lana," a teacher said, "you got any of that broiled fish?"

"Lana," said the memo on the wall, "a reminder that we will need coffee and Danish for parent tours next week."

"Mama," said the little boy. "I'm hungry. What's to eat?"

Mama, that's what the young ones call me. Three hundred and fifty kids needin' me here every day . . . but all of 'em needin' together can't never need me like he did. He'd some in at midnight, I'd have his dinner ready. He'd wake up at five a.m. and say, "Lana, get me a cuppa tea," I'd get up and do it. He'd travel, I'd pack up and cook in his hotel suite. Made sure he got all the live enzymes. Cooked without butter to save the calories—he had to allow for his sweet tooth. Made him cookies and cakes, then hid 'em so he wouldn't eat 'em all at once. He'd swallow what I made so fast I'd wonder if he had teeth in his stomach. Then he's go back to his cabin, and I'd worry about the cold from the air-conditionin' hittin' his chest, he kept it so high. What a beautiful man. I'd feed his kids at camp, break up their fights—they treated me like a mother. Nobody else couldn't a did what I did for that man.

She looked up and saw the first- and second-graders fill the cafeteria like a burst of happy swallows. They swarmed at her legs and tugged at her white bell-bottom trousers. "Mama, do you have cookies? Mama, can we have a cookie?" She told them she couldn't do that, stroked their heads, then grinned and sneaked them each a big one.

One time, man read my cards and looked at me funny. He said, "There's more of Ali's cards showin' than yours." That scared me—I'd almost lost myself to him. All I thought of

was Ali. But he gave so much of himself to the world, I told myself, he needs someone to take care of him. And that was me. Veronica, his third wife, she sat there combin' her hair while Earnie Shavers was punchin' on him, but I couldn't bear it. I had to get up and go back to my hotel room, where I prayed and screamed so long, God had to let him win. Psychic told me that in another life, I was his mother. Gets me to wanna cry, thinkin' about him. But I won't though. No, I won't.

She did a little samba around the butcher block, disappeared into the pantry and reappeared bopping out a bongo beat on a shiny ice bucket. When she leaned to dip a spoon and test the soup, her gold earrings shook. She straightened and pushed her big eyeglasses back up her steam-slick nose.

A teenage boy entered with a gift—a pair of stuffed grape leaves. She laughed from her belly and thanked him. A teenage girl said goodbye and kissed her on the cheek. "You be a nice girl," she said softly to the girl.

Even when I was 15, back in Bessemer, Alabama, I still kept my dolls on my bed. My first husband pushed them off and said I wouldn't need 'em now that I had a real one in my belly. Guess I got that motherin' instinct—can't get rid of it. Been takin' care of people all my life. Took care of my mother 'fore she died. Raised up my two little girls. Cooked for Malcolm X, for Elijah Muhammad and then for Ali. Funny thing, people trust you when you feed 'em, and folks always seem to trust me. Sitting on buses, I end up telling strangers next to me what foods they need to eat. I read nutrition books all the time when I'm layin' alone in bed.

At four o'clock she took off her white work shoes with a sigh, slipped on her sneakers and overcoat and walked out into the chill. She wedged inside the 101 uptown bus, left the million-dollar condos of the Upper East Side behind and went home to Harlem. She stopped at the post office, then sat over coffee at the Twin Donut Shop, the way she does every evening, and read her mail. Soon she would return to her apartment—her daughters live in Chicago and Miami and she is divorced—and draw a bath. "Hey, how you doin', Lana?" someone called to her. "Doin' great," she said. "Doin' great."

Course, maybe if you looked closer, you'd see the hurt in my eyes. Know what it feels like to think of somebody all the time, and suddenly they ain't there? Like losin' a child. Maybe he's sick because he ain't eatin' right. Maybe he ain't getting' the right enzymes. I see other people 'round him now. Why we ain't there? We the ones made sure he was champ. Don't wanna say my life's empty . . . no, but . . . I have dreams about him. One where he's sick and doesn't want nothin' to do with me. Then he's all better and he's so happy to see me. Sometimes I think about that poem I wrote when he was young. Wrote that somebody like that could never live to be old.

I love him, but sometimes I get mad at him, too. People say that after workin' with him all those years, I shouldn't need for nothin' . . . and I'm flat broke. If they'd only have set up a retirement fund for us, we'd have no problems now. He used to say he was gonna buy me a house when he retired. If I'd asked him, he'd a done it. But I never asked for nothin'. And maybe that's best. Maybe if I had money I'd lose my love for people.

Some days, though, I just have to hear his voice. I call him, ask him what he's eatin'. People ask me all the time how he's doin'. Know how that feels, when people ask you how's your child, and you don't know what to say?

The Masseur

The gate to the fence that surrounded the little yellow house in northern Miami was locked. "Sarria!" I called from the sidewalk. "Sarria!" From inside the house a dog barked, then a second dog barked, a third, a fourth. And then the whole house exploded and shook with barking, a dozen, no, two dozen different timbres and pitches, the baritone bark of the big dogs, the staccato yelp of small ones, the frenzied howl of the thin and high-strung. My knuckles whitened on the chain-link fence; how many could there be? "Sarria!" I cried again—he *had* to be in there, people said he was a shut-in—but my shout was hopelessly lost in the din.

I swallowed hard. Such a sweet old man, everyone had told me. I began to scale the fence.

This the dogs seemed to sense and take as an insult; the whole house seemed to snap and snarl and salivate. My eyes darted, my stomach clenched. I shifted onto the balls of my feet, approached the door, reached toward it from a few feet away and knocked—my God, I could not even hear my own rapping. *Bang!* The door shuddered, but not from my knocking. *Bang-bang!* The metal meshing put up inside to protect the windows shook as the beasts hurled themselves at me.

I counted the strides it would take to flee back to the fence—how could the gentle old man live *here*?—then held my breath, reached over a bush and rapped on a bedroom window. *"Sarriiiiiaaaa!"* In reply came the asylum howl, the door thumping as if about to splinter, the flash of teeth and eyeballs and fur in the window. I ran back to the fence and had just jabbed a toe in the meshing when, weakly, beneath the fury, came a muffled human grunt.

Five long minutes passed. Giving up, I saw the rush of snarling black. I froze, then whirled, clawing to climb. *"Negrita!"* I heard someone call. *"Ven! Ven!"* The dog hesitated, charged again, hesitated. I looked back. The old man—thank God!—was reaching out to wave me forward.

His hands, splayed from long, long arms, were broad and black and powerful from years of hacking Cuban sugarcane. I remembered them, working endlessly up and down the smooth ripples of Ali's body, rubbing until he drifted off to sleep on the table and then rubbing some more out of love. His hands I remembered, but I could not remember *him.*

His shoulders hunched, his head poking turtlelike from those shoulders, Luis Sarria moved in hobbling increments toward the steps in front of the house. He sat, and the bottom of his puppy-chewed pantleg hitched up to show the swathes of tape that wrapped his left leg. It had been chronically ulcerated since he stepped on a sea snail while fishing as a boy, but now the wound had grown threatening. At the gym near his home, where he worked until a year ago when the leg became too painful, they wondered if the germs carried by the great pack of dogs inside his house were what kept reinfecting it; and they wondered how much longer the 76-year-old man would last.

His wife, Esther, a Jamaican with small, happy-sad eyes, came out and sat next to him. Sarria picked up the black dog and hugged it to his chest. "She is his favorite," his wife said, "because she never wants to come back in the house, and so he gets to lift her like a baby."

They are childless, she explained, and need money badly, barely making it each month on Social Security. The gentle old man can neither visit friends because of his leg, nor have them in because of his dogs. "They would rip people up," his wife said. "There are 25 of them."

"But why keep so many?" I asked.

She shrugged. "They say Liberace left 25 dogs."

"How could there be room for them all in your house?

"They live in the living room and one of the bedrooms," she said. "We live in our bedroom now. We had to move all the furniture out of the living room because they were destroying it. They broke the record player chasing rats. They dug up Sarria's garden. Dogs eat pumpkins. Did you know that?"

"How can you afford to feed them all?"

"We can't. I spend five dollars a day to buy chicken backs, turkey parts, rice. I mix it with their dog food. We spoil them. But dogs are better than people. Sarria loves to caress them."

Sarria rose gradually and hobbled to the house holding the black dog. "He is sad," she said, watching him go. "Because he cannot work, he is losing force." She glanced at the fence. "If Ali would come to that gate and say, 'Let's go to Manila,' Sarria would be young again."

I remembered how reporters used to gather in Ali's dressing room after a workout, recording every word from the champion's lips, moving then to the cornerman, Angelo Dundee, or perhaps to the street poet, Bundini Brown, or to Dr. Pacheco. Never did anyone exchange a word with Ali's *real* trainer, as some insiders called Sarria. It was almost as if no one even saw him. "Even in Spanish," said Dundee, "Sarria was quiet."

He had flown to America in 1960 to train Cuban welterweight Luis Rodriguez and never returned to his homeland, yet he never learned English. He felt safer that way, his lips opening only wide enough to accommodate his pipe, and Ali seemed to like it, too. Surrounded so many days by con men, jive men, press men and yes men, Ali cherished the morning hour and the afternoon hour on the table with the man who felt no need to speak. For 16 years, the man physically closest to the most quoted talker of his era barely understood a word.

Sometimes Ali would babble at Sarria senselessly, pretending he spoke perfect Spanish, and then in mid–mumbo jumbo blurt out *"Maricón!"* and Sarria's eyes would bug with mock horror. Everyone loved the silent old one. They swore his fingers knew the secret—how to break up fat on the champion's body and make it disappear. "And the exercises he put Ali through each morning! Sarria was the reason Muhammad got like this," Dundee said, forming a V with his hands. "He added years to Ali's boxing life."

The extra years brought extra beatings. And, likely, the Parkinson's syndrome. "I used to ask God to help me introduce power into him through my hands," Sarria said in Spanish, sitting once more on the front step. He rubbed his face. "Never did I think this could happen to him. I feel like crying when I see him, but that would not be good for him to see. To tell a boxer to stop fighting is an insult. I did not have the strength to tell him, but I wish to God I had."

"Oh, Sarria," said his wife. "You have never talked."

"If I had spoken more, I might have said things I should not have. Perhaps they would have said, 'This Cuban talks too much,' and I would have been sent away. . . ." Or perhaps he would be standing in Sarria's Health Spa on Fifth Avenue, massaging corporate lumbars for $75 an hour.

He ran his fingers across a paw print on his pants and spoke softly of Ali. "Ambitious people . . . people who talk a lot . . . perhaps *this* is what happens to them."

Behind us, the dogs began to snarl and thump again. "Shhhhh," Sarria pleaded. "Shhhhh."

"Sarria," I said, "how did you get so many dogs?"

From his pocket he pulled three photographs. Two of them were yellowed ones of him and Ali, clipped from newspapers. The other was a color glossy of a little girl. Tears misted his eyes, then his wife's. And the two of them took turns explaining the story of the 25 dogs.

Fourteen years ago they had taken in the three-day-old daughter of a relative who was unable to raise her. For 11 years she gave them someone to hug and care for, to take to ballet lessons and help with homework, to fill the hole left when Ali departed their lives. And then, just like *that*, the relative reappeared and took her away. "Oh, how Sarria cried," said his wife. She turned away and clamped her lips.

"Just before she left us," she went on, "the girl brought home a stray dog. We named it Alfi, and then she brought home a second one—we named it Kelly. When she left, we couldn't give away her dogs, you see. And then they started to make babies. . . ."

The Bodyguard

Clanking and jangling with walkie-talkie, nightstick, pistol and keys, Officer Howard (Pat) Patterson swung his 220-pound body out of patrol car No. 511 on the far south side of Chicago, and the shouting match began.

"Officer, this mother's in my face."

"You reported a battery? What's your name, ma'am?" Patterson asked calmly.

"Miss Jones. I went to jail for this motherf-----, and now . . ."

"I didn't touch her!" hollered the man. "I called her a name!"

"I might kill him!"

"Wait a minute, both of you."

"She got my chain, officer!"

"You motherf-----! I was locked up last summer for your honkie ass."

"Did he hit you, Miss Jones?"

"No, but he was in my face!"

"She pulled the chain off my neck. I want my chain!"

"Look," said Patterson. "You assault him, miss, and I'll lock *you* up. You're both high. Sir, you go take a walk. Let her cool off. And you stop screaming like that, Miss Jones."

Officer Patterson stepped back to his car and shook his head. "Lot of police would put them both in jail," he said. "I know before I was Ali's bodyguard, I'd put folks in jail 10 times faster than I do now. Now I just try to help them solve their problems and send them home. My attitude's different since seeing the world and rubbing shoulders with Ali."

When the comet ride with Ali began, Patterson was a 31-year-old cop on the streets of Chicago. When it ended, he was a 45-year-old cop on the streets of Chicago. He had two children, a loving wife, a close-knit family, 50 scrapbooks and a couple of walls of photographs that a ghetto kid never dreamed he would have, and for all that he was grateful.

He got the bodyguard job through a chance meeting. The day he was assigned to protect the leader of the Black Muslim movement in America, Elijah Muhammad, back in the mid-'60s, he stuck a gun into the face coming out of the darkness: Herbert Muhammad, Elijah's son and Ali's manager. Herbert wanted just such a businesslike fellow to protect his boxer, and Patterson became the Bodyguard. He worked primarily during the weeks of fights until 1974, when he was put on permanent loan to Ali by Chicago mayor Richard Daley.

Whenever they met, Ali made a game of guessing where Patterson's gun was hidden. One time it might be the Colt Diamondback strapped to his ankle, the next time, the

9-mm automatic tucked under his suit coat; then again, if it was cold enough for an overcoat, the Colt *and* a .38 would be buried in his pockets. Upon reaching Ali's hotel suite, the Bodyguard would hide the pistols in a flower vase or beneath a sofa cushion, so he would always have one near, along with the shotgun he kept in a closet or under the bed. In a briefcase he carried as much as $50,000 in cash—spending money for the champ.

His protective instinct was fierce. At Yankee Stadium on the night of the fight against Ken Norton in 1976, he had a $400 leather suit ripped to shreds while fighting off a mob from the fender of Ali's limo. He turned down four-figure bribes from people desperate to get past his checkpoint in hotel hallways and see Ali. When Ali entered a public bathroom, Patterson went, too. "If anything at all happened to Muhammad," he said, "I figured it would be my fault."

During fights, he always kept his hand clamped over the water bottle so no one could sabotage Ali. But the Bodyguard had to sit on the corner stool and watch helplessly when his man needed protection most, in the ring when the end was near. "Watching him get hit was like watching someone stick my mama with a knife," Patterson said. "Ali fights stopped being a party. I tried to tell him to quit. . . ."

He drove the patrol car through the streets as he reminisced, head continually swiveling, eyes sweeping, ears listening for his number on the radio. The recruit he was training listened to the stories silently. Now and then a wino or a pimp called from the sidewalk, "Hey, Patty, how's Muhammad?"

"Traveling with Ali opened up the whole world for me," said the Bodyguard. "I'll admit it, I was afraid of flying before I got on that first airplane to meet him in Toronto. I never thought of going to other countries. Now I feel like there's nothing I can't do; my wife and I travel all the time.

"With him I saw that people all over are the same—trying to educate their kids and get enough to eat—just like us. Only most of them don't have as much as we do. That changed me, too. I used to worry about being a success, getting a promotion. Now that's not important. Seeing how somebody as powerful as Ali never used force to get things done, I learned from that. I'm not a police officer anymore. I'm a *peace* officer. I'd rather drive a drunk home or give somebody five dollars to solve an argument than stick them in jail. People need help, not jail."

Not long ago, he was in London with a tour group when a disheveled, unbathed man approached and asked for money. The others averted their eyes and edged away. "There's a sucker," some said when Patterson gave the beggar a bill and talked with him, but they didn't understand. He wasn't safeguarding a man anymore, he was safeguarding an idea.

"Whenever he saw someone old or sick or in trouble," said the Bodyguard, "Ali always wanted to help them. He'd say, 'Who knows? Some day I might be that way.' "

GUARDIAN Pat Patterson was entrusted with protecting the world's most dangerous man. **283**

The Manager

The last man to enter the Chicago mosque was short and round and rumpled. His sport coat was two sizes too baggy, his shirttail spilled out across the seat of his pants. His shoes were unbuckled, and his face was stubbled with whiskers. He looked not at all like the man who had reached into his pocket for a million dollars to buy the land and build the mosque he stood in.

The others at prayer stood near the front. He slipped off his shoes, padded to the back and dropped to his knees behind a pillar. Few were aware of it, but he remembered well a passage in Muslim scripture advising worshippers to pray behind an object, an obstruction for the devil.

All his life Herbert Muhammad has hidden behind pillars. As a young man he was the quiet, respectful houseman and chauffeur for his powerful father, Elijah Muhammad. Then he became the manager of Muhammad Ali, taking 33% of Ali's multimillion-dollar purses but remaining so obscure that bouncers at Ali workouts sometimes barred his entry to the gym. "I never wanted to be a leader," he said. "I never wanted to be a target. My role is to support those in the lead."

Now he was 58, and he had trouble. His pillar was crumbling, his point man fading away. His dream of building 49 more mosques like this first one, using the money Ali and he could generate, was drifting further and further from his reach. Ali slurred words and shook and didn't want to be seen on television. Ali didn't care about making money anymore.

Herbert remained Ali's manager, and he wasn't going to give up his dream without a fight. Beneath the untucked shirt, unshaven face and tufts of black hair was a man burning with determination not to be forgotten when the Muslim history in America is written. Perhaps not equal to his father nor to his younger brother Wallace, whom Elijah anointed as his successor, but close. "Fifty mosques," said Herbert. "Allah said if you build him a mosque in this life, he'll build you a paradise in the next life. My father established 200 mosques, my brother 250. But they didn't *pay* for them. I want to *pay* for 50. That would make my father proud. Every day my wife tells me to relax. How can I? I want to go till I drop. If I can't do something meaningful, take me now."

He sighed. The Muslim movement had changed since Elijah died in 1975; it had dropped the black separatist thrust and become rounder, softer—more *Herbert*. Big-name athletes weren't changing their names to Abdul and Rashad as they did in the '60s and '70s. The glamour years were gone, and now it would take the quiet, behind-the-scenes work—the kind Herbert was cut out for—to keep the movement growing.

"Seemed like we were always doing something back when Muhammad was fighting," he said. "Building buildings, schools, starting mosques, buying buses, helping people.

Now everything has quieted down with Ali, but I still got the taste of it in my mouth."

The irony was pungent. For years the Manager tried to restrain Ali. Now Ali was restraining the Manager. "I'd beg him not to be so proud, not to mess around with women, not to say, 'I am the greatest,' " Herbert said. " 'I am the greatest' was an insult to God—in our prayers, we say '*Allâhu akbar*,' God is the greatest. That was when I was trying to make him more meek and religious. Back then I had to run to keep up with him when he *walked*. But this sickness stopped him dead in his tracks. Now everything's in slow motion. Now he's a hundred times more religious and meek than I ever thought he'd be. His whole life is his prayers. But he doesn't seem to care about anything. . . ."

The Manager had ushered in the era of million-dollar sports contracts, brilliantly playing promoters Don King and Bob Arum off against each other. Now he has an agreement for 25% of the cut if he negotiates a product deal with Ali. "If he wanted it and he wasn't sick, he could be making $20 million to $30 million a year in endorsements," said Herbert. "He's probably making a couple a hundred thousand. Last year I made $500 from him."

Still, the Manager keeps busy. Between his five trips to the mosque each day, he occasionally brokers deals for Third World sellers and runs a catering business in Chicago. But Ali was, and is, the key, and Herbert knows it.

Now and then the fighter leaves his 88-acre farm, which Al Capone once owned, in Berrien Springs, Mich., and makes the two-hour drive to meet Herbert at a Chicago hotel coffee shop. Ali genuinely liked Herbert and his easy laugh: He was the only non–family member Ali said he would ask along if he could take only five people to the moon. On one visit to the city, Ali sat in the coffee shop as the Manager made plans, listening with blank eyes as if the world of money and publicity was one from which he had died and floated far away. And the Manager, sharp and angular beneath the round body and the baggy sport coat with the elbow patches, tried everything to wake him. If Ali were dead, could Herbert feel completely alive?

"I tell him, 'Joe Frazier ain't sitting around,' " he said. " 'If you lost some weight and took your medicine, you could make a lot of money. You could even fight.' I know he can't fight, but I say it just to motivate him. He won't take his medicine, he hates to depend on anything. I think his problem is getting worse. He's shaking more. Sometimes it's hard to be in his presence, like someone sick in your family. I love that man. He is quicker to help a stranger, he has more inner compassion than any human being I've ever met. But I'm afraid he's losing the values of this earth. Allah said to do everything in your power to seek an afterlife, but not to neglect your share on this earth. Ali gave away that big house of his in Los Angeles, he gave away cars. He's giving up things *too* easy. I don't want to push him, but I have got to make him realistic. His mother, his father, his eight children, what will he do about their expenses, the kids' college educations? And he shouldn't dress the way I dress. He should have a suit and tie, and he should have his hair groomed, because he represents something to people.

"He says, 'I don't need no car, I'll just ride a bike.' I say, 'That's as crazy as a guy making $400 a week driving a Cadillac.' One night when we stayed over in Chicago, he slept on the floor of the mosque instead of getting a hotel. I told him, 'People are going to think you've lost all your marbles or your money—and neither one is good.' The whole world rallied around Islam as a universal religion because of Muhammad Ali. But if he doesn't watch it, he's going to become a monk."

One day last summer the Manager received a call from Mexico City. It was Ali, seeking counsel: Should he chance a new form of brain surgery that might cure his illness? Two of the 18 patients who had undergone the operation—in which adrenal cells are placed inside the brain to help make dopamine, a brain chemical essential to controlling voluntary body movement—had died shortly thereafter, but others had shown marked improvement. Ali might be Ali again!

Ali's fourth wife, Yolanda, cried on the telephone and begged him not to risk it. Herbert Muhammad closed his eyes and thought. He so hated to see Ali hurt, he used to keep his head down and pray during fights.

"I felt if he put his trust totally in God, the operation would be a success," said Herbert. He looked down at his hands. "But I didn't tell him that. If he turned out like a vegetable, it would be seen as my decision. People would think I said yes just because I wanted more paychecks from Ali. So I told him to listen to everybody but to make up his own mind."

Ali decided to wait until American doctors had become more familiar with the surgery. Part of him was afraid to be what he was again, filled with an energy that needed lights and action and other people's eyes. The illness, he sensed, was a protection against himself. And because of this, the Manager closed in on 60 feeling the way Ali did toward the end of his career, still able to visualize himself doing what he wanted to do, but unable to do it.

"Not just 50 mosques," said Herbert Muhammad. "But 50 mosques with day-care centers and schools and old-folks' homes attached to them. I keep telling Ali, Let's get back in the race. How could I have ever dreamed I'd have to beg Muhammad Ali to *go*?"

The Motivator

The scene: a small motel room in downtown Los Angeles that costs, at monthly rates, $5.83 a night. A little bit of afternoon light makes it through the curtains, falling on a tablecloth etched with the words GOD—MOTHER—SON. On top of the television stands a small *statue of Buddha, its head hidden by a man's cap. Four packs of playing cards and a Bible lie on the head of the bed; tin dinner plates are set on a small table. Affixed to a mirror are a photograph of a young Muhammad Ali and a leaflet for a play entitled* Muhammad Ali Forever.

On the bed, propped against a pillow, is a 57-year-old black man, slightly chubby, with black wooly hair on the sides of his head and, on the top, a big bald spot with a tiny tuft of hair growing at the very front. As he talks, his eyes go wide and wild . . . then far away . . . then wet with tears.

His name is Drew (Bundini) Brown, the ghetto poet who motivated Ali and maddened him, who invented the phrase, "Float like a butterfly, sting like a bee" and who played bit parts in The Color Purple *and* Shaft; *who licked Ali's mouthpiece before sliding it in but never said a yes to him he didn't mean; who could engage the champion in long discussions of nature and God and man, then lie in the hotel pool before a fight and have his white woman, Easy, drop cherries in his mouth; who, when he felt good, charged two $300 bottles of wine at dinner to Ali's expense account and then made Ali laugh it off; and who, when he felt bad, drank rum and shot bullets into the night sky at the mountain training camp in Pennsylvania—a man stretched taut and twanging between the fact that he was an animal and the fact that he was a spirit.*

Oh yes. A visitor sits in a chair near the window of the motel room, but often Bundini Brown talks as if he is ranting to a crowd on a street corner—or as if he is completely alone:

> *The old master painter from the faraway hills,*
> *Who pained the violets and the daffodils,*
> *Said the next champ gonna come from Louisville.*

I made that up 'fore we was even champion. Things just exploded in my head back then. Guess that's why Ali loved me. I could help him create new things. See, he never did talk that much. People didn't know that about him, 'less'n they slept overnight and caught him wakin' up. All that talkin' was just for the cameras and writers, to build a crowd. He was quiet as can be, same as now. But now people think he's not talkin' 'cause of the Parkinson's, which is a lie.

I remember when he fought Jerry Quarry, after that long layoff. Going from the locker room to the ring, my feet wasn't even touchin' the ground. I looked down and tried to touch, but I couldn't get 'em to. Like I was walkin' into my past. Me and the champ was so close, I'd think, *Get off the ropes*—and he'd get off the ropes! Man, it made chill bumps run up my legs. We were in Manila, fightin' Frazier. The champ came back to the corner crossin' his legs. Tenth or 11th round, I forget. Angelo said,

"Our boy is through." I said, "You're goddam wrong, my baby ain't through!" I was deeply in love with him. Ali tried to fire me every day, but how he gonna fire me when God gave me my job? So I stood on the apron of the ring, and I said out loud, "God! If Joe Frazier wins, his mother wins, his father wins, his kids win. Nobody else! But if Muhammad lose—God!—we *all* lose. Little boys, men women, black and white. Muhammad lose, the world lose!"

And you know what? The nigger got up fresh as a daisy. Everybody seen it! Got up fresh, man, *fresh*! And beat up on Frazier so bad Frazier couldn't come out after the 14th round! God put us together for a reason, and we shook up the world!

(He picks at a thread on the bedspread.) People'd see us back then and say, "It's so nice seein' y'all together." We made a lot of people happy. I was a soldier. *(His hands are shaking. He reaches down to the floor, pours a glass of rum as his eyes begin to fill with tears.)* I was happy then. It'd be good for Muhammad if I could be with him again. Be good for me, too. Then I wouldn't drink as much. By me being alone I drink a lot. Always did say I could motivate him out of this sickness, if me and the champ was together. He needs the medical thing, too, but he needs someone who truly loves him. If we were together again, more of the God would come out of me. *(His voice is almost inaudible.)* Things used to explode in my head. . . . I'm kind of runnin' out now. . . .

He asked me to go stay on the farm with him. *(His eyes flare, he starts to shout.)* What you goin' to do, put me to pasture? I ain't no horse! I don't want no handouts! I got plans! Big things gonna happen for me! I gotta get me a job, make some money, take care of my own family 'fore I go with him. If I don't love my own babies, how in hell I gonna love somebody else's?

First thing I'd do if I had some money, I'd go to the Bahamas and see my baby. King Solomon Brown's his name. Made him at Ali's last fight, with a woman I met down there. He was born on the seventh day until the seventh month. There's seven archangels and seven colors in the rainbow, you know.

I brought him to America and lived with him until he was one. Then he went back to the Bahamas with his mother. Didn't see him for a year and a half, then I went back. Wanted to see if he'd remember me. I said, "A-B-C-D-E-F-G—dock—dock" *(he makes a sound with his tongue and the roof of his mouth)*—that's what I always used to teach him—and he remembered! He ran and leaped into my arms—I mean jumped!—and we hugged, and it wasn't like I was huggin' somebody else, we was one body, we was one! *(He wraps his arms around himself and closes his eyes.)* I'll never forget that hug. Couldn't bring him back to America, I had no house for him to come back to. Stayed eight weeks and went broke. Came back and after that I'd see kids on the street and think of my kid and start to cry. . . . Why don't you get up and leave now? Put two eggs in your shoes and beat it. You stirrin' up things, you know. *(The visitor starts to stand.)*

I'll make some money. I'll get a home he can come to, and put him in school. Got two grandchildren, too, and I wanna be near 'em. They're by my son, Drew, he's a jet pilot in the Persian Gulf. And I have another son, Ronnie, here in Los Angeles. One son black, one son white, born a day apart. And then Solomon. I'm a boymaker. Don't see my kids like I want to. Can't go back to my babies till I got somethin' to give 'em. Right now, I'm broke. I said *broke*, not poor, there's a difference. *(He glances across the room and speaks softly.)* I know one thing. You get used to good food and a clean bed, hard to get used to somethin' else. Why don't you leave now? Please?

(He rises and goes to the door, shredding a piece of bread and tossing it outside to the pigeons.) People don't know it, but feedin' the birds is like paintin' a picture. . . . Some people think Muhammad's broke, too. He ain't broke. He's broken-hearted. He hasn't found himself in what he really wants to do. Maybe he just be in the freezer for a few years. Maybe he's going through this so he has time to think. Last time I was with him, his 15-year-old son said to him, "Daddy, Bundini is your only friend, the only one that doesn't give up on you." Muhammad looked at me, and we started cryin'. But this is not the end for Ali. Somethin' good gonna happen or him. Maybe not while he's still alive on this earth, but Ali gonna *live* for a long time, if you know what I mean. Like my kids, even when I'm gone, I'm gonna be livin' in 'em. . . . if I can be around 'em enough to put my spirit into 'em. Go fishin' with 'em. There you go again, you got me talkin' about it. Didn't I ask you to leave? *(The visitor reaches for his shoulder bag.)*

It ain't nothin' for me to get up and walk down the street and have 15 people yell, "Hey, Bundini, where's the champ?" That one reason I stay in my room. *(He pauses and looks at the visitor.)* You think I'm alone, don't you? Soon as you leave, God's gonna sit in that chair. I call him Shorty. He-ha, you like that, don't you? By callin' him that, means I ain't got no prejudice about religions. I was born on a doorstep with a note 'cross my chest. It read, "Do the best you can for him, world." I had to suck the first nipple come along. I didn't run away from home—I been runnin' *to* home. I'm runnin' to God. And the nearest I can find to God is people. And all around me people are fightin' for money. And I'm trying' to find out what makes apples and peaches and lemons, what makes the sun shine. What is the act of life? We all just trancin' through? Why can't we care for one another? There's a lady that come out of church the other day and got shot in the head. I want to know what the hell is goin' on. God, take me home if you ain't gonna give me no answer. Take me home now. If you're ready to die, you're ready to live. Kiss your family each day like you're not comin' back. I want to keep my dimples deep as long as I'm here. I want to see people smile like you just did.

(His lips smile, but his eyes are wet and shining.) The smarter you get, the lonelier you get. Why is it? When you learn how to live, it's time to die. That's kind of peculiar. When you learn how to drive, they take away the car. I've finally realized you need to be near your kids, that you need to help 'em live better 'n you did, that you can live on by feedin' your spirit into your babies. But now I ain't got no money and I can't be near 'em. Back when I was with the champ, I could fly to 'em anytime. See, I was in the Navy when I was 13 and the Merchant Marine when I was 15, and they was the happiest days of my life, 'cause I was alone and didn't have no one to worry about. But now I'm alone and it brings me misery. . . . C'mon now, get on up and leave. Talkin' to you is like talkin' to myself. . . .

See this bald spot on my head? Looks like a footprint, don't it? That come from me walkin' on my head. Don't you think I know I'm my own worst enemy? I suffer a lot. If my kids only knew how I hurt. But I can't let 'em know, it might come out in anger. And 'fore I see 'em, I gotta have somethin' to give 'em. I owe $9,000 'fore I can get my stuff out of storage. *(He bites his lip and looks away.)* One storage place already done auctioned off all the pictures of Ali an' me, all my trophies and memories from back then. Strangers have 'em all. . . . *(A long silence passes.)* Now the other storage place, the one that has all Ali's robes from every fight we ever fought, every pair of trunks we fought in, lot of jockstraps, too, enough stuff to fill a museum—I owe that place $9,000, and I'm talkin' to 'em nice so they won't auction that off, too, but I don't think they'll wait much longer. Sure I know how much that stuff's worth, but I can't sell it. That's not right. I want that stuff to be in my babies' dens some day. That's what I'm gonna give my babies. I can't just sell it. . . . *(His head drops, he looks up from under his brow.)* You know somebody'll pay now?

(He rubs his face and stares at the TV set.) You stirrin' it up again. Go on, now. You know if you just keep sittin' there, I'll keep talkin'. Pretty please? *(He gets to his feet.)* You can come back and visit me. We friends now. I can't go out, I gotta stay by the phone. I'm waitin' on something real big, and I ain't gonna get caught off-guard. Somethin' big gonna happen, you wait and see. . . .

A few days later, Bundini Brown fell in his motel room and was found paralyzed from the neck down by a cleaning woman. And then he died.

Seven years ago, when the group broke camp at Deer Lake for the final time, everyone contributed money for a plaque that would include all their names. They left the task to Bundini Brown and departed.

Today the camp has become a home for unwed mothers. In front of the log-cabin gym, where babies squeal and crawl, stands a tall slab of gray granite, chiseled with 16 names and surrounded by flowers. Bundini Brown had bought a tombstone.

♦

MARKING TIME A commemorative stone at Deer Lake enshrines the entourage *(over).*

Acknowledgments

MUHAMMAD ALI IS SPORTS ILLUSTRATED'S MOST photographed and written-about subject; this tribute draws from the cumulative efforts of several generations of SI writers, editors and photographers too numerous to be individually thanked. To all of you who toiled with grace on the magazines that provided the source material from which this book was assembled: our deepest gratitude. Besides those credited on the contents pages and throughout the book, other members of the staff found time to contribute: Rob Fleder, Linda Verigan, Stefanie Kaufman, Jodi Napolitani, Eugene Menez, Rich Donnelly, Joy Birdsong, Helen Stauder and the gracious and thorough SI imaging department. Special thanks also to Terry McDonell, who conceived this project and provided steady corner work all the way to the final bell.

We are also grateful for permission to reprint the following copyrighted material:
I'M A LITTLE SOMETHING SPECIAL ©1964 by Cassius Clay
ALI TAKES A CROWN—AND A CAUSE ©1967 by Angelo Dundee with Tex Maule
THE WORLD CHAMPION IS REFUSED A MEAL ©1965 by George Plimpton
MAN IN THE MIRROR ©1970 by George Plimpton
BREAKING A DATE FOR THE DANCE ©1974 by George Plimpton